AF564520

# Celluloid to Digital

## India's Film Society Movement

V. K. Cherian

7/22, Ansari Road, Darya Ganj, New Delhi
Tel.: +91-11-4077 5252, 2327 3880
E-mail: orders@atlanticbooks.com
Web: www.atlanticbooks.com



**Published by Atlantic Publishers & Distributors (P) Ltd 2024**



Disclaimer

- The author and the publisher have taken every effort to the maximum of their skill, expertise and knowledge to provide correct material in the book. Even then if some mistakes persist in the content of the book, the publisher does not take responsibility for the same. The publisher shall have no liability to any person or entity with respect to any loss or damage caused, or alleged to have been caused directly or indirectly, by the information contained in this book.
- The author has fully tried to follow the copyright law. However, if any work is found to be similar, it is unintentional and the same should not be used as defamatory or to file legal suit against the author.
- If the readers find any mistakes, we shall be grateful to them for pointing out those to us so that these can be corrected in the next edition.
- All disputes are subject to the jurisdiction of Delhi courts only.

Printed & bound in India by Atlantic Print Services

*To the Centenarians of*
*Indian Film Society Movement, Satyajit Ray,*
*Marie Seton, Chidananda Das Gupta,*
*Vijaya Mulay and Mrinal Sen (2020-23)*

And

*To my late parents—Thankamma (Mary)*
*Kurian & Philipose Kurian*

*Who inspired me to look at the world differently!*

# Introduction

V. K. Cherian's treatise on the Film Society Movement—a predominantly post-independence voluntary initiative in our country—charts the sporadic beginnings, its enthusiastic course of growth and the excitements and travails of sustenance over a period of nearly seven decades.

At a time when the cinema of Europe and the East were inaccessible to the *cinephiles* of our sub-continent, film societies provided us with the special privilege of watching, relishing, debating and writing about the very best of world cinema. We got enriched in the process with the aesthetic experience of the most nascent of all art forms.

At the dawn of independence, our national leaders had the vision and commitment to build up a nation of enlightened citizens capable of accessing and appreciating what was new in world culture, thereby enabling and encouraging them to contribute their might to the world in return.

Realising cinema's intrinsic capability to duplicate and distribute widely, the US was quick to market it worldwide as an article of immense commercial potential. In the Soviet Union, where the early American productions (D. W. Griffith's *The Birth of a Nation* and so on) were studied and analysed by stalwarts like Pudovkin and Eisenstein in their 'Labs', it was eventually developed into an effective tool for propagating and consolidating the gains of the Bolshevik revolution ('For us, Cinema is the most of all arts,' proclaimed V. I.. Lenin in 1917). No wonder, in India, Cinema was brought under the Ministry of Information and Broadcasting. Nazi Germany used cinema

(Leni Riefenstahl's *Triumph of the Will* and so on) as a means of unmitigated propaganda.

It was in the Soviet Union and Europe that cinema was treated as an art form in the league of painting, theatre and literature. Many well-known artists of the period saw it as an extension of painting. All the early 20th century movements and trends in painting (expressionism, impressionism etc.) were applied to cinema with fantastic results.

The European masters put cinema on such a high pedestal that it gained a unique status, to be seen and appreciated and studied seriously. Thus, film clubs were born, mainly patronised by artists and intellectuals in Paris, London and elsewhere. They would debate and analyse films for their content and form, technique and aesthetics.

In India, we followed the British, and first in Bombay (1942) and then in Calcutta (1947), Film Societies were set up by small groups of film enthusiasts and intellectuals. Significantly, in Calcutta, it was led by Satyajit Ray and Chidananda Das Gupta.

It was a great start, and the movement gave the right fillip and inspiration to many artists and professionals to look up to cinema as a new realm of artistic pursuit.

V. K. Cherian faithfully follows the progress of the movement with utmost care, and in the meantime uncovers the saga of passion and commitment as evidenced in the work of some of the pioneers.

It is, of course, not an easy task to register every little development that took place in each corner of this sub-continent. But the author seems to have achieved the impossible.

Until the middle of the 1960s, West Bengal had held the enviable position of having the largest number of film societies in the country. The situation soon changed. By the 1970s, Kerala overtook West Bengal and claimed the first position in the number of film societies functioning in a state.

In the last three decades, the situation slowly and steadily started to change. With the introduction of the VHS tape, many films—otherwise inaccessible—came to be circulated in the new mode. Soon the technology was to be replaced by Compact Discs, then Digital Video Discs, and lately Blu Ray Discs, each an improvement on the previous in terms of quality of image and sound reproduction. The most dreamed-of situation was finally on hand. All the classics of world cinema had become available to the genuine film enthusiast. Film societies lost the unique position of being the one and only window to world cinema.

Fortunately, the advantage of community viewing and sharing the uncanny pleasure of watching a film with like-minded people and the discussion and debate following a screening still hold their charm to this day. Film societies continue to be relevant, even with a smaller number of patrons than before.

The author's extensive research and study of the Film Society Movement has resulted in a comprehensive and impressive volume, a significant reference for those who wish to trace the roots of the off-beat cinema in our country.

I have great pleasure in introducing this book to film lovers, students and scholars.

**Adoor Gopalakrishnan**

# A Note by Shyam Benegal

I cannot recollect at what stage of my life I got addicted to the cinema. Perhaps, it all started when I saw films for the first time projected on a silent 16 mm projector, a prized possession of my father's, that he set up ceremoniously to show the films he kept making of his ten children—each of whom had a film made on them from the time they were born until the next child came along. These were films all of us loved to see and comment on. However, he tended to reserve such shows only for occasions when he had special guests over for dinner. Having a regular cinema a stone's throw away from our home also helped greatly. Indian, American and British films were shown at this cinema which was built for the army garrisoned in the cantonment where we lived. Incidentally, the cinema was also called Garrison. By the time I was in college, going to a film had become not only my main recreation, but also a chronic addiction. The twin cities of Hyderabad and Secunderabad, where I grew up, were sadly lacking in any film clubs or societies that could screen classics of world cinema like the film societies in Bombay and Calcutta.

It was the desire to see film classics from countries other than India, the UK and the USA that motivated me and some of my friends to start a film club. We called this film club rather grandly, "The Cultural Group". This was sometime in 1955-56. Having heard of *Pather Panchali,* I wrote to Satyajit Ray to ask him if we could get his film to screen at our film society. He graciously sent me an introductory letter to his producers, who in turn sent us a print quite unhesitatingly for a screening. It was with this film that the Cultural Group was inaugurated at a cinema in Secunderabad on a Sunday morning. After this, we managed quite successfully to get films for screenings practically every

Sunday morning, with films that we managed to obtain from different foreign embassies in Delhi or through their consulates in Bombay. Over the next two years, Cultural Group screenings became exceedingly popular, and the membership soared. The screenings were usually prefaced with an introduction to the film, its director and a short background to the film industry of the country of its origin and so on. This helped to prepare the audience for the cultural character, form and content of the film. At the end of each screening, there was a certain amount of time allowed for discussion.

Apart from embassies and consulates of countries, we acquired films from film distributors and sometimes even exhibitors who had prints of some great classics that were simply lying forgotten in their godowns. The easiest films to get at the time were Soviet classics such as the ones made by Pudovkin and Eisenstein, and Mark Donskoi's *Gorky Trilogy,* and even some classics of the silent era. Satyajit Ray films made until that time were special favourites, and also Hindi films such as *Dharti Ke Lal* by Khwaja Ahmed Abbas and *Neecha Nagar* by Chetan Anand. All the 1930s Prabhat film company classics were part of the Cultural Group's repertoire.

The Cultural Group came to an abrupt end when I left Hyderabad to seek a livelihood in Bombay. There was a functioning film society in the city at the time called the Bombay Film Society which had started in 1942, and had its screenings at the Eros Mini Theatre from time to time. As it faded away, a new and dynamic film society was started by Mr Gopal Dutia called *Anandam* in 1959. Five years later, yet another film society called *Film Forum* initiated by the filmmaker Basu Chatterji became active both in the city as well as the suburbs of the city.

In the late 1960s, Sudhir Nandgaonkar and some of his colleagues started the *Prabhat Chitra Mandal* which has not only survived to this day but has grown in size and extended its activities through campus film societies in practically all the Universities of Maharashtra. This is probably among the most active film societies in the country today.

I am not sure to what extent the Film Society Movement has helped in adding to the ranks of film literates and cineastes in the country. However, one thing is certain: it has contributed to inspiring a significant number of young film enthusiasts to become filmmakers. These are among the filmmakers who have contributed to the development of the alternate or parallel cinema of the country. A substantial number of highly respected Indian filmmakers such as Satyajit Ray, Mrinal Sen, Adoor Gopalakrishnan, Aravindan, Goutam Ghose, Buddhadeb Dasgupta, Girish Karnad, Girish Kasaravalli, Jabbar Patel and scores of others are among those who benefited from the Film Society Movement.

The book on *India's Film Society Movement: its Journey and Impact* by V. K. Cherian has captured the history of the Film Society Movement in India from the advent of the Calcutta film society and the formation of the Federation of Film Societies by some of the most prominent Indian filmmakers of the time who were the pioneering spirits driving the movement. He also deals with the intervention and support that the government of the time gave to films that did not follow the conventional form of Indian Cinema, which in turn helped evolve what is termed as Alternate or *New Wave Cinema* in our country. Mr Cherian's book is a valuable addition to the somewhat spare shelf of serious books on Indian Cinema, and it is certainly among the very rare ones written about the Film Society Movement.

**Shyam Benegal**

# Contents

# List of Images

# List of Abbreviations

| | | |
|---|---|---|
| BARC | - | Bhabha Atomic Research Centre |
| BDA | - | Bangalore Development Authority |
| BFI | - | British Film Institute |
| BFS | - | Bombay Film Society. |
| BRPSE | - | Board for Reconstruction of Public Sector Enterprises |
| C&S | - | Cable & Satellite |
| CBFC | - | Central Board of Film Certification |
| CBRI | - | Central Building Research Institute |
| CDS | - | Centre for Development Studies |
| CENDIT | - | Centre for Development of Instructional Technology |
| CET | - | Centre for Educational Technology |
| CFS | - | Calcutta Film Society |
| CPI | - | Communist Party of India |
| CPI (M) | - | Communist Party of India (Marxist) |
| CPSE | - | Central Public Sector Enterprises |
| CSDS | - | Centre for Study of Developing Societies |
| CSFI | - | Children's Film Society of India |
| CSIR | - | Council of Scientific and Industrial Research |
| DD | - | Doordarshan |
| DFS | - | Delhi Film Society |
| DP I | - | Director of Public Instruction |
| DTH | - | Direct to Home |

| | | |
|---|---|---|
| DVD | - | Digital Versatile Disc |
| FICC | - | Fédération Internationale des Ciné-Clubs |
| FACT | - | Fertilisers And Chemicals Travancore Limited |
| FFC | - | Film Finance Corporation |
| FFSI | - | Federation of Film Societies of India |
| FICCI | - | Federation of Indian Chamber of Commerce and Industry |
| FSM | - | Film Society Movement |
| FTII | - | Film and Television Institute of India |
| I&B | - | Information and Broadcasting |
| ICAF | - | International Cine Appreciation Forum |
| ICCR | - | Indian Council for Cultural Relations |
| ICS | - | Indian Civil Service |
| IFFI | - | International Film Festival of India |
| IFFK | - | International Film Festival of Kerala |
| IFFS | - | International Federation of Film Societies |
| IFSoN | - | Indian Film Society News |
| IIMC | - | Indian Institute of Mass Communications |
| IIM | - | Indian Institute of Management |
| IIT | - | Indian Institute of Technology |
| IMPEC | - | Indian Motion Picture Export Corporation |
| IPTA | - | Indian People's Theatre Association |
| IPTV | - | Internet Protocol Television |
| ISRO | - | Indian Space Research Organisation |
| IT | - | Information Technology |
| JNU | - | Jawaharlal Nehru University |
| Keltron | - | Kerala State Electronic Corporation Ltd. |
| KPAC | - | Kerala Peoples Arts Club |
| KSFDC | - | Kerala State Film Development Corporation Ltd. |
| LCD | – | Liquid Crystal Display |
| MD | - | Maryland |

MFS - Madras Film Society
MOA - Memorandum of Association
MOMA - Museum of Modern Art
MPEG - The Moving Picture Experts Group is a working group of authorities that was formed by ISO and IEC to set standards for audio and video compression and transmission.
MSO - Multi System Operators
NASSCOM - National Association of Software and Services Companies
NCERT - National Council for Education and Research
NCERT - National Council for Educational Research and Training
NFAI - National Film Archive of India
NFDC - National Film Development Corporation
NFHM - National Film Heritage Mission
NGO - Non-Governmental Organisation
NIAVE - National Institute of Audio-Visual Education
NMIC - National Museum of Indian Cinema
NRI - Non-Resident Indian
OHSL - Open Health Systems Laboratory
OTT - Over the Top Technology
OUP - Oxford University Press
PCM - Prabhat Chitra Mandal
PIL - Public Interest Litigation
PM - Prime Minister
RTI - Right to Information
SAHMAT - Safdar Hashmi Memorial Trust
SITE - Satellite Instructional and Television Experiment
SRFTII - Satyajit Ray Film and Television Institute of India
TFO - Talking Films Online

| | | |
|---|---|---|
| TV | - | Television |
| UCLA | - | University of California and Los Angeles |
| UFC | - | University Film Council |
| UGC | - | University Grants Commission |
| UK | - | United Kingdom |
| UNESCO | - | United Nations Educational Scientific and Cultural Organisation |
| UNICEF | - | United Nations Children's Fund |
| USIS | - | United States Information Service |
| USSR | - | Union of Soviet Socialist Republics |
| VCD | - | Video Compact Disk |
| VC | - | Vice Chancellor |

# Preface to the Second Edition

The first edition of the book was well received, going by the reviews and national and international interest in it. This could be due to the absence of an authentic historical narrative of the Film Society Movement that drastically changed the Indian film scene, be its mentoring, the appreciation, technology, aesthetics and themes of films, though there is a compilation of documents published by FFSI itself, which was very useful for me as an author. I find that similar books that were written in the UK and other countries when the digital wave in films began to swallow old ways of seeing and appreciating films.

The multi-city launch of the book gave me more data and insights about the Film Society Movement and the people associated. I knew I had omitted *Celluloid*, the Delhi University Film Society which contributed more than the DFS of Delhi to serious films. I also wanted to bring in FSM activities of Northeast, and was surprised to find an old friend as President of the Guwahati Cine Club. I heard about Raman Raju, the FFSI secretary in the 1980s, who is now in charge of the Chidananda Das Gupta Foundation in Kolkata. I was introduced to an online film society—TFO—which has weekly screenings and discussions. I found *Banner* Film Society of Thiruvananthapuram has a day of each month dedicated to curated screening of films and attracting *cinephiles*. I realised how technology was changing the viewing habits of people, as OTT, YouTube and Internet Archive began to emerge as alternate film platforms for connoisseurs in post-pandemic years of 2020-21. However, the online film society TFO is testimony to the fact that the post-screening interactions between *rasiks* unearth the various layers of meaning of each film, which was the film society's essential function. This is an international trend corroborated by Dr Swarnavel Eswaran of Michigan State University, USA.

Community viewing may be a thing of the past, but group discussions lead to a better understanding and appreciation of the films. This makes the original goal of the film societies contemporary even today. Hence, I decided to update and add more insights to the old and new formats of the Film Society Movement in the revised book, giving it a contemporary relevance, not just historical aspects. The updating of the book was undertaken not just about historical aspects, but also to see the film society movement from the post-pandemic digital world, and hence, many questions have arisen—the answers to which will only come in the future, as things evolve. Meanwhile, Nehruvian policies in films which brought about a sea of changes in Indian films were given a quiet burial by the government of the day.

*Akka,* Vijaya Mulay, who gave continuous support to me to unearth various facets of FSM died in 2019, and we celebrated the birth centenary of Satyajit Ray during the pandemic in 2021, along with both *Akka* and Chidandanda Das Gupta. Marie Seton had her birth centenary in 2010, and in 2023, we celebrate Mrinal Sen's $100^{th}$ birth anniversary, reminding us of the lives dedicated to good film culture in India. The book throws light onto the role and contributions of centenarians and hosts of others in making a new film culture in India, which is now next only to Hollywood.

The revised book is a tribute to all of them, and an examination of how the flames lit by them are still a guiding light for generations and years to come.

Let me thank filmmaker Goutam Ghose, Raman Raju and Robin Banerjee of Kolkata, Amitab Ghosh, Secretary of FFSI, Gita Viswanath of TFO, Pankaj Butalia, Deepak Jain of Delhi, Dr Swarnavel Eswaran of Michigan State University, USA, Biju, Venu (ex Films division) from Thiruvananthapuram, Madhurima Sen Barua of Guwahati, Theodore Bhaskaran of Bangalore, who helped me add more information and insights to the revised book. Thanks to old friends Lola Nayar, Sujatha Shakeel and Amit Sen Gupta who helped me as my copy editors with valuable suggestions.

**V. K. Cherian**

# Preface to the First Edition

After 30 years of a life full of hustle and bustle in New Delhi as a media and communications professional, I began to frequent Thiruvananthapuram, the capital city of Kerala, from 2010. The city was the cradle of the Film Society Movement which sprouted in the state 50 years ago, and I was part of it as a student. My frequent visits to the city, (thanks to my flat there) led to the revival of old friendships from the film societies, the media and films. I was curious to find out whether the Film Society Movement was still active or not, and found that it existed in a new format and had new patrons. I also noted that veterans like Adoor Gopalakrishnan, M. F. Thomas, Kulathoor Bhaskaran Nair and Vijayakrishnan were not active with the Movement in Kerala and a new leadership had taken over. I met Adoor, whom I knew from my *Chitralekha* days in the 1970s. He talked about the plight of the Film Society Movement in India and Marie Seton, arousing my inherent journalistic curiosity and that led me to plan the book with a pan-India embrace. Until then, I never thought I would end up writing a book on the history and travails of the movement across India.

I travelled to all the major film centres, starting with Kolkata, Pune, Bangalore, Chennai and Hyderabad, meeting film society activists, both former as well as current ones. Thanks to U. Radhakrishnan, the former secretary of the Federation of Film Societies of India (FFSI) in the northern region, I could track almost all old and new players across India. Soon, I caught up with old friends from the film societies in Delhi and Kolkata and had discussions. At Pune, I went through documents in the National Film Archive of India (NFAI). Here, I met P. K. Nair and had a discussion with him on the state of film societies. P. K. Nair has always been a surprise for me with his deep commitment to good films. Nair *saab* (sir) is a unique person who has never made a film but knows everything about films and has inspired three generations towards a 'good film' culture. Till his death in 2016, he stayed around NFAI, which he created from scratch, like a guardian angel.

I have been meeting Gautam Kaul, a police officer, at the International Film Festival of India (IFFI) in Delhi, even when he was heading the Special Protection Force during the regime of Prime Minister Rajiv Gandhi. Kaul led me to his friend and colleague in the Film Society Movement, Anil Srivastava, whom I had seen as Delhi's first video technology evangelist in the mid-1980s. He had immigrated to the USA with his wife, Shampa (daughter of Karuna Banerjee, the lead actress in Ray's first movie *Pather Panchali*). I met the couple when they were visiting India.

I was surprised to know that in Kolkata, my Indian Institute of Mass Communication (IIMC) colleague engineer-turned-professor Asoke Bhattacharya, who was the Director of Adult, Continuing Education and Extension, Centre of Jadavpur University and a former Director of Roopkala Kendro, film and social communication institute of the Government of West Bengal, (a brainchild of Satyajit Ray -the name was given by him- and Buddhadeb Bhattacharya, the former Chief Minister of West Bengal), was also the treasurer of the historic Calcutta Film Society.

That meant an easy gateway to the history of the city's Film Society Movement for me, with all the right introductions. A visit to the maestro Satyajit Ray's home to meet his son was like taking a pilgrimage. I saw the now-empty big chair where Ray used to sit, surrounded by books. At that moment, I regretted never having met the great man, despite Safdar Hashmi, my friend, pushing me to do so in the 1980s. A visit to the CFS office at Bharat Bhavan, meeting Mrinal Sen, Sajjal Dutta of Cine Central at the *Ganashakthi* office and dinner with the old film buff and writer Abhijit Ghosh Dastidar at Calcutta Club, were all a part of the perks of enquiry into the Film Society

Movement. Meeting *Akka*, Vijaya Mulay, was an eye opener into the enormous political and governmental patronage which the movement enjoyed. Akka was a good friend of Marie Seton, the evangelist who drummed up the movement and also of Prime Minister Indira Gandhi who extended patronage to the movement and pushed it to what it is today. At 94, *Akka* continues to be as energetic as ever with her sharp memory.

I had been occasionally meeting Bikram Singh, an ex-Indian Railway Service officer-turned filmmaker before his demise in 2013. Singh was associated with the Delhi Film Society (DFS), Film Censor Board and the 1980 Film Enquiry Committee. He enlightened me on the enormous effort undertaken by the government till 1984, to create the New Indian Cinema. He shared with me the Dr. Shivarama Karanth film enquiry committee report of 1981 and asked me to look up the 1955 Film Seminar documents. Thanks to Malayalam film artist Sajitha Madathil, who joined *Sangeet Natak Akademi* by then, I obtained the entire edited volume.

However, my first visit to NFAI Pune and its library was a huge disappointment, as a library official even denied having books of Marie Seton there. Despite spending three days, I was unable to get what I wanted. It was only during my second visit that I obtained all that I wanted and much more. Thanks to Nair *saab* and Arti Karkanis, I found old documents and press clippings, which were a treasure house of information and spoke volumes of the rise, decline and state of the Film Society Movement. I could validate many anecdotes, which I had heard from various players during the past five years that I invested in my research for this book.

For those of us who were born in free India, and have only heard about the Freedom Movement or remember the 'Make in India' effort of Chacha Nehru, connecting the dots of the 1950s and 1960s was like revisiting history. I have heard and met most stalwarts who played an instrumental role in the Film Society Movement from 1975 onwards, but never sat down to talk about their work and the movement itself. Chelavoor Venu, whom I helped to procure Hungarian films in the early 1980s, recognised me on a phone call after almost 25 years, when a common friend, filmmaker T. V. Chandran, connected us. One person I missed in the search in Kerala was Chinta Ravi, filmmaker and writer, who grew up with Venu and his *Aswini* Film Society in Kozhikode. In memoriam, I must mention that Ravi was an inspiration for a lot of us in our quest for a better worldview.

My search for the last book written by Chidu *da* was quite a handful as it was out of print and even the second hands were highly-priced on various shopping websites. Thanks to Geedha, a research scholar from Jawaharlal Nehru University (JNU) who helped me procure the book by Chidu *da* as well as the thesis on the Film Society Movement by Abhija Ghosh.

When I finished the book, I realised that what I had done was an inquiry into the deep passion and worldview that I carried all my life, on good films and appreciation of art in general. The book indeed is a look at the social, political, systemic and personal influences and a movement which forced me into such a passion.

In the process, if I can get to the origin, progress, decline, trials, tribulations and future of the Film Society Movement, with its players and their success, failures and survival tactics, I have achieved my goal.

I remain thankful to filmmaker and *Karnavar* (head man) of the film fraternity, Adoor Gopalakrishnan, who read the first draft and made immensely valuable suggestions and wrote an introduction. Shyam Benegal, the eminent filmmaker, also spared his valuable time to look at the contents and write a small note for the book. Thanks to my senior friends, Vijaya Mulay (Akka), Anil Srivastava and Gautam Kaul for writing short notes for the book. A special thanks to the late P. K. Nair and Bikram Singh, M. F. Thomas, Asoke Bhattacharya and U. Radhakrishnan for their valuable suggestions and encouragement in every phase of writing this book.

My search for old photographs of the history of the film society movement was equally laborious. But for the 84-year-old *young* enthusiast Mr Pradipta Sankar Sen, the executive President of CFS, went through the CFS photo-archive to give, this book would not have the touch of that Golden period. So was Ram Rahman of SAHMAT, who introduced me to Jean Bhownagary's family, ensuring a profile of the man and rare pictures of him and his work. Thanks to Meera Sahib, Adoor's first assistant director of years, I could get a rare picture of the studio complex of *Chitralekha* Film Cooperative. I must also thank FFSI-Keralam's Sasi Kumar for ensuring copyrighted pictures of many filmmakers, as my efforts to get them from NFAI failed miserably. Professor Satish Bahadur's son, Apurva Bahadur and his sister and Shyama Vananrse from Pune and my former Editor, YC Halan (Financial Express), Arti Karkanis of NFAI and Mahesh Rangarajan (former director Teen Murti) for their valuable help in accessing historical documents and photos.

I am also thankful to the following eminent personalities for their interviews/discussions, valuable inputs and suggestions; Mrinal Sen, Adoor Gopalakrishnan, Shyam Benegal, Girish Kasaravalli, Kumar Sahni, T.V. Chandran, Vijay Mulay, K. Bikram Singh, Khalid Mohammed, Shoojit Sircar, P. K. Nair Shashidharan and Arti Karkanis (NFAI), Samik Bandyopadhyay (art and film writer), Anil Srivastava and Shampa Banerjee (USA), Peter Sutoris (UK) Sudhir Nandgoakar (PCM-Mumbai), Pradipta Sanker Sen and Ashoke Bhattacharya (CFS), Sajal Datta (Cine Central), Mihir Bhattacharya, formerly Jadavpur University (Kolkata), Kulathoor Bhaskaran Nair, M. F. Thomas, Meera Sahib, George Mathew (*Chalachitra*), Dr Rajakrishnan, Sunny Joseph, K. R. Manoj, V. Sasikumar, C.S. Venkiteswaran (Thiruvananthapuram) Venu Chelavoor, Nara Hari Rao (Former FFSI President) and Prakash Belavadi (*Suchitra* Bangalore), Y. C. Halan (DFS), Gautam Kaul (DFS-FFSI), U. Radhakrishnan (DMFS-Delhi), Partha Chatterjee, Deepak Roy, Abhijit Gosh Dastidar, Vijayakrishnan, K. N. Shaji (film writers), Shyamala Vanarse and Apurva Bahadur (Pune), Govindaraj, Jan Morach, Faizabad, N. K. Sharma and Ram Rehman (SAHMAT), Janine Bharucha (Paris), S. Jayachandran Nair (Ex-Editor of Malayalam Varika), V. K. Joseph, Mohan Kumar, FFSI Keralam and Satish Sehegal, artist, Delhi.

This note would simply remain incomplete, if I do not express my deep gratitude to Sunmita Shinde, who took the painstaking effort, despite her busy schedule, to go through each page, checking the flow of the chapters and initial editing of the manuscript. Karuna John, a family friend, further chiselled my copy and a big hug to her too.

A big thanks to the team at SAGE for their professional handling of the publishing of the book.

I am delighted that the book is being published coinciding with the 60th anniversary of the release of *Pather Panchali*. The book is also my humble tribute to the great maestro of Indian films, Satyajit Ray.

To all my readers, I sincerely hope that you enjoy reading the book as much as I have enjoyed researching and penning it down for you.

**V. K. Cherian**

# 1
# India Awaits a *Pather Panchali*

The British Film Institute and its legendary film journal *Sight and Sound*, in 2022, requested its panel of 1,600 plus influential international film critics, academics, distributors, writers, curators, archivists, and programmers—almost double the number of participants in 2012—to select the best film ever made. The decadal voting, which BFI started in 1952, saw the selection of Austrian lady filmmaker Chantal Akerman's film *Jeanne Dielman, 23 quai du Commerce, 1080 Bruxelles,* in 2022, as the best film ever made.[1]

For Indians, however, there is one film which remains at the pinnacle of the top 50—Satyajit Ray's timeless classic *Pather Panchali*. With its human document touching the hearts of millions of people across continents over generations, the 1955 film still adorns the celebrated annals of the world's top list as the 35th best film ever produced.

*"I dunno anymore what a good film is, even less what the best is, but I know which ones I like best, depending on the days, in no particular order. This one for the boy, for his grandma who waters the weeds by the house, for Ravi Shankar's music, for the spotting of his complaint after his big loss, for the photography, for the sensuality of the countryside, for the sadness of childhood and all the hope of it,"* wrote German director, Volker Schlöndorff, while voting for the Ray film as his first choice of best-ever film.[2]

**Figure 1.1.** Poster of *Pather Panchali*

Reams of analysis have been written about the film over the years. Indian and foreign critics have looked at the film from all perspectives and adjudged it as one of the best from India. Some have ridiculed it as a depiction of India's poverty and misery before the entire world. Ray's contemporary, Mrinal Sen recalled: "Certain Friday in 1956, came as a surprise, the biggest of all big surprises—*a coup d'etat*, so to speak, conceived and staged almost conspiratorially."[3] For the country, the advent of *Pather Panchali* was a watershed in the history of Indian films dividing it as the period before and after *Pather Panchali*. The film is still rated as one of the global best among the top 50 in the ratings of the prestigious journal *Sight and Sound* for decades. It bagged both national and international awards in a row raising the profile of Indian films and also has broken all box office records of the period as far as earnings are concerned. The film, made with a mere Rs 1.50 lakh budget, earned over $50,000 from the USA alone, as per rough estimates.

Unquestionably, this film was the first to put India firmly on the world map. Although films were being shown and even produced in India since colonial times after the Lumiere Brothers invented the medium, no other film has made it into the history of global films the way Ray's first film has. The fact that the film is made by the founder of the first major Indian Film Society of independent India, the Calcutta Film Society (CFS), makes it even more historic. It also highlights the contribution of new Indian films by the Film Society Movement, which flourished following the national and international honours bagged by *Pather Panchali*.

> "The international interest in Indian cinema which *Pather Panchali* had created continues to grow. Indian films are now eagerly invited by major international film festivals," noted a report of the working group on a National Policy for films, headed by Dr. Shivarama Karanth in 1980, affixing the government committee's stamp of approval for the film as "milestone among Indian films".[4]

## History of Film Appreciation

Film as a medium originated in the West soon after the industrial revolution, when the age-old poetry and materiality of science were fueling the industry with newer inventions. The medium assimilated the qualities of poetry, art, theatre and music through technology, and had easy packaging formats for transportation across the globe. Within a few years of its advent, the magic of cinema entered India, captivating the minds of many to venture into the art and craft of filmmaking. By the time India got freedom from its colonial masters, the country had developed its own film industry, dishing out mythological and historical stories year after year, attracting more people to the cinema theatres, and making the region the third largest in filmmaking, next to the USA and Europe.

Alongside the development of the Indian Film Industry, there was a parallel development of the medium and its studies and even appreciation as an art form. These flourished in the film centres, especially in Bombay (now Mumbai) and Calcutta (now Kolkata). According to Vijaya Mulay, founder of Patna Film Society and also the first Joint Secretary of the Federation of Film Society of India (FFSI), "It first happened (the first film society) in The Amateur Cine Society of India, which was started by Ferenc Berko, a cameraman of Hungarian origin who

> was serving in the British Army unit. For creating healthy and good cinema, it was necessary to create *rasiks* from the populace."[5]

P. K. Nair, Director of the first National Film Archive of India (NFAI), recounted about the origin of film societies in India[6]:

> The first official film society in India, the Bombay Film Society, was started in 1940 with the blessing and support of the colonial rulers, but obviously with different intentions. Namely, to expose budding Indian documentary filmmakers to the best of world documentary, especially the works of Grierson, Wright, Jennings and others, so that they could be engaged to make effective war effort films for the Raj.

Ferenc Berko registered his film society in 1943, under the Societies Registration Act of Bombay. The society started with nine members and conducted one film show a month. The half-yearly membership fee was Rs 12/-. Gradually, the strength increased to 60 members by 1961. The best attractions of this film society were the discussions that Borka used to keep the members enthralled. "The Bombay Film Society (of Borka) did signal service to all true lovers of cinema in Bombay by holding shows of films with outstanding, technical, historical, artistic merit, initiating discussions about films and promoting the Film Society Movement," wrote Shanti P Chowdhury from the Calcutta Film Society.[7]

## What Is a Film Society All About?

The first conference of the Federation of the Film Societies of India (FFSI) held in 1967, defined the Film Society Movement as "...is an international, intellectual, non-political and cultural movement dedicated to the study of cinema as a serious art form."

"By screening, discussing, reading and writing about good cinema all over the world, they created a higher level of artistic taste, and this builds up to a better and bigger audience for good films within the country," commented Chidananda Das Gupta, one of the founders of Calcutta Film Society along with the celebrated filmmaker Satyajit Ray.[8]

The document of the National Film Archives of India (NFAI), *How to form a film society*, defined:

> A film society can be defined as a non-profit cultural organization, formed to encourage the appreciation of cinema both as an art and as a medium of information and education, by means of showing films, discussing them, and supplying its members with information about cinema.

The Film Society Movement originated in France during the period between the two world wars, just as the films originated there. Soon after the Second World War, an international association was set up in 1947 in Cannes (France), among the groups of film societies in countries throughout the world and called *Fédération Internationale des Ciné-Clubs (F.I.C.C.)*. It has now taken the shape of an international body for film societies, namely the International Federation of Film Societies (IFFS), an organisation supported by UNESCO (United Nations Educational Scientific and Cultural Organisation).

The term 'film club' appeared for the first time in April 1907, with the creation of Edmond Benoit-Levy's 'Film Club'. Located at 5, Boulevard Montmartre, Paris, the film club was to preserve and place at the disposal of its members all cinematographic documents and productions existing. It was also equipped with a projection room. The website of the International Federation of Film Societies described its version of the origin of the film society.

The Italian film theoretician, Ricciotto Canudo, who had been living in Paris since 1921, founded one of the earliest film societies, initiating the academic study of the film as a medium and as an art. After the First World War, film director and film critic Louis Delluc founded a film society, among the earliest pioneers, and an important film magazine, *Cinéa*.

In 1930, Jean Vigo founded the first film club in Nice, Les Amis du Cinéma. In 1935, Henri Langlois and Georges Franju founded the film society *Cercle du Cinema,* which became the *Cinémathèque française* in 1936, and it aimed to show and preserve old films.

After the Second World War, the movement of ciné clubs boomed. In 1945, the Film Society of Annecy was founded, and from here originated the Annecy International Animated Film Festival. In 1948, André Bazin, together with Jean-Charles Tacchella, Doniol-Valcroze, Astruc, Claude Mauriac, René Clément and, Pierre Kast, founded the avant-gardefilm society 'Objectif 49' with Jean Cocteau as its President. This film society became the cradle of the *Nouvelle Vague*. Objectif 49 organised the *Festival du Film Maudit* which took place in Biarritz in 1949.[9]

The first film society of the United Kingdom was established in London in 1925 by a group of left-wing intellectuals interested in films from Europe which could not be screened in public cinemas for political reasons. It was called the Film Society, but is often referred to as the London Film Society, as it was followed by many others in the next 15 years. These included the Edinburgh Film Guild (1929, still in existence), the Salford Workers' Film Society (1930; this became the Manchester and Salford Film Society, still in existence) and many others.[10]

Film societies have been extremely influential in fostering film cultures in numerous countries, celebrating non-commercial cinema and film as art, and promoting film appreciation and cineliteracy. This activity has been instrumental in encouraging varied forms of film practice (the British Documentary Movement, the *Nouvelle Vague*, New American Cinema, New Indian Cinema, etc.) and in the development of film studies as a discipline, says a definition of a film society.[11]

## Search for New Idioms in Films

Independent India energized the Indians with artistic lineages and motivated the film buff into forming film societies to study and contribute to the field in a meaningful way. The first one was the Calcutta Film Society (CFS), which was founded on October 5, 1947, when the 19 founding members met in a garret in South Calcutta. Prominent among the founders were Satyajit Ray, Chidananda Das Gupta, Hari S. Das Gupta, Hiran Sanyal and Radha Mohan Bhattacharya.

The founding fathers of the film society wanted to create an ambience for "intelligent filmmaking." Their activities included the screening of outstanding feature films and documentaries which were generally outside the commercial circuit. They also held discussions on such films and planned to bring out a journal on them. They even wanted to make 16 mm documentaries. "It was a period of discovery. Suddenly we saw what cinema could mean and how different it could be from what went under its name," wrote Chidananda Das Gupta, whose garret hosted the first meeting of CFS.[12]

**Figure 1.2.** Jean Renoir at CFS, 1949

Satyajit Ray, a commercial artist with a British advertising firm and a Tagorian family background, was bitten by the film bug. He was experimenting with his scripts and conventional producers in Tollywood, of Calcutta.

Marie Seton, in her official biography of the filmmaker[13], noted:

> Following the cancellation of the contract for the script of *Home and the World*, Ray's interest in cinema increased rather than diminished. It was stimulated by the return of Hari Das Gupta from Hollywood, who was to become known as a maker of documentary films and for the formation of the Calcutta Film Society.

Nation-building in all spheres, including culture, was weighing heavily on the film industry, and a quest for an Indian idiom in films began earnestly after the country attained its freedom from the British Raj in 1947. Prime Minister Jawaharlal

Nehru, an Oxford scholar, freedom fighter, and writer of many insightful books on India and its history, had already initiated many steps to build institutions in various cultural fields, including films. The government had constituted an expert committee on films with S. K. Patil as the Chairman, ably assisted by the likes of V. Shantaram and B. N. Sircar. As opposed to the earlier Rangachariar Committee, during the British Raj, which deliberated only on film censorship, this committee under Patil had the mandate to explore the development of the film industry as a whole.

In its recommendation, the Patil Committee observed:

> In our view, remedy lies neither in *Laissez-faire*, nor in regimentation, but curing all the various elements of their defects and deficiencies and ensuring, that they combine and cooperate in a joint endeavor to make this valuable medium a useful and healthy instrument of both entertainment and education, as well as a means of upliftment and progress, rather than degeneration and decay.[14]

The year was 1951, and the Indian film industry owes its further development to Patil's insightful and futuristic recommendations. Till the Patil Committee report, the Government of India had never considered films as a medium that needed detailed attention from the State apparatus. Despite all its mass appeal, the medium was not perceived as an art form worth consideration or given status equivalent to other art forms. The entire production, funding and structure of the film industry were considered almost barbaric by the State, as the funding was considered to be from black money and the people associated were not from related regular cultural fields. Hence, the sanctioning of films for exhibition and censorship is under the Union List (7th Schedule of the Indian Constitution) and its actual exhibition and taxes were on the State List, ensuring a double control on the production and exhibition of films.[15]

Needless to say, the government of the day accepted the recommendations of the Patil Committee and went about implementing its suggestions.

The first act was to flag off the International Film Festival of India (IFFI), in 1952 itself. An Indo-French person, Jehangir (Jean) S. Bhownagary, working with UNESCO in Paris, was appointed at the Indian Information Ministry as an advisor to plan the Indian International Film Festivals and establish foundations of the institutions crucial for the development of Indian films. The government had identified the country's film industry, which had by then emerged as the world's third-largest filmmaking centre, as one of its cultural priorities.

As Ray was running around to complete the making of *Pather Panchali*, Jean Bhownagary was planning to make India the first Asian country to have its own international film festival.

Bhownagary and Asok Mitra, the then Secretary of Information and Broadcasting Ministry, are credited with the actual implementation of S. K. Patil's committee report on the promotion of films and film-based institutions like Film and Television Institute of India (FTII), National Film Archives of India (NFAI), Film Finance Corporation (FFC) and International Film Festival of India (IFFI), which have contributed to tectonic changes in Indian cinema over 75 years.

Recalling his first meeting with Bhownagary in New Delhi in the 1950s, P. K. Nair, who built the NFAI from scratch, said, "He asked me to wait and apply for the 'archives job' in the soon-to-be-established Film Institute at Pune."[16]Nair, who was an apprentice with many studios and eminent directors of Bombay during this period, had gone to meet Bhownagary to seek a role in the exciting new plans of this Indo-French for Indian films. "Everyone was excited about building a new nation from scratch. We never knew if what we were doing would be a success, but we made an honest effort," noted Vijaya Mulay, who later held many posts related to films with the Government of India for promotions as well as for policy making.[17]

Bhownagary and his team did flag off the International Film Festival of India (IFFI), which is an annual event in Goa now.

Prime Minister Jawaharlal Nehru said in his message to the first International Film Festival of India held in Bombay, from January 14 to February 1, in 1952:[18]

> I hope that films which are just sensational or melodramatic or as such make capital out of crime will not be encouraged. If our film industry keeps this ideal before it, it will encourage good taste and help pave its own way, in the building of new India.

The festival moved to Madras, New Delhi and Calcutta during the same year, opening a new window to the world of filmmaking, other than that of English-speaking countries, to the Indian audience. Nehru was sure that the festival, which also had an exhibition on film equipment, would help Indian films, both with content as well as technology. "The Festival and the Exhibition will bring new ideas from other countries. I hope that we shall profit by these ideas," Nehru hoped.[19]

"This festival here offers a very good chance to artists, technicians, and to the general public as well, to know and study the best productions of so many other countries...In fact, this is one of the best opportunities for wide cultural exchange which is sure to result in mutual advantage," R. R. Diwakar, the then Minister of State for Information and Broadcasting, pointed out in his inaugural speech of the first International Film Festival of India.[20]

## *Chalachitra Akademi*: An Unrealised Dream

Having defined his idea of culture, the scholar-statesman Nehru went on to propose a *Chalachitra Akademi* to promote his ideas. He had already elucidated his notion of a cultured mind in his April 9, 1950 speech at the inauguration of the Indian Council for Cultural Relations (ICCR), New Delhi:

> Culture, if any value, must have a certain depth. It must also have a certain dynamic character. After all, culture depends on a vast number of factors. If we leave out what might be called the basic mould that was given to it in the early stages of nation's or people's growth, it is affected by geography, by climate and by all kinds of other factors.[21]

Prime Minister Nehru had already constituted academies for arts, literature, music and dance and fine arts at the central level. As a scholar and author of great repute, he was also the president of the *Sahitya Akademi*. As the *Sahitya* (Literature)

Akademi President, he urged *Sangeet Natak Akademi* (Music and Dance) to organise a seminar for laying down the foundations of the *Chalachitra Akademi* so that it could promote good films with the Indian cultural stamp on it.

Though even today an 'academy for films' remains a pipedream for the film fraternity, Nehru had made his intentions clear even before a film like *Pather Panchali* had hit the Indian film scene surprising everyone. At a film seminar organised in 1955 at the *Sangeet Natak Akademi* in New Delhi, Nehru delved into his idea of the relationship between films and audiences stating, "it is melodrama that interests large numbers of people, whether in India, England, America or elsewhere. Public taste, to some extent, moulds what is presented to it. At the same time, what is presented should mould public taste." It was attended by the who's who of the then film industry from all regions of India. Devika Rani and Prithviraj Kapoor were the Directors of the seminar and Nehru's daughter Indira Gandhi was its Social Secretary.[22]

**Figure 1.3.** Nehru inaugurates the first film seminar, 1955

The *Sangeet Natak Akademi* of India recognised the independent strength of films. "Film was a distinct form with a separate artistic individuality," declared PV Rajamannar, the first Chairman of the *Akademi*, at the seminar.[23]

The planning and conduct of the seminar were placed almost entirely in the hands of reputed artists and other professionals of the film fraternity. As Joint and Executive Director of the seminar, actor Devika Rani Roerich played an instrumental role in organising the event, working in tandem with her Joint director and actor Prithviraj Kapoor. One could see a young Raj Kapoor, Prithviraj Kapoor's son, as a silent participant in many of the photographs of the seminar sessions. Other film personalities like Bimal Roy, K. A. Abbas, a Leftist critic, filmmaker and the scriptwriter of Raj Kapoor films, later actively participated in the seminar.

The seminar, which enjoyed the involvement of every sector of the film industry and all principal aspects of filmmaking from all zonal centres, was "well structured" and ensured an extensive and detailed discussion on the state of contemporary cinema. The seminar saw filmmaker Bimal Roy urging the government for entertainment tax exemptions for good films.

> The Government can exempt the 12 best pictures of a year from entertainment tax, or the best picture of a year from entertainment tax, or the best picture of a year could be awarded a lump sum amount which may inspire the producer concerned to pursue his good services to the society.

The veteran filmmaker's suggestion was implemented by the government, as the film policies unfolded later.[24]

In his inaugural address, Prime Minister Jawaharlal Nehru stated:

> I see a great future, a glorious future, for Indian films. Before long, I expect Indian films to be exhibited to crowded houses all over the world, and they will earn not only money for our country but also a reputation for beauty, goodness and truth. India must and will make its distinctive contribution to the film art of the world and I am confident it will.[25]

For Nehru, cinema was a medium of public influence and he wanted the budding republic to take serious note of it. He also declared that the government cannot be a mute witness to the trends in the film industry. The Prime Minister stated at the seminar[26]:

> You may consider it in terms of high art, well and good, but regardless of that, in terms of moulding... the people of

> the country, the new generation; it is of high importance... It has to be treated realistically as something of the highest importance, a government must be intimately concerned with it.

Years later, Dr. Shivarama Karanth Committee on Films, instituted by the then Prime Minister Indira Gandhi, recommended the formation of a *Chalachitra* (Film) *Akademi* to the government. Just like the unfulfilled dream of the first Prime Minister, his daughter's effort too did not meet with success; though many State Governments were taking the route of *Chalachitra Akademies* to promote regional cinemas. Curiously enough, the only other political figure who addressed the seminar was the then Indian Ambassador to the United Nations (1952—62), VK Krishna Menon. Menon emphasised the employment opportunities films could create across India from production to screening. He was keen to see Indian films reach the masses in the villages. "Until we can really take entertainment into the fields of rural India and be able to understand the response of the villagers, there can be no universal development in this direction," Menon reminded the film fraternity. The 10th session of the seminar saw Krishna Menon asking the fraternity to host similar seminars in other metro cities promoting the participation of local talents and he proposed an organisation for the assessment of public opinion.

Krishna Menon told participants at the seminar[27]:

> At the present moment, all your assessments of public response are merely guesswork. You must study how to condition that response, how to educate that response. You cannot do it all of a sudden. It is a gradual process of cultivating and educating public taste itself.

Krishna Menon stopped short of uttering the words 'film society'!

Nehru, who was also the President of the *Sahitya Akademi* in those days, took his cultural role very seriously. He had earlier called India's High Commissioner and his friend VK Krishna Menon in London to find an expert of British origin to evangelise on the educational quality in films. Menon, in turn, asked his (High Commissioner's) social secretary, Pamela Cullen, to search for the right candidate for Nehru's assignment, even before arriving in India to take over as the Defence Minister.

## Arrival of Marie Seton—the Guru of Film Appreciation

As Satyajit Ray, having flagged off the Calcutta Film Society with his friends, was busy shooting and running around to complete his first film *Pather Panchali* in 1955, Cullen, was finalising an old *India League (28)* associate of Krishna Menon and a British Film Institute scholar, Marie Seton, for Nehru's film assignment. She had just come back from the erstwhile Soviet Union, after a couple of years' association with the legendary Soviet filmmaker Sergei Eisenstein, and was invited for a lecture tour in India on film appreciation. The tour was to be conducted by the Ministry of Education in association with the British Film Institute (BFI). Marie, an activist of the British Labour Party, had once "barged" into Mahatma Gandhi for a meeting. She was excited about going to India and being a part of the young nation's efforts to build a new film culture.

**Figure 1.4.** Marie Seton

"I first met Marie Seton in 1955 when the Indian Ministry of Education, in association with the BFI, commissioned her to lecture on film appreciation at many of India's flourishing film societies," Pamela Cullen wrote later.[29]

Marie Seton and her friends from the BFI later played a major role in promoting *Pather Panchali* in the Western world, not that Ray was a greenhorn to the London film scene. Marie had arrived in India soon after the seminar of 1955 to become a lifelong family friend of the Nehrus (both father and daughter). With the International Film Festival in 1952, the Seminar of 1955 and the arrival of Marie Seton, Prime Minister Nehru earnestly took up the effort to give Indian cinema the new directions it needed, as recommended by the S. K. Patil committee.

Marie Seton remained an *Indophile* all her life till her demise in 1985. She was single-handedly responsible for drumming up and giving the sporadic flicker of film societies across a few centres the shape of a national movement. Her multi-city lectures and the excitement created by the success of *Pather Panchali* resulted in the formation of The Federation of Film Societies of India (FFSI) in 1959. *Pather Panchali*, the film which ensured India a place on the world film map, was just about the time when *Rashomon* of Akira Kurosawa (Japan) took the world of films by surprise. Both Ray and Kurosawa became the torch bearers of the new Asian cinema of those days.

Seton's first booklet remains the first effort by the Indian Government towards giving films an academic orientation. She wrote in the first chapter of her booklet[30]:

> The first subject of the seminars—Film Appreciation, introduced the audience to the history of cinematic development. It showed how the film medium had been freed from theatre traditions and had developed a technique of presentation which was suited to the artistic possibilities of the motion picture camera. It also presented cinema from an international perspective and showed that in general, a film, like a novel or play, becomes universal in its appeal (a) when it presents an important social or

political theme, and (b) when it is nationally true to the country where it is created.

Seton had written the booklet after a series of lectures across various cities in India. Her tour in India was not just for lectures, but also for screening 35 films and film extracts which she brought to be shown to the audience in India, in order to develop a taste for good films from the point of view of international cinema. Seton wrote two more booklets which were published by the National Centre for Educational Research and Technology, titled *Film as an Art* and *The Art of Five Directors, Film Appreciation.*

**Figure 1.5.** Film Appreciation by Marie Seton

There is no doubt that the terms 'film appreciation' and 'film society' were made popular in India by Marie Seton. She can be described as the first evangelist for film appreciation who gave shape to the Film Society Movement, thereby spreading the excitement of a new art among the urbanites of India during the 1960s and 70s.

What was the role and objective of 'film appreciation,' a concept which spread like wildfire in those days, among the educated youth of India? Broadly, it was defined as the following by an NFAI document on the subject years later: *How to look at films differently than what you are accustomed to, and to help one to find out the hidden layers of a well-made film and in the process, lift your enjoyment to a higher plane.*[31]

Based on these definitions, since 1967, NFAI along with the FTII, Pune, organises a Film Appreciation workshop for a month as part of its effort to promote good film culture in India. NFAI also circulated a document *How to form a film society* to interested groups.

From 1956 to 1985, Marie visited India several times. In 1984, she was awarded the *Padma Bhushan*, the third highest national honour by the Government of India, for her contributions to India and Indian films. "Indira Gandhi's sons, Rajiv and Sanjay, used to stay in her London house, when they were admitted for some short-term educational courses in London," says Vijaya Mulay, who was a close friend of Marie.[32] Prof. Satish Bahadur, the first academic initiator of film studies in India and first professor of Film Appreciation at FTII, was handpicked by Marie Seton, from St. Johns College, Agra, during one of her lecture tours across Indian cities.

### *Pather Panchali*: Defining India's Idiom in Films!

In short, just as India awaited the film *Raja Harishchandra* to join the new medium of the Industrial Revolution during the British Raj, the new democratic republic was preparing itself for the arrival of a film like *Pather Panchali* in its cultural horizon and to have its own idiom in the world of films. The first show of Ray's film in New York organised by the Indian Embassy was after a sitar recital, sending out the message of the film as a true cultural product from India.

Though skeptics tried to deride the film as selling Indian poverty abroad, Prime Minister Nehru himself defended *Pather Panchali* explaining and questioning, "What is wrong about showing India's poverty? Everyone knows that we are a poor country. The question is: are we Indians sensitive to our poverty or insensitive to it? Ray has shown it with an extraordinary sense of beauty and sensitiveness."[33]

Needless to say, the Prime Minister and his daughter, Indira Gandhi, became lifelong connoisseurs of such films and always promoted filmmakers making films like *Pather Panchali*. Ray's first film won the Best Human Document award at the Cannes Film Festival and several national and international awards, making the CFS founder a global celebrity in films.

The nation and the Calcutta Film Society celebrate *Pather Panchali* and the anniversary of its public screening every year. Film enthusiasts of the country realised that Ray's first film was not just a *Song of the Road* but was indeed a song of the times. The film gave a new face to Indian cinema and sparked off a tremendous interest in not just *Pather Panchali*, but in a whole new genre of meaningful films. The entire Film Society Movement got a jumpstart in many places with the screening of the first film of Ray. The world began to acknowledge Ray's film as the advent of New Indian Cinema. The film and its director were historically identified as pioneers of the meaningful cinema movement in India. Satyajit Ray continued to be not just the lifelong President of the Federation of Film Societies of India but remains the sole stalwart of the new Indian films.

Marie Seton[34] wrote:

> Where there is such a response to discussion of cinema and an interest in films which are not in accord with the conventional entertainment film, it is reasonable to suppose that there is a growing public of a higher and more cultural character. The success of the Bengali film, *Pather Panchali*, is also indicative of this trend.

Ephraim Katz[35] wrote:

> *Pather Panchali* introduced Indian cinema to the West as cataclysmically as Kurosawa's *Rashomon* had done for

> Japanese films. A human document of timeless simplicity and exquisite beauty.

Malayalam film-maker Adoor Gopalakrishnan, who dedicated an entire chapter on *Pather Panchali* in his first collection of articles on films, stated:

> No one ever thought there will be a narrative on the folklore of life and a celebration of life itself this way on celluloid, and that is why the *Pather Panchali* will be remembered as the harbinger of change in Indian cinema.[36]

Adoor, incidentally, was also a harbinger of the new film culture with his *Chitralekha* Film Society/ Co-operative and is considered a worthy successor of Ray and his genre of films.

The experience of Shyam Benegal, Adoor's contemporary, was no different. Benegal recalled his first experience of *Pather Panchali*: "The experience was indescribable. As the expression goes, 'it simply blew my mind'".[37] Benegal had seen *Pather Panchali* during a visit to Calcutta in 1955. He saw it over and over again, after the first show, by buying tickets continuously after each show. Such was his excitement!

Years later, Ray's own film society colleague, Das Gupta explained the excitement which *Pather Panchali* created in India and abroad:

> Political independence and the beginnings of film appreciation are thus fused in my memory. Indeed, there was more than a trace of messianic fervor in our attitude to film. A new cinema, we thought, would emerge as an art and social force. A country like India, with its honeycomb of identities defined by language, religion and a host of other criteria, would need social engineering of some scale to wield itself into a nation, and cinema would be an ideal force to supply the motivation.[38]

Looking back, Das Gupta, who was the prime mover behind the CFS and FFSI, remains prophetic even today. Das Gupta walked his talk all his life, leading the Film Society Movement and the quest for India's idiom in films through his writings and films, entering the hall of fame of the builders of modern India. For the government, looking to mould the taste of Indian films and filmgoers to a higher plane, *Pather Panchali* was *manna* from heaven. The world began to see the new wave in Indian films, rather Indian films firmly perched themselves on the global map with Ray's first film.

For Ray, without the screenings of CFS, visit of Jean Renoir, the shooting of the film *River*, and films like *Battleship Potemkin,* by Russian legendary filmmaker Sergei Eisenstein, and the Italian neo-realist film, *Bicycle Thieves,* by Vittorio De Sica (1948), which he saw in post-World War-II London, *Pather Panchali* would not have found its place in history. Ray, who was in London for six months in 1950, saw 99 films as a member of the London Film Club, which changed his outlook on films entirely.[39] The first film of the first film society organization of independent India also became the first film to make into world film history for its new path-breaking approach to filmmaking. Hence, the film became the song and toast of the times, just as its title indicates '*Song of the Road*'—*Pather Panchali,* for the Indian film society movement too.

## Film as an Art

Along with the Ray film, his colleagues from CFS began to educate the public on the need to look at films as any other art form, raising the medium's status to a new level. But for the analysis of the Ray film by Das Gupta, Marie Seton and later Professor Satish Bahadur, the film *Pather Panchali* would not have perched itself at the highest annals of the world film history for over seven decades. Das Gupta was a star film critic of the prestigious daily *The Statesman,* for years and wrote extensively on the evolution of Indian film as an art, in tune with the developing aesthetic tastes of the world. He inspired a generation of new critics, who went on to write and analyse films using global aesthetic tools of the medium and contemporary arts, raising the medium to a higher art form, attracting the attention of the general, cultural and intellectual to the arena of film. Till then, films as such did not arouse the curiosity of the traditional cultural fields, as the medium was yet to evolve on its own, past the curiosity of the new medium.

The film societies didn't just spark off a new creativity in films, but also contributed better film critics, film writers, and historians, as they remained the sole avenue for exposure to better films and filmmakers of the world. The exposure to new trends in film-making and novel genres opened a new stream of film appreciation and studies. Along with the film screenings, the groups distributed pamphlets and other reading materials about the films and sometimes one of the members introducing the film even gave background stories about the film-maker and the film itself, placing the film in its true cultural context. Many of the film societies brought out journals in their regions, spreading the new film culture among youngsters and other cultural enthusiasts.

The first film quarterly, a serious academic journal on films, was also brought out by CFS, under the guidance of Marie Seton and Das Gupta, soon after its revival following the roaring success of *Pather Panchali.* Years later, Calcutta's Jadavpur University became the first to offer a degree and post-graduate course in film studies, taking film appreciation and studies to a different level. Today, over 200 universities in India offer various courses on film studies. Many film institutes have sprung up across India, to cater to the increasing fold of film-makers and technicians.

*Pather Panchali* and its makers put the country's films into a serious aesthetic and academic route, which years later Das Gupta analysed as two streams of the medium itself: the *Desi* and *Margi. Desi* indicates the popular mass culture and *Margi* the classic culture. The film societies represented the Margi part of the film culture and over a period of time influenced the Desi culture, even raising the standard of popular Indian films, which equal the best of the film industry be it European or American, and strongly resisted a Hollywood takeover of Indian films.

The ongoing interplay of *Margi* and *Desi* culture of Indian films overturned the viewing habits of Indians. It rose from eighty percent foreign films in 1950 to over ninety percent Indian films by 2022, and that too in all Indian languages, a dream which the founding fathers of the country were keen to achieve with their interventions in the film field, like lending active support to the film societies, during the first two decades of independent India.

(No history of the Indian Film Society Movement is complete without the history and development of cinema as a medium in India and understanding the significance of *Pather Panchali* and its historic position. See Annexure I)

## Notes

1. http://www.bfi.org.uk/news/50-greatest-films-all-time
2. https://www.bfi.org.uk/sight-and-sound/greatest-films-all-time/all-voters
3. CFS Silver Jubilee brochure of *Pather Panchali's* release. 1980.
4. Ministry of I&B, *Report of the Working Group on National Film Policy*(New Delhi: Ministry of I&B, GOI, May 1980), p. 9.
5. H. N. Narahari Rao, ed., *The Film Society Movement in India*(Mumbai: Asian Film Foundation, 2009), p. vi.
6. *Article –a collection of P. K. Nair from NFAI.*
7. H. N. Narahari Rao, ed., *The Film Society Movement in India* (Mumbai: Asian Film Foundation, 2009), p.25.
8. H. N. Narahari Rao, ed., *The Film Society Movement in India, (Mumbai: Asian Film Foundation*, 2009),pp.19-20.
9. https://en.wikipedia.org/wiki/Film_society#France
10. *https://en.wikipedia.org/wiki/British_Federation_of_Film_Societies*
11. *Oxford Dictionary of Film Studies*,p.174.
12. Chidananda Das Gupta, *Talking about Films* (New Delhi: Orient Longman, 1981), p. vii
13. Marie Seton,*Portrait of a Director*(New Delhi: Penguin, 2003).
14. S. K. Patil Committee report, 1951, p. 185, para 523.
15. Rangachariar Committee 1913 and Patil Committee 1951 of Government of India.
16. Interview with P. K. Nair.
17. Interview with Vijaya Mulay.
18. *Collected works of Nehru* (New Delhi: Publications Division, I&B Ministry, GOI) p. 311.
19. *ibid*
20. https://archive.pib.gov.in/archive/ArchiveFirstPhase/INFORMATION%20ND%20BOARDCASTING/1952/INF-1952-01-24_204.pdf
21. Ibid-19

22. R. M. Ray,*Indian Cinema in Retrospect: speeches of the 1955 seminar*(New Delhi: SangeetNatak Akademi, 1956 and 2009), p. 234.
23. Ibid., p.234.
24. Ibid., p.234.
25. Ibid., p.234.
26. Ibid., p.234.
27. Ibid., p.234.
28. https://en.wikipedia.org/wiki/India_League
29. Marie Seton, *Preface of Portrait of a Director: Satyajit Ray*(New Delhi: Penguin, 2003).*30.* Ministry of Education, *Film as an Educational Force in India*(New Delhi: Ministry of Education, 1956).
31. *https://cherianwrites.blogspot.in/2016/02/typical-film-appreciation-course-by.html*
32. Interview with Vijaya Mulay.
33. Booklet CFS, *Pather Panchali's* anniversary, 2012.
34. Marie Seton, *The film as an educational force in India* (New Delhi: Ministry of Education, 1956).35.The Macmillan International Film Encyclopedia(1998).
36. Kerala Bhasha Institute *World of Cinema in Malayalam* (Thiruvananthapuram: Kerala Bhasha Institute, 1983).
37. Sandeep Ray, ed., *Deep* (Delhi: Harper Collins, 2011).
38. Chidananda Das Gupta, *Seeing is Believing* (Viking, 2008).
39. Marie Seton, *Portrait of a Director—Satyajit Ray* (New Delhi: Penguin, 2003) p.-55.

# 2
# From Calcutta Film Society to the Federation of Film Societies of India

Building a new India was the buzzword in the country in every sector, be it democratic institutions, the economy, the realm of culture or new media such as films, in the years after its independence from colonial rule. *Tryst with Destiny* was a speech delivered by Jawaharlal Nehru, the first prime minister, to the Indian Constituent Assembly in Parliament, on the eve of India's Independence, towards midnight on August 15, 1947, which reminded the people of India of bigger challenges in the future in building a new nation.

Nehru wondered in his speech:[1] "The achievement we celebrate today is but a step, an opening of opportunity, to the greater triumphs and achievements that await us. Are we brave enough and wise enough to grasp this opportunity and accept the challenge of the future?" Citizens in each sphere, including films, were getting ready with their answers, inspired by the fresh atmosphere of optimism in the country.

Chidananda Das Gupta, reflecting on the advent of the first film society of independent India:[2]

> India's Independence somehow launched me into an irrepressible enthusiasm for cinema. It was in October 1947 that some of us, including Satyajit Ray, got together and started the Calcutta Film Society (CFS) in an attic in Ballygunge, where I used to live. It was a period of

discovery. Suddenly, we saw what cinema could mean and how different it could be from what went under its name.

Das Gupta, along with his old-time friend, Satyajit Ray, did not just stop short of organising a new forum called CFS, but went on to pave the way for a Film Society Movement contributing to an entirely new concept and vision of New Indian Cinema in the following decades. CFS, in its inception, was blessed with prominent academicians and cultural figures from Calcutta. The chairman of the Executive Committee was Hiran K. Sanyal and joint honorary secretaries were Satyajit Ray and Chidananda Das Gupta.

LOUIS MALLE - AT CFS

**Figure 2.1.** French filmmaker, Louis Malle, at CFS

Decades later, Das Gupta, the trailblazer behind the Indian Film Society Movement, concluded that the quest of film enthusiasts was no different from that of the freedom fighters and leaders of the country. He pointed out in the report given by the Film Enquiry Committee of the Government of India in 1951, headed by S. K. Patil which concluded that "the film industry was incapable of reforming itself", and proposed far-reaching changes through new institutions. "Nothing but a new cinema would suffice," he wrote.[3]

Ray's contemporary, Mrinal Sen, too, noted the entry of CFS in the post-independence years.

Mrinal Sen, who turned 93 in May 2015, told the author, recalling his entry into films:[4]

> ...I have been reading lots of books on cinema which were made available to me, mostly from the National Library; it used to be called the Imperial Library during the British period. After Independence, it was renamed as the National Library. That is how I tried to understand films. After that, when the film society started here (CFS), it was basically two persons, Satyajit Ray and Chidananda Das Gupta; there were others too. But they were the main force. I am no historian, but let me tell you that this was the first film society born in India.

## The Infancy and Revival of CFS

The CFS had an impressive kick-off with Jean Renoir's visit. Later, a Russian maestro, Vsevold Pudovkin, also visited and interacted with its members, making the society the leading cultural outfit in Calcutta. CFS was started as a unit of 25 people, but by 1952, it grew to a 50-member society. The first film to be screened was the film, *María Candelaria,* a Mexican romantic film made in 1943, directed by Emilio Fernández and starring Dolores del Río and Pedro Armendáriz. "Everything was haphazard, without fixed places and fixed programmes. One film we saw on the balcony of Ray's house. Some meetings were held in my little attic I had in Kolkata, very near Ray's house... We had about 50 members and not all of them paid their subscription," Das Gupta told an interviewer.[5]

Ray and Das Gupta discovered a French film, *Dance of Life*, abandoned with a distributor, and they screened it for the members. The CFS members took the tickets for the film, *Kalpana,* and organised a discussion on what is called an experimental film by Uday Shankar, the dance maestro.

By the late 1940s, the foreign diplomatic missions began to establish their consulates in the city and CFS organised many film screenings with them. The British Information Centre helped them screen many of the best documentaries of the Second World War. CFS members could thus experience the best of non-fiction films which John Grierson pioneered in Britain.

The turning point for CFS and Ray happened when the Hollywood-based French filmmaker Jean Renoir visited Calcutta to shoot his film, *The River*, in 1948. CFS hosted Renoir for a discussion on films and Ray interviewed him for the film magazine, *Sequence*. After seeing *Bicycle Thieves* of Vittoria DeSica in London, where Ray went as part of his work with D. J. Keymer, an advertisement agency, he wrote: "DeSica, not De Mille, US filmmaker, must be our role model."

CFS also imported USSR maestro Sergei Eisenstein's film, *Battleship Potemkin*, from London and had to discuss with the local censors and the Calcutta police to screen the classic. "Ray was so enamoured by the 16 mm print of *Potemkin* that he created his own background score from his collection of LPs when he saw it for the 15th time," said Samik Bandyopadhyay, a critic and his family friend.[6]

As Ray was engaged for three years in the making of *Pather Panchali*, after his arrival back from London, the CFS had its first hiccup leading to a break in the first part during the 1950s.

The success of *Pather Panchali* and the excitement and controversies that it created led to the revival of the society in 1956, that too with a journal, *The Indian Film Quarterly*. The CFS founder's path-breaking film pumped fresh adrenalin to the budding film society movement in India, which was eventually nurtured by the central government, and patronised by none other than Prime Minister Jawaharlal Nehru and his daughter Indira Gandhi, ensuring over four decades of continuous governmental and political patronage to the movement.

**Figure 2.2.** Satyajit Ray at the CFS revival gathering

Pradipta Sen, who was president of the CFS in 2012, recollected:

> There were primarily three reasons for the re-starting of the CFS; impact and excitement about the success of *Pather Panchali*, frequent visits of Marie Seton, a British film expert, and the growing number of film buffs in the city. From 250 members, the revived CFS grew to 2,500 members in five years and remained so till the 80s.

"As the journal of the CFS, it represents and becomes the instrument of a new movement to promote the growth of better cinema and better audience," the editorial of the first issue of *The Indian Film Quarterly* of January-March-1957 had declared, said Sen, now in his 90s, a media person who was part of the revival of CFS, while he recalled the golden days of the society.[8]

The CFS celebrates the August anniversary of its release of *Pather Panchali* almost every year, as the film and its success not just revived the CFS, but the entire film society movement of India. Indeed, the celebration had become a part of the cultural mosaic of Calcutta and of the city's proud Bengali cultural enthusiasts. "By 1956, with the success of *Pather Panchali*, first at home and then abroad, the film society scene opened out and took on an almost formidable aspect. Enthusiasm for cinema became respectable and a wide range of people rushed into film societies," Das Gupta noted.[9] Cinema, as it existed in India, was till then looked down upon by practitioners of other cultural forms, be it in theatre or dance dramas or literature.

## Film Societies in Other Cities

Little did Das Gupta realise that there were many small groups waiting to explore the new media, the cinema, in many other parts of the country, following the excitement created by *Pather Panchali*. While Bombay already had its own film society to acquaint the filmmakers with the theoretical and technical aspects of the emerging medium and was screening and discussing films from other countries, other urban centres were equally eager to join the bandwagon.

New Delhi, Patna, Lucknow, Roorkee, Bhopal and Chennai slowly got into the 'excitement mode' with the film societies, exposing themselves to the experiments in this new medium happening outside India.

### The Delhi Film Society

Muriel Wasi, one of the founders of Delhi Film Society, in 1981, wrote[10]:

> It seems so long ago, but it was only about 25 years ago that the Delhi Film Society (DFS) was founded by a small group of people—not more than 12—who were anxious to see outstanding films that were not ordinarily screened in commercial cinema halls. These founding persons were professionals, journalists, businessmen, administrators, diplomats—but their common interest was cinema and the special thing that cinema could do to criticize life.

The Delhi Film Society (DFS), founded in 1956, was one of the most privileged film societies in the country. The international embassies had their headquarters in the capital. The ministries, the prime minister, bureaucrats, academics, journalists and artists, among other influential people, promoting such films, had their offices in Delhi. The last president of the now-defunct DFS was an Indian Police Service officer (retired), Gautam Kaul, who was also Indira Gandhi's cousin. A Hungarian film marked the first screening of the Delhi Film Society.

Marie Seton continued to be an inspirational presence for film enthusiasts in the capital, as she was a guest of Indira Gandhi at her home. Some of the early members of the DFS included dignitaries such as Indira Gandhi, Aruna Asaf Ali and I. K. Gujral (who went on to become prime minister). By the early 1980s, the society, which started with 15 members in 1956, had attracted over 2000 film buffs in its fold. Nehru's close aide, Defense Minister Krishna Menon, and a host of other VVIPs were regulars or guests at the DFS.

The DFS was at its peak during the 1980s and the frequency of films shown was almost five to seven in a month. Gradually, an uncanny message went around that uncensored films were shown, and this led to the beginning of the decline of the DFS. Later, in the 1990s, the film society movement became dormant because of two reasons: the advent of TV and the liberal import of films.

The censoring policy also became liberal, said Y. C. Halan, who served as both president and secretary of DFS in the 1970s and 80s[11]. Membership was not available to the students, like this author, in 1980, as DFS was full of 'elite' members, and we were left to the mercy of various cultural centres of the diplomatic missions in the capital.

As long as it lasted and flourished, the strength of DFS was its elitist membership as well as leadership, with the who's who in the government and power centres. It also attracted people who were serious about pursuing a career in film. Many of them became filmmakers like Pankaj Butalia, Gopi Gajwani and Bikram Singh. Many were politically and culturally powerful like Aruna Asaf Ali, Vijay Mulay, Usha Bhagat and Gautam Kaul. These people ensured that only serious members joined DFS.

The DFS initially had limited its membership to 250 and then extended the limit to 500; in 1980, it had grown to over 2,500 members. There is an unconfirmed story that even Rajiv Gandhi, the son of the then Prime Minister, was denied membership.

Memberships were awarded after an interview in those days. The entry barriers helped to build up a quality membership. However, the waning of initial enthusiasm for uncensored films, and with the advent of video and television, and the lack of official patronage, slowly put a curtain on DFS.

### Bhopal's International Film Club

Anil Srivastava, a technocrat, who was also a founder of the Lucknow Film Society, recounted:

> My involvement with the film society movement started with the International Film Club in high school (St. Josephs' Convent, Bhopal) in 1959. The father of two of my classmates, Saleem and Parvez Romani, had used a Bell & Howell 16 mm film projector. We used this to start showing films and started a film society on 4th August 1959. We began with 16 mm film distributors like MGM, Columbia and NEIF Film Club. Tagore's birth centennial

(1961) was coming up and from the newspapers we learnt about Satyajit Ray and his new film, *Teen Kanya,* based on Tagore stories, and Tagore documentary.

**Figure 2.3.** PM Nehru visits the Bhopal International Film Club

He went on to work with companies like Apple in the USA, after founding the first trust that promoted video and related technologies in a big way. He also founded the Centre for Development of Information Technology (CENDIT), way back in the 1980s. CENDIT happened, even before India climbed on to the information technology bandwagon; Anil was among the founding fathers of National Association of Software and Services Companies (NASSCOM), the industry body of India's IT companies, before he immigrated to Mexico and then the USA[12].

Anil Srivastava had the distinction of forming the first teenagers' film club way back in 1959 in Bhopal, where Prime Minister Jawaharlal Nehru was a guest. He also became a disciple of Marie Seton, the first official 'evangelist' of the film society movement in India. "I still have the long letters which Marie used to write," he said.

A report in the *National Herald* in 1961 recorded all of it when the club made its first short film. "The teenage film unit of the International Film Club of Bhopal has produced its first-ever documentary made by youngsters under 17," the report said, featuring a photo of the production unit.[13]

Taroon Kumar Bhaduri, the journalist father of actor Jaya Bhaduri Bachchan, was a patron of this film club. The first of the films shown was *Pather Panchali*. Anil, whose life and work centred on films, later married Shampa Banerjee, the daughter of Ray's first film's leading lady, great actress Karuna Banerjee. Shampa Banerjee acted remarkably as the little Durga in *Pather Panchali*.

## The Lucknow Film Society

Marie Seton, who had not only inspired people in Delhi, but in Bhopal as well, had a young follower, Anil Srivastava, who went on to become one of the founders of the Lucknow Film Society.

Remembering the early days of the Lucknow Film Society,[14] Anil Srivastava, said:

> I had finished my High School. My father's two-year posting in Bhopal was coming to an end. We were going back to Lucknow. I told Marie that I was very unhappy about having to leave Bhopal. She told me about Professor Kailashnath Kaul, director of the National Botanical Gardens (now National Botanical Research Institute) and suggested that I should meet him about starting a film society in Lucknow.

**Figure 2.4.** Vijaya Mulay and Anil Srivastava, with a Polish diplomat in Lucknow

Kaul was the brother of Kamala Nehru, wife of Jawaharlal Nehru, and mother of Indira Gandhi. Professor Kaul's son, Gautam Kaul, along with Anil, had become the beacons of the Film Society movement in Delhi and remained ardent film buffs. Gautam was also the office bearer of the DFS, before the regular screenings stopped.

Sheila Kaul later became a central minister and Gautam Kaul became the president of the Federation of Film Societies of India (FFSI). Anil recounted his nostalgic memories:

> Marie had spoken to Professor Kaul in Delhi. I still remember vividly my meeting with Professor Kaul and his words about how the botanical garden was a place for nurturing the intellect and human culture. Walking through the botanical garden, he spoke of films and his stay at Royal Botanic Gardens, in between bending down, pointing and describing the plants along our path. Films, he talked about, and plants he described; they seemed equally to preoccupy his thinking. He had a beautiful small film auditorium in the garden which was the venue for most of the Lucknow Film Society's screenings. I don't know how the group came together. One person led to another and we all met at Professor Kaul's home. It was decided to start the Lucknow Film Society with Sheila Kaul as the President, and Wendy Vora, Devendra Mishra (father of filmmaker Sudhir Mishra); journalist CS Pandit, Harbans Mathur, KN Kacker and me as members. I was not even 18 but was treated as an adult. I was asked to be the joint secretary of the society.

## The Madras Film Society

At the same time, post-*Pather Panchali*, the Madras Film Society (MFS) was founded in October 1957, putting South India on the nation's film society map. Ammu Swaminadhan, a politician and mother of Mrinalini Sarabhai, and Captain Lakshmi Sehgal, were the founder-presidents of MFS. Being the first film society in Southern India, it played a stellar role in inspiring other cities of the region to form their own film societies.

K. S. Govindaraj, who was one of the founder members of the MFS, is presently the executive vice president. The MFS which, is nearing the 60th year of its existence, was started with a Rs 12 annual subscription, and today the subscription is Rs 700 per annum.

"Many film personalities have benefited from our screening of international films. The filmmakers, K Balachander, Kamala Haasan, Singeetham Srinivasa Rao, Muktha Srinivasan, SP Muthuraman, Balu Mahendra, and popular actors Suhasini and Nazar were MFS's regular guests at the screenings," recalled Govindaraj[15].

Film Historian Theodore Bhaskaran who was a member of MFS in the 80s, said he used to attend its screenings but was told that some financial frauds happened, and MFS became dysfunctional later. "In Madras we had American Centre and they used to do a lot of screenings, I have seen films festivals with retrospectives of many film-makers like John Hopkins. There was a Directors' Council and it used to function from American Centre auditorium and I used to see actor filmmaker Kamala Haasan there", Bhaskaran recalled. The eminent historian lamented the attitude of the leaders of the South Indian film city. "They did not encourage the film society movement but also degraded it; some of them wrote articles openly against the movement", he pointed out. After all, the movement was asking for corrective measures from mainstream industry and most of these film people were also political leaders from the 80sand upto the 2010s and they never encouraged such corrective forces.

MFS screened films in collaboration with the US Information Service and other consulates in old Madras and remained as an upper-middle-class activity, as the popular films took over the taste of the masses, while two chief ministers in the state came from the film industry itself.

## The Bombay Film Society

RE Hawkins, former general manager of the Oxford University Press, in 1981, reminiscence about the period in the FFSI's journal as follows:

> We normally had our screenings at 9.15 pm at Eros cinema. Ferenc Berko, our founder, was an enthusiast who at the end of the show would start a lively discussion in the miniature theatre where we met often, the one above the Eros Cinema–a discussion which would be continued in homes and cafes.

Hawkins, indeed, was the last chairman of the Bombay Film Society (BFS) which was founded by Berko in 1937. He was also the vice president of the new FFSI in 1959. The last general body meeting of the Society was held on May 22, 1962, and was attended by many film buffs, including V.M.Vijakar and Jag Mohan (joint secretaries), V.N. Raji (treasurer) Tina Khote, S.T. Berkeley-Hill, K.L. Khandpur, M.V. Krishnaswamy, Sudharshan Sharma and A. Bhaskara Rao. Jag Mohan, Khandapur and Krishnaswamy remained ardent film society activists till the end of their lives.

Jag Mohan, a leading light of the BFS[16], observed:

> The BFS was an offshoot of the Second World War, when a group of serious-minded Britishers, mostly from the services stationed in Bombay, along with a few Indians, wanted some diversion. Typical of the British and elitist approach to films prevalent at that point of time, the members had drinks and dinner before seeing the films.

The BFS merged with the K. A. Abbas-led *Film Forum,* whose contribution to Hindi films is immense, in terms of creating a spectrum of filmmakers and writers.

## The Patna Film Society

In Patna, the UK-educated Vijaya Mulay and her friends, who were regulars at the morning shows of English films in the city, decided to have their own club to view films of their choice. "In a way, these half-empty morning shows proved a boon to the 15 or 20 of us who founded the Patna Film Society in 1951," said Mulay who went on to become one of the leading lights behind the FFSI from 1959 onwards. She remained the finest and most enduring icon of the film society movement till her death in May 2019.

Mulay was bitten by the cinema bug while she was a student at Leeds University in the UK on a government scholarship. She was a member of the University Film Society at Leeds, way back in 1947. On her return from the UK, she was posted by the government at Patna from 1949 to 1954; her passion for cinema made her persuade her friends to form the Patna Film Society (PFS) in 1952. The president of PFS was Professor Devi Chatterjee and Mulay (fondly called Akka) was the secretary and Arun Roy Chaudhuri was the joint secretary.

"Among the founder members were Akbar Imam, Kumar Durganand Sinha, Sita Sharan Srivastava, Gyan Chandra, N. S. Thapa (who later became the chief producer of the Films Division)." PFS was also flagged off with the screening of *Battleship Potemkin*.

"We all knew each other very well and after the show there used to be passionate and almost endless discussions," Mulay remembered the good old days. After she moved to Delhi, the PFS suffered many setbacks and was closed down in the 1960s. Later, in 1974, the Cine Society of Patna was formed, and they continued to screen films, keeping Patna on the film society map of the country.[17]

### The Roorkee Film Society

Y. C. Halan, a Delhi University academic turned editor, who was also the secretary and president of the DFS explained about how he got into the Film Society Movement:

> I was in Roorkee at the Central Building Research Institute (CBRI) in the early 1960. My uncle was the president of the Roorkee Film Society. I watched a Kurosawa film and realised how different it was. I was told that the best films, particularly non-commercial, from foreign countries, were not shown in India. Also films from non-English speaking countries were never shown in India. Those were the days when foreign films were not freely allowed. Such films were brought in by the embassies and were routed through film societies. The film society movement was at its peak as important persons like Usha Bhagat, social secretary to Indira Gandhi, and serious film buffs were interested in

watching such films. Since these people were influential, the best films from the best directors were brought in by the embassies and shown to members.

The Roorkee Film Society, which was also among the first few to form the FFSI, was established by academics; it was almost a campus film club of the Central Road Research Institute (CBRI). A.K. Rahman, who, later, became a scientist at the CSIR in New Delhi, was the man behind the Roorkee Film Society.[18]

## Agra and Faizabad Film Societies

Though the film societies in Agra and Faizabad came up soon after the formation of FFSI in 1959, they are considered to be pioneers in the northern region.

Professor Satish Bahadur, who organized the Film Club, recalled in one of his notes:

> Based in the Institute of Social Sciences and the Institute of Linguistics and Hindi Studies, the Agra University Film Club had about 150 post-graduate student-members. Almost all of them came from a middle-class, urban or rural background, and almost none of them had any background of film appreciation; commercial Hindi cinema was all they had hitherto watched, or popular Hollywood films.

The society functioned from 1960 to 1963 and ceased to exist after the professor went to FTII as a staffer. Going by the description of Professor Bahadur about the Agra Film Club, it was indeed a new experiment in film appreciation in the town of the Taj Mahal across the river Yamuna, with a flourishing education hub and a skilled world-class leather industry of brilliant local craftspeople.[19]

The experiment, which was a totally indigenous and voluntary activity by Prof. Bahadur, impressed Marie Seton and she insisted on making Prof. Bahadur the first Indian professor of Film Appreciation at the FTII, Pune. The professor took his post as a life-long mission and trained almost two generations of filmmakers and film buffs through the FTII course, with a highly acclaimed, annual, one-month residency run by him and

P. K. Nair of the National Film Archive of India (NFAI) from 1967 onwards.

The Faizabad Film Society was established by a family which ran the newspaper *Hum Aap*, recalled senior journalist Madhukar Upadhaya, who belongs to the town. Despite repeated calls to individuals in the temple town of Ayodhya, details of this society were not forthcoming, though there was an Ayodhya Film Society, but not affiliated to FFSI, functioning in the town during the 2010s.

## Political and Governmental Patronage

Both Nehru and Indira Gandhi, who was the Information and Broadcasting Minister in Nehru's successor's government, and later the prime minister for over one-and-a-half decade, remained patrons of the new and emerging film culture, extending their total support to the film society movement from 1950 onwards. Most of the initiatives of the government in films coincided with the advent and growth of film societies in the urban centres of India.

**Figure 2.5.** Satyajit Ray with Michelangelo Antonioni and Kurosawa at the Taj IFFI, 1977

Nehru's tryst with films was kicked off by the submission of the first Film Enquiry Report led by S. K. Patil to the government in 1951. The committee had made wide- ranging recommendations with a view to effect far-reaching changes in Indian cinema, which had emerged as a popular and meaningful mass medium by then. The Indian film industry was the second largest in number in the world, only second to Hollywood by the

1950s, though most of the luminaries in traditional and classical arts and its connoisseurs did not choose to touch films even by a barge pole. Films did not find a place in the list of coveted arts among Indian artists, just as music, theatre, literature and arts, and there was no wider social acceptance of film as an art form.

The first agenda of the central government was to showcase the best of world cinema to Indians so that it could attract the best of artistic minds of the period. They had to depend on global Indians to undertake this, and hence a search was on right earnestly to get evangelists for the new Indian films. In 1951 itself, Nehru, on the advice of Indira Gandhi, brought in Jean Bhownagary, a French Indian,from UNESCO in Paris, as an advisor to the Ministry of Information and Broadcasting to flag off the India International Film Festivals, which have become an annual feature now. The S. K. Patil committee in 1950 had made recommendations for many institutions to make Indian films world-class. Bhownagary, who enjoyed the confidence of Nehru and Indira Gandhi following the successful conduct of the India International Film Festival in 1952, was entrusted with the task of ensuring that the institutions which the Patil Committee recommended were established. The I&B Ministry had an enlightened secretary Asok Mitra, who moved the government machinery to build the institutions as recommended by the S. K. Patil Committee. These institutions included the Film and Television Institute of India (FTII), Film Finance Corporation (FFC) and National Film Archive of India (NFAI).

Nehru had also initiated the formation of a '*Chalachitra Akademi*' through a major seminar in Delhi in 1955, even before Marie Seton was brought in 1956 to emphasise the new film culture. Marie could not have done what she did without the complete support from Nehru and his daughter.

Anil Srivastava, a veteran of the movement, fondly recollected the involvement of Nehru as far back as in 1959:[20]

> *Chacha* Nehru was the universal uncle. We wrote to him about our film club in Bhopal. Our film projector was old and rickety. He was visiting Bhopal so it was natural to ask our beloved 'uncle' to gift us a new film projector.

> Lo and behold, he wrote back and promised to meet us. Marie Seton was a guest at Nehru's residence in Teen Murti Bhavan. On his return to Delhi, he mentioned us to Marie and that brought me into the fold of the larger Indian Film Society Movement.

Both Marie and Indira Gandhi, who had developed a great personal friendship by then, initiated the formation of the FFSI in 1959, following Marie's successful all-India lecture tour on Film Appreciation with a few films from British Film Institute. Marie stayed with the Nehrus at the PM's official residence in Teen Murti Bhawan, Delhi, and even penned a biography of Pandit Nehru[21]. Indira Gandhi remained in the post of vice president of FFSI, till she became a minister under Prime Minister Lal Bahadur Shastri.

Indira Gandhi was so intensely involved in the campaign for a new film culture that she even asked Marie to show films to her sons and their friends at Teen Murti, so as to mould their minds and so that they could become more sensitive towards the emerging film culture.

There were two major film enquiry committees under Nehru and Indira Gandhi. "All film policies of independent India began about that time (1947—61), so you can certainly imply that it was a Nehruvian policy initiative," said Shyam Benegal, eminent filmmaker and director of the popular TV series, Discovery of India, based on the writings of by Nehru[22].

K. A. Abbas, a veteran filmmaker, in his autobiography, describes an incident after the preview of the director's film, *Munna*, in the basement of the theatre in the Rashtrapati Bhavan. He was invited by Nehru for a breakfast chat along with a leading actor, a boy. Later, Abbas got a telegram from Nehru stating: "I liked the film and consider it good from many points of view. It was a simple story artistically told without too much embellishment or overstatement."[23] Abbas, who initiated neo-realist cinema in India through his film *Dharti Ke Lal* in 1946, was another confidant of Nehru and Indira Gandhi in the film field. Abbas was also the successful screenplay writer for many of the hit films of Raj Kapoor.

Indira Gandhi remained an ardent supporter of the film society movement and extended her political patronage in her official capacities, first as the I&B Minister and later as the Prime Minister. She remained an ardent admirer of new Indian cinema till her death, ensuring that FTII, FFC and NFAI had the best of professionals manning them. The appointment of film-maker Ritwik Ghatak as vice-principal of FTII was at the instance of Indira Gandhi, on the recommendation of Satyajit Ray.

The FFC's golden era produced the landmark *New Wave* films of Mrinal Sen, Mani Kaul, Kumar Shahani, Adoor Gopalakrishnan—all under her patronage. From playing an important role in the formation of FFSI in 1959, to the formation of the Film Enquiry Committee headed by eminent cultural icon, Dr. Shivarama Karanth remained part of the new film culture of India all her life. She brought in Jean Bhownagary from Paris in 1951 to mount the first India International Film Festival, which opened a new vista of diplomatic missions as a source for the finest films from across the world. The new avenue, which opened up a non-commercial route for getting the best of films from each country, still remains as the biggest source of global films to film society networks.

The Cold War between the West and the Eastern bloc countries ensured that the Indian film society movement benefited from a free supply of films from these countries who were vying to influence Indian minds in the cultural field. The FFSI network had a free supply of such films for the affiliated film societies and could be screened without entertainment taxes.

With the active support of Indira Gandhi and Bhownagary, the head of the Films Division could mentor a new Indian documentary culture in the country, introducing a new genre of independent filmmakers like Sukh Dev and painter M. F. Husain, who went on to make their mark globally.

Indira Gandhi's special interest in the budding film society movement was evident from the word 'go'. When she became a minister, and later prime minister, she deputed Usha Bhagat, her social secretary, as the joint secretary of FFSI, keeping a close eye on the activities of the movement. "As I remember, the Federation had at that time (1961) only nine film societies affiliated to it. The office, consisting of a dilapidated typewriter and a few files, was carried on in a portion of the garage in my house," Bhagat recalled in 1981, in an article in IFSON, the journal of DFS[24].

By sanctioning special film import provisions to FFSI, ensuring entertainment tax, censorship exemptions to the screenings and an annual grant, Nehru and Indira Gandhi patronised the film society movement. The formation of the Federation of Film Societies of India on December 13, 1959, was inspired by Indira Gandhi, with the active support of the government. An ICS officer drafted the memorandum of understanding. Later, in 1960, Nehru's confidant, a former finance secretary and the then chairman of the University Grants Commission (UGC), C.D. Deshmukh, was prompted to form a University Film Council with a former I&B Minister R.R. Diwakar as its Chairman.

Apart from institutional support from the government, both Nehru and Indira Gandhi extended their personal support, whenever the need arose, for the new Indian filmmakers. In 1956, *Pather Panchali*, which is the first product of the Indian film society culture, and directed by the promoter of the first major film society of independent India, ran into controversies over the depiction of poverty; the prime minister stepped in to publicly hail its cinematic treatment of the subject of poverty with its aesthetic qualities.

It appeared that Nehru, who pushed his agenda of a new Indian idiom in films, saw the success of *Pather Panchali* as an endorsement of his views for the new film culture in India. "What is wrong about showing India's poverty? Everyone knows that we are a poor country. The question is: are we Indians sensitive to our poverty or insensitive to it? Ray has shown it (poverty) with an extraordinary sense of beauty and sensitivity," said Nehru about *Pather Panchali*[25].

The personal support and involvement of India Gandhi to new the Indian film culture was total. So much so that MS Sathyu's epic film, *Garam Hawa,* got clearance for public shows from none other than Indira Gandhi, after a preview at the Rashtrapati Bhavan screening hall. The censors in those days had rejected the film which remains a cinematic landmark in depicting the complex India-Pakistan divide and the question of Hindu-Muslim identities in independent India. David Lean's controversial film *Doctor Zhivago* was also cleared by Indira Gandhi with minimum cuts to "safeguard" India's relationship with the then Soviet Union, after a preview.

Combined with the liberal political thoughts of Nehru and the parallel efforts of the Leftist Indian People's Theatre Association (IPTA), the movement towards new films and film appreciation got a further push. The Communist Party of India (CPI) had identified cinema as an important medium for influencing people's thoughts towards their political and social ideologies. They identified K. A. Abbas, who had already written screenplays and was a film critic of long-standing, to make a humane document on the Bengal famine in 1946. Thus, the classic, *Dharti Ke Lal* which was in the neo-realist tradition in a post-war world was made. With his involvement in two path-breaking films in Hindi, *Naya Sansar* (1941) and *Neecha Nagar* (1946), as a screenplay writer, Abbas had made a name for himself. The tri-lingual (Hindi, Urdu and English) writer, Abbas was also among the early film critics arguing for better films since 1935 in his newspaper, *Bombay Chronicle*. Abbas remained a Leftist all his life and is credited with forming the first trade union in the Bombay film industry while promoting a film society, *Film Forum*, with the trade union.

John Wood, author of the book on the art filmmakers of India, said[26]:

> While IPTA transformed ideas of political and social reform into cultural substance, the film societies and the international film festivals allowed would-be filmmakers such as young Ritwik Ghatak and Satyajit Ray, for example, to learn from of masters such as Eisenstein, as well as the best of contemporary foreign directors, especially the Italian neo-realists and all of them were heirs of a quite different tradition of cinema from what had developed in India during the first half-century.

Thereby arrived a confluence of thoughts and subjectivity between the liberals and Leftists which gave a further impetus to the film society movement. The liberals led by Nehru patronised the movement by extending total government support so as to improve the aesthetic content of the films, and the Left saw it as an opportunity to take its agenda forward in the most popular mass medium. This caught the popular imagination of the educated classes, whereby the Leftists and liberals were ruling the political roost. Both Kerala and West Bengal, with their film societies and international film festivals, flourished, bearing testimony to this historic tradition of political patronage till the end of 2010.

### The Impact of Success of *Pather Panchali*

The universal excitement after the inspiring success of *Pather Panchali*, with its many international and national accolades and awards, and the Best Human Document Award at the Cannes Film Festival 1956, and also the Indian President's Gold and Silver Medals in1955, saw the dawn of a new genre of filmmaking in India. A new generation of sensitive and discreet audiences was born. Ray's first film created waves, and its acceptance worldwide captivated the young nation and boosted its sense of cultural pride. The world began to emphasise the birth of this genre of New Indian Cinema, in contrast to the dance-drama shows of the existing popular cinema.

Marie Seton not only added *Pather Panchali* and its director to her list of 'The Art of Five Directors—Film Appreciation,' published by NCERT, but also identified an Indian professor who took upon himself the analysis of *Pather Panchali* as a life-long mission for FTII and other students. For years, the first professor at the Film and Television Institute of India (FTII), Professor Satish Bahadur, lectured and taught film appreciation with *Pather Panchali* as his model film, thus establishing a new paradigm in academic studies on films.

Seton wrote, emphasising the need for serious film appreciation[27]:

> Very few people appreciate the greatest literature or paintings the first time they look at an example. The same is true of films. For almost everyone, an interest in film appreciation commences with their own film sense being

awakened by an exceptional film which produces in them the desire to see more examples.

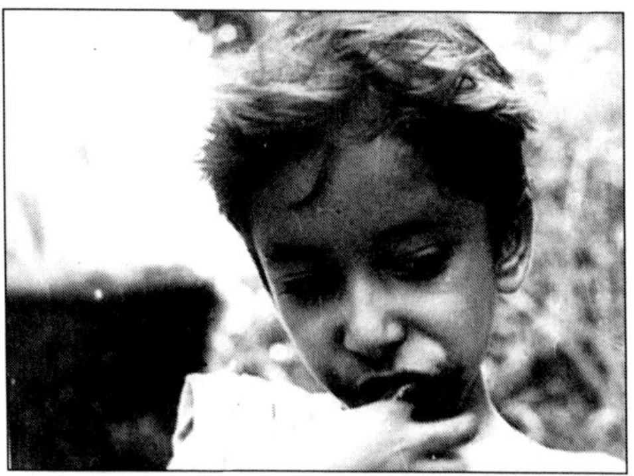

**Figure 2.6.** A still from *Pather Panchali*

In his article titled 'Everything in the film is Significant', in the prestigious British film journal *Sight and Sound* in 1955, Lindsay Anderson wrote, "*Pather Panchali* is a beautiful picture, completely fresh and personal, which required great courage and perseverance to make."

Akira Kurosawa, Ray's contemporary and great filmmaker from Japan, who put his country's films on the world map with his production, *Rashomon*, too, was excited about *Pather Panchali*. "I can never forget the excitement in my mind after seeing it for the first time. I have had several more opportunities to see the film since then and each time I felt more overwhelmed. It is the kind of cinema that flows with the serenity and nobility of a big river," said Kurosawa about Ray's first film.[28]

*Pather Panchali* had awakened India and had taken the world of films to a new height and Indian cultural enthusiasts were eager to join the new realm of new films. "After *Pather Panchali*, Ray often said he had learnt film-making by seeing films. Some of them he saw a dozen times," Chidananda Das Gupta captured the excitement of the times[29].

Meanwhile, word was out that if anyone wishes to make meaningful cinema, or be a connoisseur of such films, the first thing to do is to see as many such films as possible. And the only way out to see such films in the 50s, 60s, 70s and 80s continued to be the film society circuit, unless, of course, one was associated with a film studies organization, which happened to be only one–the FTII. No doubt, film societies increased cinematic and aesthetic awareness with the finest films from across the globe and helped construct a new film idiom and provided tools for open-ended and creative criticism. The new forum, through its programme notes, lectures, workshops and journals, paved the foundations of a new genre of film appreciation and film studies in India.

IFSON's first editor, Anil Srivastava, reflected on the entire period as follows:

> The film society, *Pather Panchali*, and the Nehruvian ethos shaped my being, and I find it difficult to talk about the underlying theme without bias. I believe it is the intersection of these three that contributed to the New Indian Cinema in its various manifestations, whether it was Mrinal Sen's *Bhuvan Shome*, Adoor Gopalakrishnan's *Anantharam*, Girish Kasaravalli's *Ghatashraddha*, Sudhir Mishra's *Hazaaron Khwaishein Aisi*, or, for that matter, the New Indian Cinema manifesto authored by Arun Kaul and Mrinal Sen.

## Formation of Federation of Film Societies of India

By the late 1950s, the country was ready for a movement called the film society, and the world for the new genre of New Indian Cinema. As Marie Seton was about to leave India after her lecture tours on cinema, the secretaries of Calcutta and Bombay film societies met her and discussed how to take the movement forward. She was more than willing to make a note and submit it to the government. That prompted the government to undertake a survey on the film society movement. M.V. Krishnaswamy, Director, Film Division, prepared a document, and Jean Bhownagary made his own suggestions and submitted them to the government. Indira Gandhi sent two of her trusted aides, Pupul Jayakar and Pritish Neogi to Calcutta and Bombay to undertake a fact-finding mission on the state of film societies. The urban spurt of film societies was ready to take off to a wider spread across the country with the blessings of the government of the day.

In her article in the first issue of *The Indian Film Quarterly*, January-March 1957, Marie Seton featured the increasing enthusiasm in the urban centres of India about films like *Pather Panchali*. "The reactions evoked by my illustrated lectures on cinema in Bombay, Delhi, Allahabad, Banares, Patna, Gaya, Calcutta, Madras, Mysore, Bangalore, Hyderabad and Ahmedabad indicate that the time is ripe for the development in India of a film society movement...."

Seton defined the aims of the film society:

> (a) to show the best feature and short film from any country, including its own national production of high merit; (b) to encourage a higher level of film appreciation through the development of discussion; (c) when a society or group of societies is sufficiently developed, for example, the Scottish Federation of Film Societies or the Venice Film Society, to publish a magazine of a critical and informative nature.[31]

Years later, the NFAI, in its circular 'How to Form a Film Society', expanded the objectives to take the initial momentum, that Seton had observed, as a national movement. The objective, as defined by the NFAI, was:

> (a) to enable its members to study the history and art of the film by exhibiting films of cultural, artistic and technical merit, especially those, which, owing to language difficulties or small box-office appeal, are not ordinarily shown commercially; (b) to encourage an intelligent and discriminating attitude towards films; (c) to encourage the production of films of artistic values; (d) to promote research on cinema; (e) to cooperate with national and international organizations having similar objects.

Undoubtedly, Seton's lecture tour series of 1955-56, and the success of *Pather Panchali* in 1955 established film societies as a new arena of cultural activity across the nation.

On December 13, 1959, seven representatives of the existing film societies met at the residence of the secretary of *Sahitya*

*Akademi*, Krishna Kripalani, and adopted a Memorandum of Association (MOA) for FFSI. Needless to say, the active involvement of the government meant that the document was vetted by MD Bhatt, an ICS officer, who was the chairman of the Film Advisory Board of the government of India. The FFSI was registered under the Societies Registration Act XXI of 1860. "*Chidu da* (Das Gupta) had come down from Calcutta and we needed to meet at a central place, and Krishna Kripalani, who had a house close to the city centre, offered to host our meeting," *Akka* (Vijaya Mulay), who was present at the meeting, recalled.[32]

At the time of the adoption of MOA, the FFSI committee of administration had Satyajit Ray as its president. The vice-presidents were Ammu Swaminadhan of the Madras Film Society, Robert E. Hawkins of the Bombay Film Society and S. Gopalan of the Delhi Film Society. The joint secretaries were Vijaya Mulay and Chidananda Das Gupta. The joint treasurers were D. Pramanick and Abdul Hassan. The members of the committee were R. Anantharaman, Rita Roy, K. L. Khandapur, Jag Mohan, A. Rehman and A. Roy Choudhury. The film societies, which signed the FFSI MOA were the Delhi Film Society, Patna Film Society, Roorkee Film Society, Bombay Film Society, Madras Film Society and Calcutta Film Society.

Indira Gandhi, who was the ruling Indian National Congress party's president, was also co-opted as the vice president of FFSI. Vijaya Mulay clearly remembered the historic day of the FFSI's formation:

> I went to Teen Murti house and told Ms. Gandhi that she must become the vice president of FFSI. She asked me who the president was and I told her it was Satyajit Ray. She readily agreed to be the vice president, and remained on the post till she became the I&B Minister of the Lal Bahadur Shastri Cabinet in 1964.

Summing up the role of the FFSI and the film society movement, Mulay said:

> The movement has definitely helped in creating awareness for good cinema and in cultivating a discerning audience for good films at a time when there was no film and

television school to teach film appreciation and discuss films, no Directorate of Film Festivals to showcase good world cinema and hardly any audience for quality films.

Recollecting his association with the historic Agra University Film Club (1960-63) which made him the first professor of Film Appreciation, Professor Satish Bahadur said in a note:

> The most important thing to do was to run the film society as a very 'serious' organisation, by giving it the appearance of being a serious organisation, so that when students came to a film society show, they were not going to any film show, but to see a film which deserved more careful attention.

Clearly, the professor was preparing the new generation for a fresh experience of cinema as an art form.[35]

Indeed, while the film society movement created the wave of New Indian Cinema, almost at the same time, Asian Cinema got noticed across the globe through Japanese masters like Akira Kurosawa whose *Rashomon* put Japanese cinema on the map of great world cinema. In fact, the initial lineup of New Indian Cinema's pioneers like Satyajit Ray, Mrinal Sen, Ritwik Ghatak, K. A. Abbas, Adoor Gopalakrishnan, Pattabhirama Reddy in Bangalore were all products or advocates of the budding film society movement.

Adoor Gopalakrishnan, the second batch (1963) student of FTII, who pioneered the film society movement in Kerala with his *Chitralekha*, recalled those initial days: "The aim of the film society was to spread the culture of the 'new wave' of films, film literature with publications and then produce films."[36]

## The New Wave and Nehruvian Challenge

From Guwahati in the North East, Calcutta (now Kolkata) in the East, Lucknow in the North, to Bombay (now Mumbai) in the West and Trivandrum (now Thiruvananthapuram) down South, the quest for a new Indian cinema culture had taken the shape of film societies. These innovative and creative groups were watching, discussing and debating the best of world cinema with a view to create new, meaningful and brilliant cinema which could reach out to a discerning and serious film audience across the globe. This trend finally gave India a strong presence on the global film map.

With active support and political patronage from the Congress-led government of the day, FFSI grew its tentacles across India. The government had no qualms in opening its Central Film Library with the Ministry of Education to the FFSI network for renting its films for screening. The UGC promoted a University Film Council to spread film clubs in the universities. It allowed FFSI to import films and access foreign films from diplomatic missions in India directly, exempting the FFSI network from entertainment tax and censorship. The period saw the government establishing the Directorate of Film Festivals to organize national and international festivals, the Film and Television Institute of India (FTII), the NFAI and the Film Finance Corporation (FFC) to produce quality films, which the world began to term as 'New Wave' Indian films. But for the active patronage of the government of the day, this would not have been possible. Clearly, the film field had taken the challenge posed by the Nehruvians for a new India, and the film society's movement, flying on the wings of creative excellence, serious film appreciation and innovative and imaginative experiments with the new medium became a national movement.

Within the first three decades, the FFSI had four full-fledged regional offices in the North, East, West and South of the country, situated in Delhi, Calcutta, Mumbai and Madras, and there was a sub-regional office for Kerala at Thiruvananthapuram. The National Council of FFSI has 60 members elected through direct voting by the member societies once every two years. The council further elects a 15-member Central Executive Committee to run the FFSI properly.

"The Federation of Film Societies of India is a body with a statute recognised by the government of India and mostly by all the state governments as well. It has representations in several committees of the government related to cinema," states the website of the IFFS, of which Mrinal Sen and great French filmmaker Francois Truffaut were presidents.[37]

## References


1. Noteshttps://en.wikipedia.org/wiki/Tryst_with_Destiny
2. Chidananda Das Gupta,*The Cinema of Satyajit Ray*(New Delhi: NBT, 2001).
3. Chidananda Das Gupta,*Seeing is Believing*(Viking, 2008).
4. http://vkcherian.blogspot.in/2012/06/mrinal-sen-at-90-riding-wave-of.html
5. https://www.youtube.com/watch?v=QapaT0A-HMc
6. https://cherianwrites.blogspot.com/2020/07/samik-da-on-satyajit-ray.html
7. Interview with Pradipta Sen of CFS.
8. Ibid
9. Ibid.
10. H. N. Narahari Rao, *The Film Society Movement In India*(Mumbai: Asian film Foundation, 2009), p. 27.
11. https://cherianwrites.blogspot.in/2016/02/interview-with-yc-halan-past-president.html
12. https://cherianwrites.blogspot.in/2016/02/a-few-notes-for-book-towards-new-film.html
13. http://cherianwrites.blogspot.in/2016/02/national-heald-clip-film-club-of-bhopal.html
14. Ibid.
15. http://cherianwrites.blogspot.in/2016/02/interview-with-govindaraj.html
16. H. N. Narahari Rao, *The Film Society Movement In India*(Mumbai: Asian film Foundation, 2009), p.103.
17. Interview with Vijaya Mulay.
18. Ibid.
19. http://cherianwrites.blogspot.in/2016/02/interview-with-ms-shyamala-vannarse.html
20. http://cherianwrites.blogspot.in/2016/03/on-fsm-by-anilsrivastava-pioneer-and.html
21. https://en.wikipedia.org/wiki/Marie_Seton
22. http://cherianwrites.blogspot.in/2016/02/interview-with-benegal.html
23. K. A. Abbas, *I am not an Island* (Vikas, 1977), p.370.

24. H. N. Narahari Rao, *The Film Society Movement In India*(Mumbai: Asian film Foundation, 2009),. P. 49.
25. CFS Brochure. *Pather Panchali anniversary*, 2012.
26. John W Wood, *The Essential Mystery*, p. 5.
27. How to commence film appreciation- by Marie Seton, Ministry of Education.1961.
28. Ibid.
29. Chidananda Das Gupta,*The Cinema of Satyajit Ray*(New Delhi: NBT, 2001).
30. http://cherianwrites.blogspot.in/2016/03/on-fsm-by-anilsrivastava-pioneer-and.html
31. http://cherianwrites.blogspot.in/2016/02/marie-seton-from-cfs-published-in.html
32. Interview with Vijaya Mulay
33. Ibid.
34. Annexure 1.MOA FFSI.
35. Ibid.
36. http://cherianwrites.blogspot.in/2016/02/adoorgopalakrishnan-on-film-society.html
37. http://www.ficc.info/

# 3
# Pioneering Leaders of the Film Society Movement

Film Societies sprang up in India's urban centres, thanks to the quest of a few enlightened people to view the world with a big perspective, especially in cinema. They networked among similar groups across India. Besides the entertainment tax and censorship exemptions, the Central Government extended its patronage facilitating the spread of the movement till the 1980s. Just as in Bombay, Calcutta, Patna, Bhopal, Lucknow, Agra and Trivandrum, there were pioneers, mostly English-educated young men and women across India, to inspire their contemporaries and to push these individual clubs to an organised national movement.

Looking back, many like Satyajit Ray, with the formation of the Calcutta Film Society (CFS), and Adoor Gopalakrishnan, with the founding of *Chitralekha* Film Society, literally created an audience for the kind of films they planned to make. Despite being busy filmmakers, they continued to actively promote the film societies in their regions, as they realised that nuanced and critical appreciation of their films came from the members of the film societies. Both Ray and Adoor did succeed in creating such an audience for their films and have become cultural icons of the country, winning several national and international honours.

The contributions of Indira Gandhi, Chidananda Das Gupta, Marie Seton, Vijaya Mulay, K. A. Abbas, P. K. Nair, Professor Satish Bahadur, Jehangir Bhownagary and Anil Srivastava are no less in the creation of new film culture with their individual contributions and interventions in the Film Society Movement.

The exit of the pioneers from their societies saw many of them collapsing like the CFS, *Chitralekha*, Agra Film Society, and even the Jodhpur Film Society, which survived till 2000 when its founder died. Some were revived later, with the support of the pioneers. The CFS was revived and kept alive for its historic role of being the launch pad of pioneers like Ray and Das Gupta and it is still active in Kolkata. Pioneers inspired and created a group of people who took to serious film appreciation and film studies, changing the way films are perceived and made in India.

"Should film appreciation, and filmmaking for that matter, remain perpetually split between the masses and their entertainers on the one hand, and the intelligentsia and their artists on the other?" This was the question posed by many, a fact often articulated by Das Gupta in his writings.[1]

All of them tried to answer the question with their involvement with the Film Society Movement and Das Gupta even theorised the complex relation between the two streams with his concept of *margi* and *desi* in his last book, based on his experience of a lifetime, while settling the initial divides between the two groups once and for all. No history of the movement can be complete without considering the contribution of the pioneers who raised the levels of appreciation, leading to a new film culture in India.

## Satyajit Ray

If there is anyone who can be credited as a true visionary for a New Indian Cinema—with the arrival and resurrection of authentic and meaningful Indian cinema—and its culture and carries the idealism and creativity of the emerging new nation called India, it is one and only Satyajit Ray. Reams have been written about his films, but there is very little available on record, in English, on his role as a founder of CFS and as a lifelong mentor of the Film Society Movement of India. The fact that both Ray and Chidananda Das Gupta, the co-founder of CFS in 1949, and the film society evangelist Marie Seton, were his friends for life, explains yet another side of Ray who remained the lifelong President of the FFSI.

"In the year of India's independence, we formed the first film club in Calcutta, thereby shackling ourselves willingly to the task of disseminating film culture amongst the intelligentsia," Satyajit Ray wrote after about 30 years.[2] In the first two years, Ray admitted, the membership "refused to go above 25". His co-founder, Das Gupta, said that by 1952 the membership had doubled to over 52. Years later, after the success of his first film, Ray said in his Pune Film Institute convocation address: "Remember, the public itself is a species capable of change and evolution through the pressure of circumstances."[3] This, clearly, indicated his lifelong advocacy for new film culture and its acceptance by the people.

**Figure 3.1.** Satyajit Ray at CFS

From being evicted by the landlord for a meeting of film buffs, the Calcutta Film Society, run from a member's house to being honoured by Calcutta University for his first film, Ray travelled a long way to get his vision of films accepted by people. The process of acceptance included a film club, CFS, occasionally writing in local journals, eliciting the support of fellow writers and intelligentsia etc. Professor P.C. Mahalanobis of the Calcutta Statistical Institute, who went on to head the Planning Commission of India, was a mentor of CFS in its glorious days in the 1950s.

Ray is the first auteur filmmaker who put Indian cinema on the world map with his path-breaking film, *Pather Panchali,* in 1955. His passion for good films, a new cinematic idiom for the budding nation, was fuelled not just by the renaissance in Bengali culture or the screenings and discussion in CFS, which he founded with his friends, but also by the exposure to the best of world cinema in London, where he was sent while working as a commercial artist in the British advertisement firm, D. J. Keymer. He reportedly watched 90 films in three months. Films like Italian Vittorio De Sica's neo-realist classic, *Bicycle Thieves*[4], had a lasting impression on him.

Ray's exposure to world classics like the Russian film *Battleship Potemkin* by Sergei Eisenstein[5], and *Nanook of the North* by Robert Flaherty[6] at the Calcutta Film Society, and the 90 films at London, remained the best-ever education for him as a filmmaker. Later, over the years, Ray saw *Battleship* numerous times and so smitten was he by this great Russian film and its director that he told a visiting Eisenstein archive director, just before his death, that he wanted to spend a night in the great filmmaker's flat in Moscow, according to Samik Bandyopadhyay, an art/film critic from Ray's friends' circle.[7]

The cinema of Italian neo-realists[8] filmmakers like Roberto Rossellini, De Sica, and Luchino Visconti's films made a deep impression on the young Ray. "I saw half a dozen Italian films, including *Bicycle Thieves*. It was a tremendous experience," Ray was quoted in his biography penned by Marie Seton.[9] Enriching this experience with films was his exposure to Jean Renoir[10] shooting *The River* in Bengal and the interaction with Russian maestro, Vsevolod Pudovkin,[11] during his visit to Calcutta.

Ray also fired up a great interest in the New Indian Cinema Movement across the country. Narrating his entry into the Film Society Movement, Anil Srivastava, founder of the Lucknow Film Society and the Bhopal International Film Club in 1959, described the excitement of getting *Pather Panchali* to be screened in Bhopal those days. "I found Satyajit Ray's phone number and called him. He must have been flabbergasted by the unexpected call from a school kid asking him to screen the film; he asked the distributor (Aurora) to send a 35 mm print of *Pather Panchali*." Anil was a student of St. Joseph's Convent in Bhopal in 1959.[12]

A bio-sketch of Ray reads as follows:

Satyajit Ray was born on May 2, 1921, in Calcutta, to Sukumar and Suprabha Ray. He graduated from the Ballygunge Government School and studied Economics at Presidency College. He attended Kala Bhavan, the Art School at Tagore's University, Shantiniketan, during 1940-1942. Without completing the five-year course, he returned to Calcutta in 1943 to join the British-owned advertising agency, D. J. Keymer as a visualiser. Within a few years, he rose to be its art director.

In 1948, he married Bijoya Das, a former actress/singer who also happened to be his cousin. Their only offspring, Sandip, was born in 1953. In 1983, Satyajit Ray suffered a massive heart attack. He died on April 23, 1992, in Calcutta after having made some 40 films and documentaries and has numerous books and articles to his credit.[13&14]

The excitement of *Pather Panchali* continued to haunt film academia across the world. Just as *Battleship Potemkin*, Ray's first film is a must-see for any budding Indian filmmaker. The first professor of film appreciation at FTII, Pune, Professor Satish Bahadur, remained a lifelong expert on Ray's first film, as he taught one batch after another with the example of *Pather Panchali*. Such was the professor's passion in analysing *Pather Panchali* that even Ray wondered how the professor derived various levels of meaning from his films, some of which even he, as director, had never imagined.

Such was the excitement about his films and the man himself that when Ray visited Trivandrum in the 1980s for the first time and much to his surprise, there were unending receptions given to him by competing film societies and institutions. Ray had transformed his passion for good films as a young man into a movement through CFS and remained the lifelong guardian angel of India's 'New Cinema', not just with his films, but with his insightful and refreshing writings on films, and patronage to a whole generation of filmmakers.

In his writings, from the early 1940s till his death, one can see his vision of films, especially in two of his books, *Our Films Their Films*[15] and *Deep Focus*.[16] "After every screening of my film at Kolkata, he would call me home and discuss the film in detail and that was an enriching experience," said Adoor, who is considered the worthy heir to Ray's school of filmmaking[17]. Though he had a difference of opinion with the styles adopted by FTII products like Mani Kaul[18] and Kumar Shahani[19], Ray never disowned them. "He always believed the film must have a story to be told to the audience and believed he was best at it," Samik Bandyopadhyay, who saw one of the last communications between Ray and Das Gupta[20], observed.

However, being a busy filmmaker, with almost a film a year, Ray could never devote his time to CFS or the Film Society Movement. He never even previewed any of his films at the flourishing CFS but showed unfinished reels of his film *Devi* at the DFS. "He was busy and totally involved in the production of his films and could not spare time for the Film Society Movement," his son, Sandeep Ray[21] recalled those days from his South Kolkata home. But his intervention was always sought for the movement, whenever necessary.

Akka, on Ray's active guidance of the movement[22], recalled:

> We had an issue with the censoring of foreign films. The embassies would not allow us to censor films. So we went to Ms Gandhi, the then Union I&B Minister, to discuss the issue. She sought a letter from *Manikda* (Ray) and he was ever obliging as the president of FFSI. Ms Gandhi waived off censorship for film society films.

Ironically, the flood of uncensored films to the FFSI circuit attracted 'undesirable' patrons to the Film Society Movement, much to the disdain of the founder of the movement itself.

However, the flourishing Film Society Movement of the 1960s and 1970s relied heavily on the vigorous and ever-active filmmaker—Ray's works—complementing each other, taking 'New Indian Cinema' to new levels. He remained the president of FFSI from its inception in 1959 till his death in 1992.

### Indira Gandhi

It is rare for any prime minister of a country to be featured as one of the pioneers of a Film Society Movement, but the history of the Indian Film Society Movement cannot be written without Indira Gandhi. The fact that she was the official hostess of the first film seminar organised under Jawaharlal Nehru's administration and a personal friend of the Indian Film Society Movement evangelist, Marie Seton, gives a peep into her deep interest in new film culture. Though her association was short-lived with FFSI, her tenure as I&B Minister and Prime Minister witnessed the rise of New Indian Cinema, registering robust growth with FFSI becoming the toast of the urban young in the 1960s and 1970s with government patronage and backing by the public sector Film Finance Corporation, under her ministry, which produced a host of films. No other Prime Minister has ever shown such personal interest in the new film culture of India, leading to the total neglect of the genre of meaningful films. The last film enquiry commission was also in the last tenure of Indira Gandhi, though it was initiated during the days of Morarji Desai as Prime Minister.

**Figure 3.2.** Indira Gandhi with Professor Satish Bahadur at FTII

In her speech at the presentation of the National Awards for Films, on May 25, 1966, Indira Gandhi observed, "Our films seem to be all-pervasive. They are bringing villages and towns closer. In numerous other ways also, films have contributed to fostering a sense of oneness in our country." She went on to say, "A film has the quality of a work of art. It depends on the vision of its creator and on the technical mastery with which he communicates this vision in words or sound or colours or images."[23]

Indira Gandhi as Prime Minister, since 1966, had a clear vision about the directions Indian films need to take to be noticed across the globe, thanks to her early introduction to Marie Seton. In her first monograph, *The Film as an Educational Force in India*, published by the Ministry of Education in 1956, Marie Seton describes an incident involving Gandhi and a party for children. Marie Seton was asked to show films at a children's party Gandhi had organised with her two sons and their friends. That was the time when Marie Seton was touring the country lecturing on films as an educational medium to the academia and screening films of high quality. As a concerned mother, Gandhi was keen that her two sons and their friends appreciated the best of films.[24]

Later, in 1959, FFSI was formed at Gandhi's prodding, after a report by Marie Seton which was vetted by her film advisor, Jean Bhownagary, and cultural aides like Pupul Jayakar, with full government support, ensuring an annual grant from the central government, which continued till 2014.

Indira Gandhi remained a connoisseur of fine arts, including films, all her life. She had no hesitation in personally getting involved to clear good films from the conservative scissors of the film censors of her times. There is one such intervention which saved a landmark and epical film by M.S. Sathyu, *Garam Hawa*, from being abandoned. Gandhi's cousin, a key catalyst in the Film Society Movement, an IPS officer (Retd) Gautam Kaul, said it was her personal intervention which ensured that *Garam Hawa* was not a victim of censorship.

> I got a call from her saying that, 'you are a film society man,' come and see what is so objectionable in *Garam Hawa*. The film was shown in the basement theatre at the Rashtrapati Bhavan, which was the favourite screening place of the PM those days. After the screening, Ms Gandhi looked back and told me, "What is objectionable in this film--maybe the Muslim girl from a noble family romancing on the shores of Yamuna at Agra? That we will be able to handle it...is it not?"

A waiting Sathyu asked Gautam Kaul, as to what her response was. Kaul said, "It is done," ending the long uncertainty over the film's release.[25]

It was widely known that her social secretary, Usha Bhagat's major assignment was to arrange a meaningful film screening for the prime minister. Bhagat was also a secretary at DFS and later joint secretary of the FFSI-North region.

Indira Gandhi also directed the Film Finance Corporation to treat the script of a film along with the copyright as collateral while deciding to finance film production. The directive went after FFC refused to finance the script of *Bhuvan Shome*, which also got the best script award of the corporation in that year's competition. Mrinal Sen, the writer, approached the PM for her intervention. Ms Gandhi seems to have asked the concerned officials as to what the most important ingredient of the film is, to which they replied that it was the script, and, later, the copyright of the film. She directed the officials to treat both as collateral while financing a film. Thus, *Bhuvan Shome* was financed by FFC and is considered the film which re-energised the New Cinema after *Pather Panchali,* bringing in a new generation of FTII-trained filmmakers like Mani Kaul, Kumar Shahani and Adoor Gopalakrishnan into the limelight.

Not just Mrinal Sen, Sathyu or Vijaya Mulay, her contemporary, had lots to share about Indira Gandhi's personal involvement in the success of the movement, be it exempting film society films from censorship, or the import of films for the FFSI network, grants for FFSI functioning, and even trying to save FFC Chairman B.K. Karanjia from Sanjay Gandhi's wrath. Gandhi remained solidly behind the movement, good cinema and its proponents.

So was the strength of a circular initiated by Gandhi as I&B Minister, the *Chitralekha* film co-operative in Thiruvananthapuram benefited from it after four decades in settling the Rs 1.5 million loans from the state government. The circular in the 1960s had advised the State governments to grant space to film societies to build alternate cinema halls in each district. *Chitralekha*, which began its operations in the late 60s, had procured land in the North Kerala town of Thalaserry for such a cinema hall. The appreciated land value ensured that the cooperative could sell it and pay off its debts by 2010.[26]

Even during the turbulent times of the Emergency in the 1970s, when Sanjay Gandhi and I&B Minister V.C. Shukla were forcing FFC Chairman BK Karanjia to quit, Indira Gandhi invited the FFC chairman over tea to hear his version and bargain a compromise. Karanjia described the incident vividly:

> Although I had not met the PM before, I knew her to be a staunch supporter, even before she became the minister for information and broadcasting, of what the Film Finance Corporation stood for and what it was trying to do as a trendsetter and leavening force within the film industry. On one occasion when the Union Finance Minister Morarji Desai had questioned the non-return of some of the loans advanced by the FFC, she had written to him: 'The FFC does not have an investment angle... Even more important is the promotional aspect...' These words became the FFC's credo.

Though she could not save Karanjia from the wrath of V.C. Shukla, who was the 'Goebbels' of a dictatorial Sanjay Gandhi, the former FFC chairman and editor of *Filmfare* magazine gives full credit to Ms. Gandhi for her intervention. "In contrast to Shukla, she was extremely courteous and gracious throughout the interview," the veteran editor recalled in his autobiography.[27]

The International Film Festival of India in 1977 saw India hosting two maestros: Akira Kurosawa and Michelangelo Antonioni. This was during the infamous emergency days.

Indira Gandhi kept her commitment to good films all her life. She was the last to receive Film Enquiry Committees of the government, which led to the altering of many government policies on films. In her speech at the Golden Jubilee celebrations of Indian cinema in 1981, she stressed that "a good film, like any other good art, should be an experience". She pointed out that "Cinema is entertainment. It is no less important an instrument of social change. And I believe that there is no dichotomy between the two."[28]

It was during her tenure that India's film institutions like the FFC, which later became NFDC, the Film Institute of India (FTII), National Film Archive of India (NFAI) and Children's Films Society of India (CFSI) were established. Her unfettered support ensured that the Films Division of India pioneered a documentary film movement in India too.

Whatever be her political legacy in the nation's history, Indira Gandhi remained an ardent connoisseur of good films, who extended political and governmental patronage to the Film Society Movement and initiated policies and institutions to ensure the production and appreciation of meaningful films, thereby giving a new direction to the crass commercial film sector of India. No other prime minister, including her father, Nehru, patronised the new film movement of India in the manner she did.[29]

**Figure 3.3.** Marie Seton speaking at CFS, 1956

## Marie Seton

If anyone can be described as a pioneering evangelist of the Film Society Movement in India and the New India Cinema of the 1950s, 1960s and 1970s, it is the one and only Marie Seton, the chain-smoking, saree-draped, British socialist, film scholar and lifelong *Indophile*. She was not just a film scholar, a family friend of the Nehrus and a coveted guest of Indira Gandhi at Nehru's Teen Murti Bhawan residence, but a true campaigner who ignited activists and film lovers across India, fuelling a new film culture.

Marie's deep relationship with the Nehru-Gandhis and Indian cinema led her to pen down the biography of Nehru and New India's cinema star, Satyajit Ray, apart from Paul Robson, the black American musician, and the pioneer of Soviet films, Sergei Eisenstein.

Marie Seton, with her memorandum to the then government, single-handedly evangelised and transformed the scattered interests in film societies in the urban centres of India into a national movement. Her suggestions for an FFSI were accepted by Indira Gandhi with political and governmental patronage from her father Prime Minister Jawaharlal Nehru in 1959.

Professor Satish Bahadur in an article in *The Hindu*, paying his tribute to Marie Seton's birth centenary in 2010[30], wrote:

> Marie Seton, the renowned film critic from the UK, who played a very important role in promoting the Film Society Movement in India, made her first visit to India in 1955-56 on an invitation from the Audio-Visual Department of the Ministry of Education, Government of India. After her first visit, Marie Seton developed such an attraction for India, she virtually became a citizen of this country, having toured the length and breadth of this vast land and befriended almost everyone she worked with.

Pamela Cullen wrote in the obituary of Marie Seton in *Sight and Sound*[31]:

> Her involvement with India was perhaps one of the most interesting and important facets of her life; an involvement which, although going back almost a hundred years through family connections in the days of the British Raj – of which Marie would have no part– started for her in 1955 when the ministry of education with the British Film Institute asked her to travel all over India lecturing on film appreciation...With her provocative and stimulating

lecturers, she breathed new life into India's flagging film society movement.

Pamela Cullen, the then social secretary of High Commissioner Krishna Menon, said:

> I first met Marie Seton in 1955 when the Indian Ministry of Education, in association with the British Film Institute, commissioned her to lecture on film appreciation at many of India's flourishing film societies... She was known as a very feisty, formidable lady who did not suffer fools gladly...I discovered she was an extraordinary, stimulating, witty person with words and ideas tumbling out of her lips with hardly a pause.[32]

In 1959, soon after the formation of FFSI, responding to an editorial on the Film Society Movement, Marie wrote in the Letters to the Editor column, which appeared on Christmas Day, that the movement was the most satisfying work she had done in many countries. "Of all the work I have done in many countries, the most rewarding has been in India, because the people are so responsive in India," Marie noted while appreciating *The Times of India*'s editorial on the budding Film Society Movement in the late 1950s.[33]

There was no one in those days in the academic field, media and film fraternity who had not heard of or met Marie Seton. Pradipta Sen of the CFS credits her with the revival of the then-defunct CFS in 1956. Adoor Gopalakrishnan remembers her from his days in the FTII in 1962. Kumar Shahani recollects the screening of her version of Eisenstein's film, *Quiva Mexico*, in FTII in the 60s. In Delhi, Vijaya Mulay, Marie's contemporary, fondly remembered the lively chats in her drawing room with her and film society enthusiasts.

Marie was the one who ensured *Pather Panchali* got the full support of the government of India. In the words of Ray himself, "There were some ministers who had taken objection to the film on the ground for being a true picture of unadulterated poverty. According to Ray, "She (Marie) immediately wrote a letter to the ministry praising the film and saying if it came to that it fully deserved to be shown abroad. A few months later, Nehru saw the film."[34]

In 1956, Marie submitted her findings to the government on how to launch the National Adult Literacy Campaign. Of the important recommendations in her report, the need for the establishment of film clubs in urban and semi-urban centres and universities was included so as to quicken the pace of literacy. Her findings were published as a monograph, *Film as an Educational Force in India* by the Ministry of Education in 1956.

Marie, with her proximity to Nehru and Indira Gandhi, was the key figure in the formation of FFSI. Based on her report about the film societies across a few centres, the government encouraged the formation of an all-India association to give it a national footprint. Marie's report was vetted by the I&B ministry and an enquiry by Pupul Jayakar, Gandhi's cultural advisor, led to the registration of FFSI in December 1959. Marie also kept up public interventions for a new film culture through her writings and multi-city lecturers with select film screenings in the 1950s and 1960s. The Ministry of Education, where she was an advisor for adult literacy, published a few of her monographs which included *The Art of Five Directors*, *Film Appreciation, Film as an Art and Film Appreciation.*

To Marie's credit is a monograph of her mentor, V. K. Krishna Menon, who was the High Commissioner in London and instrumental in making her a lifelong *Indophile*. No wonder, she visited the family house *(tharavadu)* of Menon when she was in Kerala as a part of the lecture tour in India. Adoor Gopalakrishnan remembers the incident very clearly. "My colleague at *Chitralekha* Film Cooperative, Bhaskaran Nair, took her to Menon's family house in North Kerala."

According to Professor Satish Bahadur, she was also the advisor to the University Film Council (UFC) which was set up by UGC in 1960. However, the project got stuck in a bureaucratic web and never took off, remaining the biggest missed opportunity for the Film Society Movement in India. Marie, along with Professor Bahadur, flagged off a summer Film Appreciation course at FTII, which was immensely popular among the academia and film buffs across India till 2019.

Despite her failing health, Marie was involved with the production of *Gandhi* by Richard Attenborough and played an important role in the selection of Ben Kingsley who played Gandhi in the film. According to Cullen, Marie was "deeply upset" with the assassination of her friend Indira Gandhi in 1984, the year the government honoured her with the Padma Bhushan for her contribution to the country in its formative years as a free nation. Rajiv Gandhi, who stayed at Marie's home in London as a student, condoled her death stating that "...she was a fine friend who reached out to people, effortlessly crossing the generation gap and any kind of cultural barrier."

Later, Marie's estate was handled by Cullen, says Vijaya Mulay, her friend and fellow film society activist. On her death, she was cremated, on her own wish, and the plaque in Golders Green Crematorium reads: Marie Seton Hesson, *Padma Bhushan*, and Citizen of the World. (35)

**Figure 3.4.** Chidananda Das Gupta

## Chidananda Das Gupta

Chidu *da*, as Chidananda Das Gupta was fondly called by friends and admirers, was unquestionably the brain trust of the Film Society Movement. Five years after the formation of FFSI, one of its secretaries, Das Gupta wrote in an article "By screening, discussing, reading, and writing about good cinema all over the world, they create a higher level of artistic taste and thus build up a better and bigger audience for good films within the country."[36]

By 1983, analysing the growth of two decades of the movement, Das Gupta listed a few survival models, as the movement had reached its peak by then and had become the toast of many urban centres in India. "If they—film societies—are to survive, the film societies must therefore turn more to the development of Film Culture on a large scale and provide a stable nucleus for products of the New Cinema in India," the veteran said, noting that the movement was already losing its steam of the 1960s and 1970s.[37]

Born in 1921, veteran film critic and historian Chidananda Das Gupta, wrote over 2,000 articles on cinema in various periodicals. Das Gupta along with Ray started the *Indian Film Quarterly* in 1957, and he was also one of the prime movers behind the formation of the FFSI in 1959.

Das Gupta is also known for his essays and translations of the works of Rabindranath Tagore, Manik Bandyopadhyay and Jibananda Das. It was Das Gupta who rendered the English translation of the famous Bengali poem, *Banalata Sen*, composed by Jibananda Das.[38]

The year 1947 saw the beginning of a new dawn as Das Gupta, along with Satyajit Ray and Hari Sadhan Gupta, founded the CFS. The forming of CFS had a lasting impact on Ray, as well as others like Mrinal Sen and Ritwik Ghatak, as they were all gifted with an opportunity to view the best of world cinema. Both Ray and Das Gupta began to write about the need for a new film culture in Calcutta newspapers, which was dismissed by film critics and the film industry.

Das Gupta, in one of his video interviews, recalled:

> Surprisingly, within a few years, things began to change, some of the film critics began to use the words which we were using...and take a different kind of angle, particularly this happened after *Pather Panchali* of course.[39]

The stalwarts such as Das Gupta, Ray, Robert E. Hawkins, Mulay, Ammu Swaminadhan, Diptendu Pramanick, Abul Hassan and A. Roychowdury were the pioneers responsible for the formation of the FFSI. Das Gupta wrote in the *Film Quarterly* of UCLA, "Indian cinema faces the eighties, indeed the twenty-first century, with a confidence few countries can equal. As a mass medium as well as an art, it is on a continuous upswing."[40]

With his last book, *Seeing Believing,* and his theories of *Margi* (classic) and *Desi* (Popular), Das Gupta emerged as the last word in film analysis and theories of his generation of film writers. What he and Ray began as part of the new film culture had caught on, affecting all genres of filmmaking and a generation of film writers and film society activists, taking Indian films to the global stages, from the Oscar awards to prestigious international film festivals of the globe.

Das Gupta made a few feature and documentary films as well. He directed seven films, and though not celebrated as his contemporary, Ray, he has his unique place in Bengali cinema. His contributions to *Sight and Sound,* a British film magazine, and *Film Quarterly* of UCLA, have permanent archival value. He also wrote a book on Ray in 1980, *The Cinema of Satyajit Ray*, considered one of the most authentic studies of Ray's work, though their friendship became cold after his critique of Ray's second film, *Aparajito*. His body of work as a film writer and filmmaker had a deep influence on his daughter, eminent actor and filmmaker, Aparna Sen.

The year 2004 was a glorious one for Das Gupta as he was honoured with a Lifetime Achievement Award at the Osian Film Festival for his writings on cinema. He passed away on May 22, 2011, in Kolkata, succumbing to bronchopneumonia brought on by Parkinson's disease. He will always be remembered as a leading Bengali filmmaker, critic, film historian, and, above all, the 'brain' behind the Film Society Movement in India.

Marking his birth centenary, the Chidananda Das Gupta Memorial Trust was formed in 2021 by his family, friends and admirers. The Trust not only pays tribute to the person whose name the Trust bears, but also encourages debut filmmakers and practitioners of critical writings on cinema for their significant contributions in promoting meaningful cinema in India. It gives an annual award for best debut film, best writing on cinema, best costume design and conducts an annual lecture at Kolkata.[41]

### Vijaya Mulay

*Akka*, as Vijaya Mulay is known to film enthusiasts across India, was the head of the jury of writing on films in the 2012

National Film Festival of India. In her address at an award function at the Vigyan Bhavan in Delhi, unlike the other jury heads, she blasted the festival directorate. The reason, according to her, was that they have not yet differentiated between blog-writing and traditional writing in journals, forcing the jury to go through thousands of articles to select one article for the award. She ended her speech with a piece of advice, that it was time the festival directorate woke up to new media realities and sorted out this confusion, much to the surprise of the audience, which included the President of India.

That is *Akk*a for you, rebellious even in her 90s, frank and straight to the point, and wanting to reform the sectors she strongly believed in. For the Film Society Movement, she has been as important as Marie Seton, rather, she is the Indian Marie. *Akka* worked with Marie Seton to ensure the formation of the Patna Film Society, DFS and FFSI. She was instrumental in the spread of the movement as a Ministry of Education officer in the 1950s and 1960s, in the Film Censor Board, in UGC, and in SITE, the first Indian Satellite TV experiment.

**Figure 3.5.** Vijaya Mulay

Along with Ray and Chidu *da, Akka* in Delhi paved the red carpet of the government ensuring full patronage to the budding Film Society Movement from the word go. From the formation of two pioneering societies, in Delhi and Patna, to the formation of FFSI and all important landmarks of the movement, there is nothing which does not have her imprint. After Ray's death, she was also a one-time president of FFSI and earlier, vice-president of FFSI, northern region.

*Akka* recalled her initial days with film societies[42]:

> On my return (from UK-Leeds University) to Patna in 1949, I actively participated in the nascent Film Society Movement of India. Film societies were the only institutions where cinema different from the commercial run-of-the-mill kind could be seen; some of us, therefore, started the Patna Film Society. When I was appointed as the Education Officer to the Ministry of Education and moved to Delhi in 1954, I found more like-minded people to start the Delhi Film Society. Later, when eight film societies came together to form the FFSI, with Ray as its founding president, Das Gupta, the well-known film critic and founder member of the Calcutta Film Society, and I, were elected as the first joint secretaries.

In my first sitting with her at her South Delhi residence, she asked me to base my research for the book on the Film Society Movement in India.[43] She said there is a book on the official history of FFSI and asked me to unearth it. Cheerful, energetic and with a sharp memory, she shared snippets of the golden days of the movement and the friendly assemblies of people, including Marie Seton, at her house. "We were all building the new India and never thought our efforts would lead to a movement or new genre of films. But we did our part," *Akka* told me during the many long sittings I had with her before her death.

*Akka*'s insightful recollections about the period, its history and growth, lead one to the correct perspectives. Indeed, it was a deeply patriotic and visionary act of a generation which was involved in the nation-building of a young republic. The movement for her and her friends was a search for new Indian idioms in Indian films, from the British Raj legacy of the mythological and melodramas.

At Leeds University, she was initiated to the emerging medium called cinema and its possibilities in the 1940s.

She told an interviewer:

> On post-war cinema in the UK–The Workers' Unity Theatre played to full houses. Films from the Soviet Union and Eastern Europe ran often. I saw film classics, experimental films, and socialist cinema. I also gained a better perspective and understanding of cinematic art by joining the university film society. Film viewing, once a casual pastime, became my serious passion. she told an interviewer.[44]

She had returned to Patna, in 1949, where she went to work actively in the local film society. However, in 1954, Mulay shifted to New Delhi as she was appointed Education Officer. It was her love for cinema which made her stick to her passion, and, eventually, in 1959 she was instrumental in the formation of the DFS.

Vijaya Mulay's childhood was no bed of roses, as her father died early, and her mother brought up the kids with great difficulty and hard work. "*Akka*'s school friend was Ahilya Rangnekar (Randive) sister of communist leader BT Randive. This was *Akka*'s initiation into left-wing politics that lasted a lifetime, even though she stopped being a card-carrying member of the CPI after the Soviet Army overran Hungary in 1956.

"In Thane, the communists held *Prabhat Pheri* (morning street demonstrations) against British rule. They sang anti-British songs lustily on the streets; we children learnt many of these songs from *Akka*," her eldest daughter, Shree Mulay, wrote in her obituary.

> The Federation of Film Societies of India with Satyajit Ray as its president and *Akka* and Chidananda Dasgupta as its secretaries; I will not talk about this except to say that our home in Kaka Nagar was the Delhi headquarters of the FFSI. Many international film festivals were organised around the dining table. *Akka* had a ready supply of ushers amongst her three daughters and their friends. I shudder at the thought of the fire hazard the films posed while they were stored under my bed because there was no place to store them.

Tom Waugh, professor emeritus in Cinema at Concordia University, wrote in the foreword of the book, *From Rajahs and Yogis to Gandhi and Beyond:* "*Akka* put me in touch with a vibrant network of filmmakers from Kolkata to Thiruvananthapuram. Everywhere, these committed visionaries greeted me with open arms as soon as I mentioned *Akka*; they shared their work and ideas about the future of activist documentaries in India."[45]

*Akka* also played an important role in the formation of the University Film Club, the Film Censor Board, and India's first satellite Television Project SITE. She made a few documentaries as well. *Tidal Bore* was one of them, in which Satyajit Ray gave voice and was shown at the Mannheim Short Film Festival. Her short, brilliant film, *Ek Anek Aur Ekta*, made for kids in 1974, became so popular that it became a hot favourite on India's national television—Doordarshan—which telecast the film repeatedly. In 2002, she was given the Lifetime Achievement Award, at the Mumbai International Film Festival.

### Khwaja Ahmad Abbas

K. A. Abbas (Khwaja Ahmad Abbas) may be best known as the director who introduced Amitabh Bachchan, the iconic Hindi film star, to Indian films, or as the scriptwriter of filmmaker Raj Kapoor in popular Bombay film history, but his body of work in the films is much more serious and deeper than merely the popular genre. As a member of the Indian People's Theatre Association (IPTA), promoted by the Communist Party of India, Abbas was active in the film field as a film critic from the late 1930s and directed *Dharti Ke Lal* during the British Raj itself. He was one of the key figures behind the film society, Film Forum, in Bombay, along with fellow journalist and scriptwriter, VP Sathe, filmmaker Basu Chatterjee, Bikram Singh, the film critic, and Arun Kaul, who co-produced Mrinal Sen's *Bhuvan Shome*. *Film Forum* was a film society of film technicians and trade union members, unlike other thriving societies which were either too elitist or too star-stuck, arranging receptions for film stars in Bombay, etc.

**Figure 3.6.** Khwaja Ahmed Abbas

"Our industry is suffering from certain handicaps to general development and I said we need all-round general development and progress to have those handicaps removed," Abbas said at the first government seminar on a policy on films in 1955.[46]

He had also bitterly complained about the lack of cinema halls for Indian films and the domination of English films in the movie halls of Mumbai and other cities, calling for an Indian resurgence of cinema at the 1955 seminar. As a politically left-oriented cultural ideologue, Abbas was an active member of the IPTA, had directed a few films and had even organised the film technicians of Bombay under a trade union by 1955. He was also the first president of the *Film Forum*, established in 1965 with film trade unions and others like the first film society of India, the Bombay Film Society, which merged with the new powerful film society of the film city. They became Bombay's connection with FFSI as one of the largest film societies in India and had 2,500 members at one point of time. Filmmaker Govind Nihalani was a member of the *Film Forum*, as was Khalid Mohammed, who went on to become a film critic and a filmmaker. Film Forum was the most active film society showing up to seven films a month till the 1980s. Amol Palekar, the filmmaker/actor, too, was groomed at the *Film Forum*. Arun Kaul, along with Mrinal

Sen, was instrumental in the production of *Bhuvan Shome*. They also came out with a New Indian Cinema Manifesto.

Born on June 7, 1914, Abbas was a noted director, novelist, screenwriter and journalist in three languages: Urdu, Hindi and English. Abbas was born in Panipat, in the British province of Punjab, and in the home of Altaf Hussain Ali, a student of the great Urdu poet Mirza Galib. His grandfather, Khwaja Gulam Abbas, was one of the well-known rebels of the 1857 Mutiny against the British, and the first martyr of Panipat to be executed by cannon fire. Abbas's father, Ghulam-Us-Sibtain, graduated from the Aligarh Muslim University; he was a tutor to a prince and businessman who modernised Unani medicine. Abbas's mother, Masroor Khatoon, was the daughter of Sajjad Husain, an educator.[47]

Abbas made many popular and acclaimed Hindi films like *Saat Hindustani* (1969) and *Do Boond Pani* (1972), both of which bagged the National Film Award for Best Feature Film on National Integration. His movies, *Pardesi* (1957) and *Shehar Aur Sapna* (1963) were nominated at the Cannes Film Festival; the last film won the National Film Award for Best Feature Film. Abbas is considered as the harbinger of neo-realist cinema as he not only penned films catering to the parallel cinema, but he also initiated this genre of films in India within a realm of pre-Independence production. *Dharti Ke Lal* made in 1945, was produced by IPTA, the cultural organisation of CPI. He went on to establish his film production company in 1951, Naya Sansar, which consistently produced films with social and contemporary relevance, such as *Anhonee, Munna, Rahi* (1953), *Shehar Aur Sapna*(1964), *Saat Hindustani* (1969). etc.

Abbas was a prolific writer and novelist. During his illustrious career, he wrote 73 books in English, Hindi, and Urdu. His best-known work, *Inquilab*, was based on communal violence which made him a leading light among the writers of his generation. Many of his works have been translated into Russian, Italian, German, French and Arabic. He also wrote the script for many Raj Kapoor films, including *Awaara, Shri 420, Henna* and the most famous of them, *Mera Naam Joker.*

Abbas will always be known as one of the greatest producers, directors, scriptwriters and journalists of international repute. As an IPTA activist, his support for the Film Society Movement will remain etched in golden letters, as he, with the *Film Forum*, brought the Bombay film trade unions to the fold of better cinema. *Film Forum* will be part of Indian film history for contributing a few good directors like Basu Chatterjee, Basu Bhattacharya, Govind Nihalani and a host of film writers like Khalid Mohammed, who later became a filmmaker, and Bikram Singh.

**Figure 3.7.** Ammu Swaminadhan

### Ammu Swaminadhan

Ammu Swaminadhan was a freedom fighter and a Member of Parliament from the Indian National Congress, hailing from Tamil Nadu. I came across her name while searching for the origins of the Madras Film Society (MFS). She was the patron of the society carrying the Film Society Movement to the South of Vindhyas and the first vice-president of FFSI, along with Indira Gandhi.

"The MFS was formed on October 30, 1957. Ammu Swaminadhan, the mother of Advocate General Govind

Swaminadhan, was the founder president of the society," said AG Raghupathy, a founding member of FFSI and general secretary of MFS.[48]

Ammu's name came up during my research when I was trying to find out more details of the Kerala film societies. Everyone was talking about a Malayalee lady with a sweet name, Ammu Swaminadhan. Later, I was in for a big surprise when I found out that Ms Swaminathan was the mother of the famous danseuse, Mrinalini Sarabhai, and the legendary freedom fighter of the Indian National Army led by Subash Chandra Bose, Captain Laxmi Sehgal. She was also the maternal grandmother of the much-admired danseuse and social activist, Malika Sarabhai and Suhasini Ali, a trade unionist, and a politburo member of the Communist Party of India (Marxist)—CPI(M).

"My mother (Kamala Sharada Prasad) says Ammu Swaminadhan was extraordinarily beautiful and vivacious. She was later to become a member of the Constituent Assembly and the Rajya Sabha," recounted Ravi Prasad, an IITian. Kamala was in the legal team which prosecuted Gandhiji's assassin, Nathuram Godse, and was the wife of Sharada Prasad, who served as Indira Gandhi's long-time Information Advisor.

Ammu Swaminadhan belonged to a Nair family from Palghat, a northern border town between Kerala and Tamil Nadu, then part of the Madras Presidency. She was married to a Tamil Brahmin, Swaminadhan, a leading lawyer, who inherited the family's legacy of promoting young, intelligent men in education. After her marriage, Ammu went to Madras with her husband, where he made a successful career in law.

She took an active part in India's struggle for freedom and became a close disciple of Mahatma Gandhi. Her political entry was during the 1942 Quit India Movement, when, along with Manjulakshmi, Kuttimalu Ammal and others, she joined the non-violent struggle. She was arrested and sent to Vellore Jail with a sentence of two years.

She was elected Member of Parliament in 1952 and was associated with many cultural and social organisations. She went to Ethiopia, China, USA and USSR as a goodwill ambassador.

She was also selected as the 'Mother of the Year' in 1975, on the inauguration of International Women's Year.[49]

### Anil Srivastava

Evangelist is a term often used in IT technology, which I am sure, has roots in the Christian belt of the United States. In the field of technology, evangelists illustrate innovations by promoting an idea or a product to garner market attention. Much before such terms occupied the public narrative in India, Anil Srivastava, one of the founders of NASSCOM, India's IT industry body, can truly be described as an evangelist of the Film Society Movement. He organised film societies as a student in Bhopal and Lucknow and went on to edit the film society's journal, *IFSON*, while still in his 20s. He even got Prime Minister Nehru to visit his film club at Bhopal and said he stayed at Teen Murti Bhavan on one occasion, the official residence of the prime minister, as a guest of Marie Seton.

**Figure 3.8.** Anil Srivastava

My interview with Gautam Kaul, former president of FFSI and Anil's film society mate at Lucknow in the 1960s, enlightened me about Anil's role as a dynamic and committed film society activist. After re-establishing contact, I sent him a questionnaire on his involvement with the movement, as I had heard about him from other pioneering leaders of the movement, P. K. Nair and Vijaya Mulay. Let me give Anil's own version of his initial involvement with his first love as a lifelong evangelist of the new phenomenon, in his own words:

My involvement with the Film Society Movement started with the International Film Club in high school (St. Josephs' Convent, Bhopal) in 1959. The father of two of my classmates, Saleem and Parvez Romani, had a used Bell & Howell 16 mm film projector. We used this and started showing films and started a film society on 4 August, 1959. We began with 16 mm film distributors like MGM, Columbia and NEIF Film Club. Tagore's birth centennial (1961) was coming up and from the newspapers we learnt about Satyajit Ray and his *Teen Kanya* based on Tagore's stories and a documentary on Tagore.

Jaya Bhaduri was a couple of years junior, and her father, writer, journalist, and stage artist, Taroon Bhaduri, was a well-known personality in Bhopal and respected for his writings on dacoits of the Chambal Valley. Tapan Sinha was coming to Bhopal to shoot *Kshudita Pashan* (The Hungry Stone). If I remember correctly, Taroon Bhaduri was the host (or had something to do with Tapan Sinha's film) and that is when the idea of getting Satyajit Ray's film for screening in Bhopal was born.

Prime Minister Jawaharlal Nehru was coming to visit Bhopal. So, we decided to write to '*Chacha* Nehru' telling him about the International Film Club and the wonderful work we were doing and asked him to gift us a film projector.

Marie Seton, as I learnt later, was Nehru's house guest at Teen Murti Bhawan in Delhi. Nehru passed on our letter to Marie. We were surprised by a long letter from Marie Seton telling us about the Film Society Movement in the UK; Vijaya Mulay and the film societies in Bombay, Calcutta, and Delhi; and the formation of the Federation of Film Societies of India (1959).

This was the beginning of a long correspondence over the years. I have always marvelled at Marie's dedication to the Film Society Movement and her effort to bring together everyone she got to know, from Indira Gandhi and Satyajit Ray, at one end, to a kid like me, who just happened to share her interests in film.

> In the course of my correspondence with Marie, I had mentioned to her about the film we were working on. We called it, *Together We Learn*. She promptly responded with the information about the *News Chronicle* in London about a competition on films made by children, suggesting that we should enter the competition, which we did...
>
> Marie's letters were amazing; they were usually several pages long and full of news, ideas and connecting to interesting people with similar interests. Her letters talked about the film festivals that FFSI was planning; films she was getting for the private screening of Prime Minister Nehru; NIAVE (National Institute of Audio-Visual Education) of NCERT (National Council for Educational Research and Training), where she was helping with the Central Film Library and had written a couple of monographs on film study; and the wonderful man, Satish Bahadur, at Agra University, whom I must meet.
>
> For me, in faraway Bhopal, Marie's letters were my window to the wondrous world of cinema. Each letter was like a tutorial telling me about all the wonderful people and films, and, in between, she talked of contemporary India—Nehru, Indu (Indira Gandhi) and Krishna Menon.
>
> I had finished my High School. My father's two-year posting in Bhopal was coming to an end. We were going back to Lucknow. I told Marie I was very unhappy about having to leave Bhopal. She told me about Professor Kailash Nath Kaul, director of the National Botanical Garden (now it is called National Botanical Research Institute) and suggested that I should meet him about starting a film society in Lucknow.[50]

From then onwards, life was mostly about films and new technologies for Anil. Marie, the film society evangelist at the national level, found a child prodigy 'evangelist' in Anil. She, in turn, brought this to the notice of Vijaya Mulay, Chidananda Das Gupta and Satyajit Ray. Anil's involvement with the movement led to his co-founding the Lucknow Film Society. Later, he worked in close collaboration with Professor Satish Bahadur and P. K.

Nair at the FTII and the National Film Archive of India. He edited *IFSON*(Indian Film Society News); Satyajit Ray's issue of *Montage*; and *Movement* published by *Suchitra* Film Society, Bangalore.

Anil's interest in cinema has continued through his work with the Centre for Development of Instructional Technology (CENDIT), with two other film society founders of Delhi—Celluloid—to promote video as a popular technology. He led a National Film Heritage Programme, building the Indian film collection at the US Library of Congress. He collaborated with Richard Leacock on the use of 8mm film for broadcasting. He later served as UNESCO's technical advisor at the FTII, working on the use of small-band film and video for broadcasting.

He co-authored with Shampa Banerji, his wife (who acted in that wonderful role as little Durga in *Pather Panchali*), the book, *One Hundred Indian Feature Films: An Annotated Filmography.* He led the team which included P. K. Nair to create FIAF guidelines for the cataloguing of films and allied material in the film archives, using computers.

Anil Srivastava, who is settled in the USA, wrote in 2017, in a note on the movement[51]:

> Earlier, this year, I was invited to watch the re-release of the digitally mastered *Pather Panchali* on the 60th anniversary of its world premiere at the Museum of Modern Art (MOMA) in New York. I sat in the darkness, wiping my tears and reliving my viewing of the film in Bhopal. My involvement in the film society brought me to *Pather Panchali* and that was the beginning of a life-long journey of learning to be a human being and not just another animal walking on two legs.

### Professor Satish Bahadur

If someone can truly be called the *guru* of 'film appreciation' in India, it definitely is Satish Bahadur. He was not just the first academician to become a professor of film appreciation in the FTII, Pune, in 1962, but he was a lifelong promoter of the academic study of film and its appreciation as a serious subject when star-gazing of celebrity film stars was the norm of the day. With the one-month-long rigorous course at FTII, along with the National Film Archive from 1967 till his death in 2010, he nurtured academicians and film buffs across the country, making them connoisseurs of good cinema.

**Figure 3.9.** Professor Satish Bahadur

"Nothing in the film is accidental. Everything that you experience is 'put there' by the makers of the film," were his often-repeated words, recalls one of his students, Arun Khopikar. Recounting his days in the classroom presided over by Bahadur, Arun wrote:

> Bahadur *saab* made us understand how a film is 'made'. To concentrate on that, we needed to be denied the pleasure of sitting and staring hypnotised at the screen. Like a mother who applies bitter medicine to her breasts for weaning, Bahadur *saab* used cruel methods to shake us up from the somnambulist state of a film spectator. Sometimes, he would tell you the story of a film before he showed it, ruthlessly killing the pleasures of anticipation and surprise. At other times, he would project the film in half-lights and comment with his pointer at its compositional highlights. Occasionally, the film would be projected without sound and sometimes only the soundtrack was kept on for to you to analyse it.[52]

Professor Bahadur defined film appreciation as film criticism.

> A filmmaker makes a film. A spectator receives the film. These are two segments of the communications process. The critic is also a spectator but of a special kind. What a critic does has a special significance for the lay spectator and for the filmmaker, as well as for the development of the art of the film.[53]

Professor Bahadur began his career as a lecturer in economics at DAV College, Kanpur, and then shifted to St. John's College, Agra, where he founded the first university film club in India. The Agra Film Club was one of the early film clubs of India and Bahadur was its secretary. As an academician, he encouraged discussions on a film after every screening and this led to further discussions on the film from various angles. This caught the attention of Marie Seton, the British film expert, who evangelised film appreciation in the late 1950s in India.

When FTII began its operations in 1961, Professor Bahadur was persuaded by Marie Seton to join them as a professor of film appreciation, and he remained there until he retired in 1983. His close associates in the field were Vijaya Mulay and P. K. Nair, who later became the curator of the Film Archive. "Prof Bahadur remains the initiator of serious film appreciation in the country," said Adoor Gopalakrishnan, his student from the second batch of FTII.[54]

"Satish was not only the lifeblood of film appreciation, he greatly contributed to the development of filmmakers like Adoor who led the new cinema movement," says Anil Srivastava, who worked with the professor to bring out the first journal of FFSI, *IFON*.[55]

It was under him that the one-month-long film appreciation summer residencies were conducted at the FTII, along with the Film Archive. From 1967 onwards, the summer residency had been an annual feature at Pune, attracting film buffs from all shades of the academic fraternity and the Film Society Movement.

Professor Bahadur wrote about his pedagogy, as far as film appreciation is concerned, as follows:

> I have shaped myself through my conscious decision of using the classroom as a space for live interaction with

> young minds. My entire being as teacher depends on the obvious fact that I am face to face with live, young persons who are hoping to learn from what I do in the classroom. This unrelenting practice over the years has built in my system a natural respect for young students who are willing to learn. Such teaching-learning interaction in the classroom builds up confidence in a student, so that he can go beyond the mere understanding of the subject and discover his own path to learn more and more.

Over the years, the one-month residency had spread to other centres on a yearly basis. Many of the institutions and film societies have been hosting film appreciation courses of a shorter duration in various cities of India. Comparing films and literature, Bahadur insisted that there is no film culture without film criticism, just as there is no literature without literary criticism. He noted in his *Notes on Film Criticism*, "Literary Culture is not merely Literature. It is Literature plus Literary Criticism. It is Criticism which completes the communication process and makes Literature a social entity. Likewise, Film Culture is not merely films. It is Films plus Film Criticism."[56]

The Moradabad-born professor wrote extensively on the aesthetics of cinema, but he is best known for his analysis of Satyajit Ray's films. His last writing was the textual analysis of the *Apu Trilogy*. He wrote and taught Ray's early films with such critical consistency, that even Ray was quoted as wondering how critics find meanings in films which sometimes even the filmmakers have never thought of!

Though he taught for about four decades, he did not bother to write a book and his writings remain scattered. Shyamala Vanarse, his long-time associate, remarked:

> He loved to lecture and discuss films, but he was almost averse to writing. The only book he saw through was posthumously published, *A Textual Analysis of Apu Trilogy*. He wrote his lectures for AIR and wrote papers for seminars, but never really bothered about getting them into print... and his hands were full with lecture tours, courses, and routine teaching at the institute. Many people had urged him, but he would just freely pass on his notes.[57]

Professor Satish Bahadur continued serious academic work on films which Marie Seton and Chidananda Das Gupta initiated. He became the first Indian professor of film studies, making a lasting impression not just on his students, but on film buffs across India. The annual film appreciation workshop of FTII became a cornerstone of film studies for the movement.[58]

**P. K. Nair**

The founder-director of the NFAI, Parameswaran Krishnan (P. K.) Nair, retired in 1991 and chose to live in Pune, not in his Laurie Baker-designed house in his native place, Thiruvananthapuram, Kerala. Despite difficulties in moving around after a road accident, Nair *saab* (*Sir,* as he is popularly called), was involved with NFAI till his death, just as he had been from 1961 when he joined FTII as a research assistant. The reason is simple. His life is all about films and their preservation for the future. For him, the preservation of this new cultural medium and its true appreciation, and the development of a discerning audience was the mission of his life and he carried it even after his retirement.

**Figure 3.10.** P. K. Nair

Nair *saab*'s life itself is a testimony to the emergence of a new and original Indian film culture. Under his leadership, a world-class film archive was created that stores Indian films, from the first film of the country to the latest, for their historical value. "In Pune, between the Film Institute and National Film Archive, only two of them (P. K. Nair and Satish Bahadur) had complete knowledge and a definite idea about films as a cultural product. Others were mostly specialists in their fields," said Anil Srivastava, who was associated with them from the early 1960s. Indeed, he is credited with spotting *Raja Harishchandra*, the first Indian film by Dadasaheb Phalke, bought it and restored the film to be shown across India, preserving it for the future.

Together, Nair *saab* and Professor Bahadur built not just a repository of films, but systems, institutions and people for a new film culture over the years, which the filmmakers and even the film institutions are dependent upon now. This fact is best explained by an incident involving Mrinal Sen. A few years ago, Sen was invited to a retrospective of his films in early 2000 by the prestigious Cannes International Film Festival, and, to his horror, it was found that most of the prints of his films were not in a good condition. As a Member of the Parliament, he was wondering how he could go ahead. "Prime Minister Manmohan Singh heard about my plight and sanctioned funds to restore and digitise all his films through NFAI," Mrinal Sen said, recounting the historic service which NFAI has now undertaken.[59] The incident led to a massive digitisation programme involving NFAI, converting all films from analogue celluloid to digital format under the National Film Heritage Programme.

As for the film societies across the country, NFAI and P. K. Nair were the prime sources of film classics from across the world. One of my early surprises in the *Chitralekha* Film Society during the 1976-79 period was watching Ingmar Bergman's films, *Wild Strawberries, The Seventh Seal* and *Silence*; the three black and white films remain etched in my mind even today. Little did I know that it was an NFAI package which was put together by P. K. Nair for the film societies! Along with the archiving of films, Nair *saab* took upon himself the responsibility to fill the growing appetite for good films from the international circuit, other than from Hollywood, that too among the film societies across India.

Since he could preserve dance maestro, Uday Shanker's 1944 film *Kalpana*, we in *Chitralekha* could see that too. In fact, Nair *saab* had developed NFAI into an alternate film circuit source to the then popular Eastern Bloc and other diplomatic missions of various countries.

Looking back, it is now evident that Nair *saab* introduced international filmmakers like Ingmar Bergman, Akira Kurosawa, Andrzej Wajda, Miklós Jancsó, Krzysztof Zanussi, Vittorio De Sica and Federico Fellini to the film society circuit. The NFAI screenings at FTII, Pune, in the 1970s and 1980s, and the annual summer film appreciation course, were big events for film society enthusiasts and other film buffs.

By the 1980s, films of Indian stalwarts like Satyajit Ray, Ritwik Ghatak, Mrinal Sen, V. Shantaram, Raj Kapoor, and Guru Dutt were made available to FTII students, film society members, and other film study groups through the precious NFAI film library.

By the turn of the 1990s, the NFAI had spread its screening and study centres to Mumbai, Kolkata, Bangalore and Thiruvananthapuram, catering to the increasing space for good international and regional films. By 2023, all these centres developed an annual International Film Festival of their own, catering to the appetite for the latest and acclaimed films across the world. Apart from establishing a film circuit, NFAI under Nair *saab*, advised and helped establish film societies across India with the required paperwork and advisories. When the government tried to establish film clubs in universities, the UGC was asked to coordinate with NFAI.

Nair *saab* is often described as Henri Langlois of India, considering his dedicated life for archiving films in India. Henri Langlois was a French film archivist and cinephile. A pioneer of film preservation, Langlois was an influential figure in the history of cinema as the pioneer behind the *Cinematheque* of Paris. *Celluloid Man*, a 2012 documentary film directed by Shivendra Singh Dungarpur has documented the life and work of this legendary Indian archivist.

In three decades, he built the NFAI from scratch and collected films from India and abroad. His dedication to authentic and meaningful cinema ensured that NFAI now has in its collection most of the early films, including the first film of India, Dadasaheb Phalke's *Raja Harishchandra*. Some of the noteworthy films in the NFAI collection include *Kaliya Mardan*, Bombay Talkies films such as *Jeevan Naiya*, *Bandhan*, *Kangan*, *Achhut Kanya* and *Kismet*, SS Vasan's *Chandralekha* and Uday Shankar's *Kalpana*.

P. K. Nair was born in the capital of the erstwhile kingdom of Travancore, now Thiruvananthapuram, Kerala. Tamil mythological films in the early 1940s, such as K Subramaniam's *Ananthasayanam* and *Bhakta Prahlada*, sparked his early interest in films. Though his family was not appreciative of his interest, he was determined to get into films soon after his graduation from the University of Kerala in 1953. He proceeded to Bombay to pursue a career in filmmaking; little realising that he was among the few graduates pursuing such a career at that time, though he had the good fortune of working with directors like Mehboob Khan, Bimal Roy and Hrishikesh Mukherjee.

Nair *saab* recalled those days[60]:

> In Mumbai, I realised that academically I had a different bent of mind, maybe my degree in science led me to look at the emerging opportunities in the film establishment as suggested by the S. K. Patil Committee. I heard about Jean Bhownagary, a French Indian and advisor to the Ministry of I&B and went to meet him. It was he who advised me to wait and apply for the post of a researcher/archivist at FTII, which they planned to convert into a film archive.

It was at the Film Institute, Pune that P. K. Nair, along with Marie Seton and Satish Bahadur, started the annual summer film appreciation course. The programme continued till the 2020s.

The independent NFAI was established in 1964, and P. K. Nair was appointed Assistant Curator in November 1965. He was promoted as the Director of the archive in 1982. When he retired in April 1991, he had collected over 12,000 films, of which 8,000 were Indian. He had also established NFAI as an institution worthy of its stature in the international film archive circuit, in three decades of his service. The Government of India in January 2023, merged NFAI with the public sector National Film Development Corporation (NFDC) but maintained it as a separate division.

Unquestionably, Nair *saab*'s contribution to the Film Society Movement is a pioneering one. He was a supporter of the 'minority cinema,' as he later called it, against the 'majority', the more popular films, now known as Bollywood, though he never made any differentiation while archiving films. "Why do you buy all these trash films," asked a secretary at I&B Ministry, in an interaction to convince the ministry on the annual budget. Nair *saab* kept quiet, but, later, wondered aloud, "Why do you allow such trash films to be made at all!" That is Nair *saab* for you.[61]

The clash of the 'majority' and 'minority' films and their impact on quality films were always on his mind. The article he wrote in 2000 reveals it all:

> Let us not assume everyone wants to see the same kind of cinema. The market forces would naturally dictate the filmmaker to cater to the majority for his very survival. But we have to create the necessary climate for the 'Other Cinema' to survive. For a healthy society, all shades of views and expression should be allowed to flow. Just because someone doesn't want to talk to the majority, but just shares the views with a minority, who would like to listen to him? Should he be prevented from doing so? It would be a sad day for the society if all its resources are earmarked only for the majority and it doesn't care about what happens to the minority.[62]

No one has to be told where the author's heart is, after reading this article. In short, a life dedicated to promoting, archiving and supporting quality films; that was P. K. Nair, with a definite film source and support to the Film Society Movement, even in the digital era, long after he is gone.[63]

### Jehangir Bhownagary

I first heard about Jehangir Shapoorji (Jean Bhownagary) from NFAI's first director, the late P. K. Nair, and was surprised as he attributed his joining the FTII, established in 1961, as an assistant librarian to Bhownagary. "I was assisting Mumbai directors like Mehboob, when I heard about the man behind big policy decisions of the central government about films in Delhi, and I met him. Bhownagary told me that they are going to announce the recruitment for FTII and advised me to wait and apply."[64]

**Figure 3.11.** Jehangir Bhownagary

He found Nair, a science degree-holder, a good candidate for handling the preservation of films at FTII, which later became the National Film Archive. NFAI was first initiated as a film library of FTII, and it was made a separate division.

Bhownagary is also credited as the man behind the first International Film Festival of India in 1952. He was an advisor to the I&B Ministry, on deputation from UNESCO, Paris, to give a fresh outlook to Indian filmmakers, bringing to India the post-War film movements of Europe, the Soviet Union and the USA. Being a confidante of Nehru and Indira Gandhi on film matters, Bhownagary's imprint can be seen in most of the early film institutions, which include FFSI, FTII, Film Finance Corporation in the mid-60s, which later became National Film Development Corporation (NFDC) and even NFAI in 1964, apart from the Films Division, which he headed for a decade. All these film institutions were mandated to create a new film culture in the new republic and film societies were the public wing of these institutions.

"Born in Bombay on 5 March, 1921 to an Indian father and French mother, who met and settled in Paris, and then sent their son Jehangir to India for part of his education, Bhownagary constantly straddled the boundaries between Europe and India," the first detailed profile of this film man can be seen in the book, *Visions of Development* by Peter Sutoris, a Cambridge scholar who did a fine study of the Indian documentary sector from the1940s. "He came to India at the beginning of World War II to work night shifts at *Reuters*, the news agency; he was later involved in setting up the Turkish consulate, then briefly worked for Tata Sons and was a co-writer for Gujarati comedies with Adi Marzban."

The French call him Jean Bhownagary, but for India he was Jehangir.[65] He started his film career with the war-time film department of the British Raj called 'Information Films India'. In 1945, he became a scriptwriter and a commentary-writer; a year later he was promoted as the assistant producer and news editor of the *Indian News Parade*. From 1948, till his retirement in the 1980s, he worked at UNESCO in Paris, specialising in mass communication initiatives.

"The call of Europe was strong... yet, there was a wrenching back and forth between two civilisations which had started in childhood and would continue throughout my life," Bhownagary wrote later. He came to India in 1952 for the India International Film Festival, then as advisor of the I&B ministry in 1954, returning again in 1965 as deputy, and, later, to head the Films Division.

According to Sutoris, Bhownagary was "an artist, a painter, sculptor, poet, engraver, potter, award-winning filmmaker and an accomplished magician." His daughter, Janine Barucha, described Jean as a great discoverer of talent in the aesthetic arena and encouraged them to be filmmakers with a view to bringing in a fresh outlook and vision to the medium. Acclaimed documentary filmmaker, Sukh Dev[66] in the 1960s, was one of the best talents discovered by Bhownagary. Apart from Sukh Dev, who became a legend in documentary films, Shyam Benegal, Adoor Gopalakrishnan and a host of FTII graduates in the 1960s, and, even painter M. F. Husain, were offered films by the Films Division under Bhownagary.

Aware of a wide range of approaches to film, Bhownagary admired the French *New Wave*, for the individuality of its directors, looked up to the British Free Cinema Movement and found inspiration in Italian neo-realism and early Indian Parallel

Cinema. He believed that films could be used to bring together various ethnic and religious groups in India by exposing them to the commonalities in their history and culture. According to his daughter, he was "very aware that India was a young country, and very aware of being part of building it."[67]

No wonder, he was close to Nehru and Indira Gandhi, to become one among the pioneering and visionary builders of a new, democratic and secular India.

Jehangir's work in India was noticed internationally. John Grierson, the father of the British Documentary Movement, held Bhownagary in high esteem for his work in India, describing his work as "trying to change the world.". "Haven't done it yet. But, tried," Bhownagary told Grierson to that comment in one of their exchanges, noted Peter Sutoris in his book.

"Turning a heavy-handed bureaucratic operation into one with an environment amenable to openness, innovation and creativity, was no small feat and Bhownagary did indeed try," wrote Sutoris in his book.[68] Grierson, considered the father of the global documentary film movement, was in India for two months in 1971 and made recommendations for Canadian assistance for publicity funds for India's family planning programme.

In his tenure as advisor to the I&B ministry, Jehangir was the main force behind the implementation of the S. K. Patil Committee Report which suggested the creation of film institutions like FTII, NFAI, FFC, Children's Films Society and even a Film Society Movement and the formation of its federation, FFSI. Nehru and Indira Gandhi dipped heavily into the international experience of Bhownagary to modernise Indian films and create institutions to upgrade its content and technology.

Jehangir Bhowngary died in April 2004 in Paris and his friend and a former editor of *The Times of India*, the late Dileep Padgaonkar, wrote in his obituary, "Jean-Jehangir was also a ceramist, a potter, a lithographer, a painter, and above all, a gifted documentary filmmaker. The films he directed or produced all over the world for UNESCO, which he served for more than three decades, won awards at prestigious film festivals."[69]

Now the Films Division and film festivals have all merged under the National Film Development Corporation, his legacy may have further merged into the bureaucratic maze of the governmental system. However, filmmakers like Sukh Dev, N. V. K. Murthy, Pramod Pati and institutions like the National Film Archive will stand testimony to a visionary who travelled ahead of his time in building a modern film movement with its own unique and brilliant space in world cinema.

There are other pioneers who worked as secretaries of FFSI, like A. K. Dey, Raman Raju of Kolkata, Arun Kumar Pramanik, Arun Roy from Patna, Amitabh Ghosh from Jamshedpur, John Joshua of the Delhi Film Society, Arun Kaul of Film Forum, Mumbai, N. Narahari Rao of Bangalore and Adoor Gopalakrishnan in Thiruvananthapuram; they all have contributed to the growth of the Film Society Movement. However, one is forced to limit to the present list for want of space and to keep the focus on the movement, and the visionaries who gave it a national and global vision and direction.

## References


1. H. N. Narahari Rao, *The Film Society Movement In India*(Mumbai: Asian Film Foundation, 2009) p.71.
2. Satyajit Ray, *Our Films, Their films* (Orient Black Swan, 2011), p. 6.
3. Satyajit Ray, *Deep Focus* (Harper Collins, 2011), p. 49.
4. https://en.wikipedia.org/wiki/Bicycle_Thieves
5. https://en.wikipedia.org/wiki/Battleship_Potemkin
6. https://en.wikipedia.org/wiki/Nanook_of_the_North
7. https://cherianwrites.blogspot.com/2020/07/samik-da-on-satyajit-ray.html
8. http://www.bfi.org.uk/news-opinion/news-bfi/lists/10-great-italian-neorealist-films
9. Marie Seton, *Portrait of a Director: Satyajit Ray* (New Delhi: Penguin, 2003), p.55.
10. https://en.wikipedia.org/wiki/The_River_(1951_film)
11. https://en.wikipedia.org/wiki/Vsevolod_Pudovkin
12. http://cherianwrites.blogspot.in/2016/02/a-few-notes-for-book-towards-new-film.html

13. Dilip Basu, *Biography of Satyajit Ray* (http://satyajitray.ucsc.edu/biography).
14. http://www.satyajitray.org/
15. Satyajit Ray, *Our Films, Their films* (Orient Black Swan, 2011).
16. Satyajit Ray, *Deep Focus*(Harper Collins, 2011)
17. Interview with Adoor Gopalakrishnan.
18. https://en.wikipedia.org/wiki/Mani_Kaul
19. https://en.wikipedia.org/wiki/Kumar_Shahani
20. Interview with Samik Bandyopadhyay
21. https://en.wikipedia.org/wiki/Sandip_Ray
22. Interview with Vijaya Mulay.
23. *Selected Speeches of Indira Gandhi*–(New Delhi: Publication Division, Ministry of Information and Broadcasting, GOI), p. 279.
24. http://cherianwrites.blogspot.in/2016/03/marie-setons-first-booklet-edited.html
25. Interview with Gautam Kaul.
26. Based on an interview with Kulathoor Bhaskaran Nair, MD, Chitralekha Film Cooperative.
27. B. K. Karanjia, *Counting my Blessings* (Viking, 2005).
28. *Selected Speeches and Writings of Indira Gandhi* (New Delhi: Publications Division, Ministry of Information and Broadcasting, GOI), p. 378.
29. https://en.wikipedia.org/wiki/Indira_Gandhi
30. http://www.thehindu.com/arts/article148630.ece
31. *Sight and Sound*, March 1985.
32. MarieSeton, *Portrait of a Director: Satyajit Ray* (New Delhi: Penguin, 2003).
33. http://cherianwrites.blogspot.in/2016/02/marie-setons-letter-to-editor-published.html
34. H. N. Narahari Rao,*The Film Society Movement In India* (Mumbai: Asian film Foundation, 2009), p. 228.
35. https://en.wikipedia.org/wiki/Marie_Seton
36. H. N. Narahari Rao, *The Film Society Movement In India* (Mumbai: Asian film Foundation, 2009), p. 72.
37. Ibid., p. 102.
38. https://en.wikipedia.org/wiki/Chidananda_Dasgupta
39. https://www.youtube.com/watch?v=xzTDE1gtbCQ&t=23s

40. *Film Quarterly,* Fall issue journal of UCLA, 1980.
41. https://www.cdg100.com/the-trust.php
42. Vijaya Mulay, *As Others See It*(NFAI project), p. 3.
43. HN Narahari Rao, ed., *The Film Society Movement In India*(Mumbai: Asian Film Foundation, 2009).
44. https://en.wikipedia.org/wiki/Vijaya_Mulay
45. https://cherianwrites.blogspot.com/2023/03/celebration-of-life-of-vijayamulay-may.html
46. R. M. Ray, *Indian Cinema in Retrospect:Speeches of the 1955 Seminar* (Sangeet Natak Academy).
47. https://en.wikipedia.org/wiki/Khwaja_Ahmad_Abbas
48. https://cherianwrites.blogspot.com/2016/02/interview-with-govindaraj.html
49. https://en.wikipedia.org/wiki/Ammu_Swaminathan
50. https://cherianwrites.blogspot.com/2016/02/a-few-notes-for-book-towards-new-film.html
51. https://cherianwrites.blogspot.com/2016/03/on-fsm-by-anilsrivastava-pioneer-and.html
52. http://www.academia.edu/957386/White_chalk_and_Blackboard_On_the_occasion_of_Prof._Satish_Bahadurs_book_release
53. http://cherianwrites.blogspot.in/2016/02/interview-with-ms-shyamala-vannarse.html
54. Interaction with Adoor Gopalakrishnan.
55. Interaction with Anil Srivastava.
56. Ibid., p. 53.
57. Ibid., p.58.
58. https://en.wikipedia.org/wiki/Satish_Bahadur
59. https://cherianwrites.blogspot.com/2016/06/mrinal-da-interviewed.html
60. Interview with P. K. Nair.
61. Ibid., p.60.
62. https://cherianwrites.blogspot.com/2016/02/from-nfai-collection-national-cinema.html
63. https://en.wikipedia.org/wiki/P._K._Nair
64. Peter Sutoris,*Visions of Development* (Oxford University Press, 2016)
65. Ibid., p. 64.

66. https://www.thehindu.com/features/metroplus/shabnam-sukhdev-makes-documentary-on-her-father-filmmaker-s-sukhdev/article6324214.ece
67. https://cherianwrites.blogspot.com/2016/04/daughter-of-jean-man-behind-nehruvian.html
68. Ibid., p. 64.
69. https://timesofindia.indiatimes.com/home/sunday-times/all-that-matters/Jeans-magic-spell/articleshow/653690.cms

# 4
# The Networks of Films and Film Buffs

Hollywood films were the hot favourite of the best cinema houses in urban centres of the country till 1950, even after the country was free from colonial rule. During the British Raj, despite the country emerging as the third largest film production centre, the British administration clearly favoured English language films, by not allowing commercial screenings of other languages. A rough estimate is that 80 per cent of the films shown were of foreign origin and Indian language films were not so popular with the system, though there was a huge market waiting to lap it up as seen from the 1960s onwards.[1]

Filmmaker K. A. Abbas, "invoking the authority of no less a person than the Prime Minister of the country who asked us to consult among ourselves", on the first day of discussion at the Film Seminar, organised by the *Sangeet Natak Akademi* in 1955[2] lamented:

> In Bombay all big cinemas (almost all the air-conditioned cinemas) located in the finest, best and hygienic parts of the city, run pictures belonging to the foreign exhibitors. Indian films are shown in these picture houses, once a year or once in two years or three years. ...This is against our national pride and self-respect that you cannot see Indian pictures in certain Indian cinemas.

Little did Abbas realise that even after years of political freedom, the country was following the policies and practices of the Indian Cinematograph Act, 1918. The Rangachari Committee on Films during the British Raj (1927-28) had dictated that "Every characteristic of the cinema industry makes it unsuitable for provincialisation." It went on to suggest that the policies to favour English films from the UK follow a strict regime of censorship.

No wonder, Jean Renoir, the French director, advised Satyajit Ray back in 1949, while shooting at Calcutta for his film *River,* that "If you could only shake out Hollywood out of your system and evolve your own style, you would be making great films here."[3]

In the 21st century, the world film map shows that there are only a few countries, notably India and France, which still have their own film industry and films depicting the social and cultural issues of their people and are popular in their cinema houses. Both India and France have been able to counter the onslaught of Hollywood, with in-house film productions. Even in the metro cities, and most regional centres, all movie theatres treat Hindi films or regional language films as being more important than English films, as the viewers prefer their own cultural products.

The annual report of the Ministry of Information and Broadcasting of the COVID year 2020 listed a total of 4,060 films censored during the period out of which only 558 were foreign films.[4] Clearly, over the seven decades of free India, the country has been able to grow its film industry into a formidable force.

The story of the emergence of the Indian film sector as the global force from the years 1947 to 2023 is also the story of the young nation's quest for its own idiom in films, guided and patronised by two Indian Prime Ministers, Jawaharlal Nehru and Indira Gandhi. The Film Society Movement, the alternate film circuit, which the former prime ministers promoted for the outlined goal through the films, may not be in good shape today, but they seem to have achieved the goal of promoting quality films through the International Film festivals over the years and also the global spread of Bollywood films[5], the popular term for the Hindi film industry. Bollywood films give Hollywood films a run for their money in India and wherever Indians are across the globe. Some of the star directors, technicians and stars of

Bollywood are either from FTII, be it filmmakers Subash Ghai or Rajkumar Hirani or the products of the Film Society Movement like Shoojit Sircar, which the founding fathers of India supported wholeheartedly the development of Indian films.

It is said that Satyajit Ray saw over 99 films during his short stay in London, before making his first film and among them the Italian neorealist films made a deep impression on him. "He learnt most from Italian films (in London). During his voyage home, he worked on the script of *Pather Panchali* and thought of ways he could raise money to make the novel into a film," Marie Seton, his biographer described Ray's London education in films as a young art director of a British advertising firm.[6]

A writer takes to reading like a fish to water, and for a filmmaker seeing films is his/her *raison d'etre*. Film societies have been filling this role of exposing film buffs and filmmakers to the best of cinema from across the world now for decades as an exclusive channel, till the advent of Videos and DVDs in the 1990s. India is perhaps the only nation which has not seen a takeover by imported (Hollywood) films on its screen till today. This is something which India can be rightly proud of, especially in these days of globalisation when Hollywood cinema has virtually dominated the world screen. The first two decades of cinema in the country saw imported films, mostly from Europe, occupying the bulk of our screens. The figures at the end of the silent era were 80 percent imported and only the balance 20 percent being indigenous. The beginning of the 'Talkies', made it possible to see, hear and enjoy films in one's own language. This brought in a dramatic change with the imported films (by this time mainly American) getting pushed out and cinema in various Indian languages taking over.

Slowly, the ratio reversed, it became almost 98 per cent Indian and the rest foreign films (2020), and since then Indian cinema has never looked back.[7] Films in native Indian languages continue to have a hypnotic hold on the Indian masses, both within and outside the country. This continues despite the onslaught of the dominant cinema from mighty Hollywood.

P. K. Nair, analysing foreign films in India, observed:

They, Hollywood, tried to dub their films in Hindi and other Indian languages to penetrate the Indian market. Barring exceptions like *Jurassic Park* or *Titanic,* they could not make much of a breakthrough. But with costs soaring sky high and diminishing returns and a crumbling economy, can we hold on for long? This should be a matter of concern for all of us.

## Appreciation of Films as an Art

In a country, where literacy rate has been growing from 18 percent in 1951 to 74 percent in 2011[9], the political leadership from the first prime minister onwards has been identifying a deeper influence of visual media and films, in comparison to books and print media in the educational programmes. Maybe, television has taken over the role of films since the 1990s with the arrival of national TV channels, but cinema remained a major influence on people throughout the years. Realising the influence of films over other means of communication, Prime Minister Nehru had clearly set out to draw a line. "...What is presented should mould the public taste, action and reaction," Nehru's policy direction on films was clear from the word go.[10]

Nehru did appreciate the growth of the film industry over the three decades prior to 1955. "Nevertheless, they have made progress (film industry)...of course, many people criticize the quality of many of their films from their rather highbrow point of view, and their criticism from that point of view is justified, highbrow or not,"[11] the scholar statesman made his point clear to an audience that included film industry giants like Devika Rani, K. A. Abbas, S.S. Vasan and Prithviraj Kapoor and his sons. Nehru bluntly told them the melodrama, which was the hallmark of films those days, put him to sleep. He stopped short of saying that the Government had some interest in setting the agenda for the film industry, though by 1960 he was exercising it through institutions like FFSI, FTII, FFC and NFAI.

Paul Rotha, the eminent British film historian, did not consider such criticism as highbrow and went on to say, "Almost the whole potential of the cinema as an instrument of public education has been neglected by the industry's controllers in their pursuit of big returns." He emphasised, "Film appreciation is concerned with these films and enabling people to separate the chaff from the grain in cinema."[12] Marie Seton had already defined that "Film appreciation aims to cultivate a taste for the grain", through her multi-city screenings and lectures in the 1950s in India.[13]

**Figure 4.1.** The audience at the 1955 Film Seminar

The Film Society Movement pioneer, Chidananda Das Gupta, went a step further to say that appreciation of quality films was a precursor for making good films. In the introduction to his book *Cinema of Satyajit Ray*, he wrote:

> In a country fed mostly with imported escapist films and their inept local imitations, the exposure to *Battleship Potemkin*, *Nanook of the North*, *Night Mail* and *Un Carnet de bal* brought about a burning desire to tell what a great art cinema was and to prove in the shortest possible time, that great films could be made in India—films that would shake the world and change our own country.[14]

Earlier during a review of the Film Society Movement, in 1965, Das Gupta, further explained:

**Figure 4.2.** A still from *Battleship Potemkin*

> Without wishing away the difference between the art audience and the mass audience it is still possible to direct film appreciation at two objectives: to inject more cinematic technique and attitude into the commercial cinema and to make it raise its sights within reason: and to create the urge for and the climate in which genuine artistic expression becomes possible on a wider scale.[15]

All of them were pointing towards the emergence of film as an art, a serious vocation aimed to positively influence viewers, just as any other art form be it writing, painting, theatre or music. The art which developed as a by-product of the Industrial Revolution in the West came to India when there was no industry here, hence the science and art of filmmaking was seen as an extension of the countryside dance dramas in its initial years. However, the new nation, out to industrialise itself through huge public sector units, was ready to explore art and its technology seriously, with the technological sensibilities of the West where the medium originated. No wonder it was the public sector professionals in various cities who carried forward the yearning for a new kind of film appreciation through the Film Society Movement in many cities.

**Film Sources for Film Society's Pre-FFSI Days**

The success of a film society was its ability to screen a varied genre of films, Indian or foreign, not necessarily English, as Hollywood films were abundantly available in India from colonial times.

The acquisition of Sergei Eisenstein's *Battleship Potemkin* by CFS in 1948 opened up a new avenue for the film societies as far as sourcing of films for their screening was concerned. *Battleship Potemkin* ended up being shown as the first film in most of the early film societies, such as Lucknow and Patna Film Societies. There is hardly a film society member who has not seen the Russian film about an early revolutionary struggle at Odesa[16] harbour steps. It was the first film of the FFSI circuit and its classical position in film history had made it a must see.

Chidananda Das Gupta, while discussing the parallel history of Indian cinema,[17] observed:

> India's doors and windows had started to fly open. In 1948, the CFS imported a copy of *Battleship Potemkin* and showed it, dodging police restrictions, to stunning effect of its viewers. Hard on the heels of this event came Jean Renoir's recce in 1948 and for the shooting of *The River* in 1949... The shooting of The River was observed by many who were later to turn famous practitioners, such as cinematographer Subrata Mitra, art director Bansi Chandra Gupta, documentarist Harisadhan Das Gupta and so on. Roberto Rossellini came a few years later and so did John Houston, Frank Capra, V Pudovkin and Nikolai Cherkassov all names to reckon with in cinema, popular or unpopular.

The erstwhile Soviet Union, which produced films like *Battleship Potemkin*, also gave a big boost to other films from the entire Eastern bloc, where filmmaking was identified as a political act to promote their ideology. The Eastern bloc senses the appetite for non-English films in the film society circuit and was ever ready to pump in their films as part of their spreading influence over Indian intelligentsia under Prime Minister Nehru, who loved to be identified as a left-leaning socialist. Ray, himself had seen *Battleship Potemkin* over and over again and even scored his own music for this silent film, with a collection of the LP records, when he saw it for the 22nd time.[18]

The story of *Pather Panchali* being shown in Bhopal by the students led by Anil Srivastava, in the late 1950s, is yet another landmark in the history of films which excited societies. Marie Seton came to India with five films from the British Film Institute: Charlie Chaplin's *The Immigrant*, Alexander Dovshenko's *Earth*, Vsevelod Pudovkin's *Storm over Asia*, G. W. Pabst's *Kamaradechaft* (Comdradeship), Rene Clair's *Le Million* (The Million), Luchiano Emmer's *Sunday in August* and John Ford's *They Were Expendable* and *Children of Hiroshima*. This unique collection of films from the British Film Institute, with which Marie was associated, travelled with her to various metro and non-metro cities of India, giving an opportunity to the increasing film societies and some selected academics a glimpse of emerging film trends in the West.

After her lecture tour with the films, Marie wrote: "The films illustrating Film Appreciation stressed that the feature film at its best is an educational force and that dramatic films can be based upon real situation as in *They Were Expendable, Kamaradechaft* and *Children of Hiroshima*."[19]

Some of the films shown by the CFS in the first two years included the Mexican film *Portrait of Maria*, *A Cage of Nightingales* (France), *Brief Encounter* (UK, David Lean), *The Way Ahead* (UK, Carol Reed), *This Land is Mine* (Jean Renoir, France), *Counter Attack* (Hungary, Zoltan Korda), *Nanook of the North* (Robert Flaherty, USA).[20] Most of these films were either procured from the regular circuit or granted by embassies of the respective countries or from the Central Film Library of the Ministry of Education.

With the formation of the FFSI in 1959, a plan with the active involvement of the film bodies of the Central government was put into place and submitted to the government. "To begin with, some Government organisations—the Films Division or the

Board of Film Censors—should be asked to act as the importer and distributor of film societies", the first Five Year Plan of the FFSI suggested.[21] FFSI was allowed to import 16 films a year without the mandatory customs duty, provided they had enough foreign exchange to do so. Indeed, FFSI imported a few films during the period 1963-64. The Federation did get a package of films from the Colombo Film Society of Sri Lanka. The package included films like *Passion of Joan of Arc, The Last Laugh, Le Million, The Italian Straw Hat, The Cabinet of Dr Caligari, The Blue Angel* and *Metropolis*. In 1965-66, a few more films were directly imported from London. Three films were also obtained from the Swedish Embassy. All these were procured with a generous grant from the Government of India, to promote the availability of quality films for the FFSI network.

However, over a period of time, FFSI ended up being dependent on the Central Film Library of the Ministry of Education and the diplomatic missions in India, as the government grants dried up. The censor restrictions further restrained them from getting more films. In 1964, Indira Gandhi as the information minister exempted film society screenings from censorship and there was a flood of films from all diplomatic missions, especially the Eastern Bloc. Films from Poland, Hungary, Czechoslovakia, Bulgaria and Russia (Soviet Union) remained the toast of the film society circuit for a long time.

In the first five years before the formation of NFAI, FFSI was able to circulate over 70 feature films in its network.

Das Gupta, in his assessment of the first 5 years of FFSI[22], recalled:

> Direct import and an exchange through UNESCO have accounted for all of these films, the rest having been arranged with the co-operation of various foreign missions in India, notably those of France, Sweden, Mexico, Japan, West Germany, Poland, Hungary, Bulgaria, Czechoslovakia, UK, Yugoslavia, USSR and East Germany.

The nominal membership fee charged by the film societies did not allow them to hire cinema halls for 35 mm films and pay a screening fee from the normal film distribution circuit. Hence, they were mostly dependent on 16 mm film prints. Most of the cultural and educational institutions had the 16 mm projector as part of the educational tools. Since the growth and spread of film societies were around educational or cultural bodies, till the advent of Video and DVD projectors. 16 mm films and video and DVD/Blu-Ray screenings suited the fragile economics of running a film society.

### The Central Film Library to NFAI-FFSI Network and FFC

The Central Film Distribution Library had 16 mm print of 20 classic films by Sergei Eisenstein, Robert Flaherty, Vittorio De Sica, David Lean, Henri Georges Clouzat, Jean Vigo, Mark Donoskoi and Charlie Chaplin. Documentary films of John Grierson, Basil Wright, Paul Rotha and Humphrey Jennings were also available at the library, whose membership was extended to the film societies affiliated with FFSI. The early societies, the founders of the FFSI had access to these films through their contacts in the government like Vijaya Mulay and Marie Seton, both of whom were attached to the Central Ministry of Education in Delhi.

All these films were later transferred to the NFAI in the 1960s. The Information and Broadcasting Ministry took over the functions of the Central Film Library, and the films were housed at NFAI attached to the ministry and were made available for distribution to film societies. In 2014, the NFAI's distribution library had over 25 active members throughout the country, and it also organized joint screening programs on a weekly, fortnightly and monthly basis in six important centres. NFAI has over 17,000 films, 25,000 books, 10,000 film scripts, and more than 125,000 photographs. Various educational institutions, cultural organisations and film societies are members of the NFAI distribution library. "To start with, the Archive's distribution library had about 20 film classics. This unit started expanding gradually, and by the 1980s it reached a figure of over 100 titles that included both Indian and foreign classics," P. K. Nair wrote in IFSON, the official journal of FFSI in 1981.[23]

**National Film Achieve of India, Pune**

As many as 739 film societies across India were affiliated to NFAI from 1994-95 onwards to source its films for screenings. Most of them were not even affiliated to the FFSI going by the numbers. On an average 30 film societies per year were registered with NFAI and P. K. Nair, its director, satisfied himself with the conduct of each of these film societies and transported the films from the NFAI library.[24]

NFAI had also taken upon itself the promotion of film appreciation as envisaged by the founders of the film societies. The annual one-month summer course at the FTII, organised by NFAI, is a big draw even today. At the International level, NFAI supplied several Indian classics for major screening programmes to those interested in Indian films, ensuring a two-way exposure of films.

The Distribution Library dispatches films by railway, surface courier and also by air throughout the country. It is also responsible for sending films abroad with a view to popularise Indian cinema.

A number of classics like *Bicycle Thieves, Pather Panchali*, and documentaries like *Nanook of the North*, are featured in the distribution list of the film library of NFAI. All the National Award winning films are to be procured by the NFAI, apart from the panorama films of the India International film festival.

As a part of its activities under the dissemination of film culture, NFAI, with its headquarters in Pune and three Regional Offices in Bengaluru, Kolkata and Thiruvananthapuram, extended distribution library facilities to the members throughout the country. The distribution library caters to the special screenings of films from the NFAI collection. NFAI conducted joint screening programmes in Mumbai, Kolkata, Bengaluru Hyderabad, Thiruvananthapuram, Kochi, Jamshedpur and Pune till the pandemic season of 2020.

Film Finance Corporation and its contemporary version, NFDC was also a source of films for film societies as it has its own library of films which it produced over the years and also took up distribution. Various diplomatic missions continue to be another source for most recent films from non-English speaking countries.

The grey market too has emerged as a major source for film buffs. At Thiruvananthapuram, I saw a list of over 5000 films with a film critic. He told me that such films or any new films in the international circuit are available for a throwaway price in the city. A whole new grey market operates outside the city. I saw the same on a visit to Dhaka, where I could buy a collection of Ray and Ghatak movies at throwaway prices. The arrival of DVDs and CDs has completely changed the availability of films and also the very need for film societies just to see films for serious film buffs. However, stringent copyright laws over the years have checked such grey market availability of films.

## Entry of Eastern Bloc and Others: Non-English Films

In my early days in Delhi during the 1980s, I used to receive letters from film society friends from Kerala, asking me to help them to procure films from diplomatic missions of Eastern bloc countries of Poland, Hungary, Czechoslovakia, Cuba, Yugoslavia and Bulgaria. Since India was with the Eastern Bloc during the Cold War, the diplomatic missions saw the films from their countries as a good way of getting to reach the cream of Indian society. It gave them and their ideology a certain acceptability and entry to the educated strata of society.

The films of Germans, French and Japanese were also eagerly awaited in India. These films never got into the regular cinema houses and thus they had become a hot property in film society circles. In the 1980s, there was hardly anyone in the film society circuit who was not excited about the films of Jean Luc Godard[25], Werner Herzog,[26]Ferderico Fellini,[27] Ingmar Bergman,[28] Miklos Jansco,[29] Krzysztof Zanussi[30] and Akira Kurosawa[31]. Bergman, Kurosawa, Fellini, Godard, Jansco and Zanussi became cult figures among film society members and film students. An added attraction was that these films were not censored, and portrayed female nudity artistically, much to the surprise of the Indian audience.

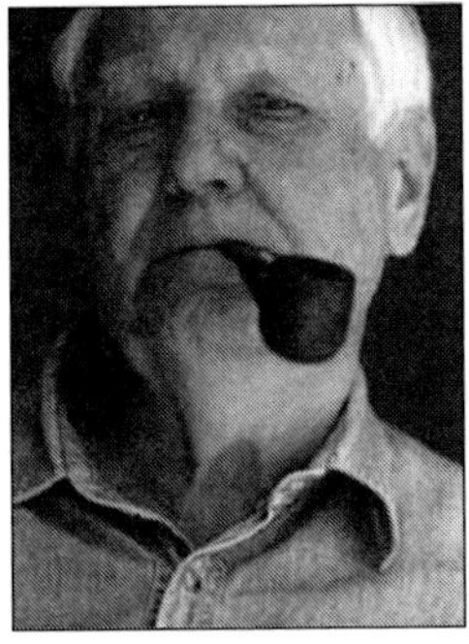

**Figure 4.3.1.** Miklos Jancso

**Figure 4.3.2.** Federico Fellini

**Figure 4.3.3.** Ingmar Bergman

**Figure 4.3.4.** Krzysztof Zanussi

**Figure 4.3.5.** Andrei Tarkovsky

The fact that the government establishments and Leftists, in general, supported the Film Society Movement wholeheartedly, as a part of their wider political agenda, made the acceptance of the Eastern Bloc films easier. The Indian International Film Festivals always had a good package of films from these countries. Most of these filmmakers were invited to visit India during the film festivals. As a journalist, I remember meeting Polish filmmaker Zanussi and Cuban filmmakers Humbarto Solas and Thomas Alea while they were on an official tour in India. Indian film critics too feasted on their films and wrote extensively for the mainline and regional media. Most of the film festival entries were detained by the diplomatic missions for wider circulation through the film societies in those days. This opened up a huge film library which was mostly available for free screening by film societies. This arrangement also suited the fragile economics of the film societies and attracted more members to the societies.

"The initial selection of the films was done by the cultural attaches of the different embassies and programme officers of the consular offices/cultural centers. The selection followed patterns like tributes to film eras, important film directors and illustrious actors and actresses," pointed out Abhijit Ghosh Dastidar in his note on the availability of films of those days. Mr Dastidar, a Kolkata-based film writer and a retired Indian postal service officer, who made it a habit to travel to all major film events in search of good films across India and the world and wrote a film column in the Kolkata-based English weekly *Frontier*. He is a regular in film society circuits of Kolkata too.[32]

The French, Canadian and Netherlands embassies were also equally supportive of the film society movement. According to Adoor Gopalakrishnan:

> The French embassy had a special audio-visual section (they had a great collection of both classic and contemporary films in 16 mm which was freely available). Canadian High Commission- National Board of Canada which produced highly experimental films, prominent among them being Normal McLaren's unique creations exploring new frontiers in cinematic expressions). Netherlands

(the Dutch) Embassy again with a large collection of documentaries significant among them being *Mirror of Holland, Zoo, Glass Rembrandt-Painter of Man,* etc., by Bret Hanstra, was another attraction for film societies. The Czech Embassy and their consulates with a large collection of the Czech New wave films in 16 mm was another source.[33]

## New Wave Films Make an Entry

The Film Institute of India (FTII) as Television was added later, which was established in1960, had started producing a line-up of well-trained and well-exposed film technicians and directors to the field. The FTII along with NFAI had also started a one-month summer film appreciation course, exposing film buffs to world cinema and starting a film appreciation course, which started off as the pioneer classroom for academic film studies in India.

The FFC, which later became NFDC, had started funding some of the FTII graduates to make films. This circuit then began to throw up a new set of filmmakers. This was in addition to filmmakers like Satyajit Ray, Ritwik Ghatak and Mrinal Sen, who had been making waves in national and international film circuits from the 1950s. Ghatak also served as the Vice Principal of FTII influencing a fresh set of young filmmakers. Adoor Gopalakrishnan, Mani Kaul, Kumar Shahani, John Abraham, Girish Kasaravalli and a host of others were joining the ranks of Ray and his colleagues from Bengal. Most of these FTII graduates made their first film with FFC funding, giving an official stamp of the government of the day to "*New Wave*" films. "My first film *Maya Darpan* did not get a regular theatre release, but was immensely popular in the film society circuit," Kumar Shahani recalled.

Although these were public sector produced films, they did not get distribution or exhibition facilities. The films of Kumar Shahani and Mani Kaul remained the toast of the film society circuit though FFC produced them. Though Adoor, John and Girish Kasaravalli got theatre releases for their films, in their regions, Shyam Benegal with his refreshingly new Hindi films and G. Aravindan with his esoteric films also began to excite the film society circuit and film festivals in India and abroad. Pattabhirama Reddy, Girish Karnad, B.V. Karanth, A.K. Kaul with his film *27 Down*, Nirad Mohapatra, Kanthi Lal Rathod, Rajendra Singh Bedi and Basu Chatterji carried forward the New Wave to their regions.

**Figure 4.4.1.** Ritwik Ghatak

**Figure 4.4.2.** Kumar Shahani

**Figure 4.4.3.** G. Aravindan

**Figure 4.4.4.** Girish Kasaravalli

This new crowd of filmmakers had captured the annual National Awards and many international awards at Cannes, Berlin and Moscow, jettisoning the regular mass appeal films from the 1970s to 2000. A new set of technicians, actors, and filmmakers entered the regular film industry from FTII, giving it a fresh outlook and technical quality. Many of them totally rejected the popular style of filmmaking, and with government patronage, they were placed as the new face of Indian films. FFC Chairman B.K. Karanjia, who patronized *New Wave films* with lavish funding, was later removed during the national emergency period of 1975-77 as few in the government felt New Wave was discrediting the glamorous popular films. However, Indira Gandhi reaffirmed her commitment to New Wave when she came back as prime minister after a three-year break by appointing a new Film Enquiry Committee under the Karnataka cultural icon Dr. Shivarama Karanth.

The New Wave in Indian films was lapped up by the film society goers, as they were exposed to quality films through the FFSI and other film circuits. This led to a new set of filmmakers being popularised by the film societies at its peak of popularity in the late 1970s and 1980s. They included Mani Kaul, Kumar Sahani, Saeed Mirza, Shyam Benegal, A.K. Kaul, Govind Nihalani in Hindi; Ritwik Ghatak, Mrinal Sen, Buddhadeb Dasgupta, Gautam Ghosh, Aparna Sen, Utpalendu Chakrabarty in Bangla; Pattabhirama Reddy, Girish Karnad, B.V. Karanth and Girish Kasaravalli in Kannada; Adoor Gopalakrishnan, G. Aravindan, John Abraham, T.V. Chandran, K.R. Mohanan and Shaji N. Karun in Malayalam; Jabbar Patel in Marathi; Jhanu Barua in Assamese and Nirad Mohapatra in Odiya. Most of them were trained in filmmaking at FTII or were products of the Film Society Movement. They were award-winning filmmakers either at the national film festivals or international film festivals. They all took the film society network and its members as their basic audience, as the films were made with aesthetic appeal and not on box office formulae. Film society membership in the 1960s, 1970s and 1980s was a connoisseur's prized possession in most urban centres of India and they feasted on these *New Wave* films, making their arrivals happening events in the media as well as public, although the box office response to most of these films was lukewarm.

Mrinal Sen, a contemporary of Satyajit Ray, explained the philosophy and economics behind his kind of filmmaking, which he believes is best appreciated by the minority audience in and outside India as follows[34]:

> You cannot expect a large number of people to see your films. Any sensible film maker, when he makes films, his films are not that reachable to everyone.... For instance, take fiction.... If you read novels.... Popular novels are very different... Even then I want to be popular... But I am a popular failure most of the time...in the box office. But then that is why my arithmetic is very simple.... I make low-budget films. People say filmmaking is an expensive process. I do not agree with them.... Not all agree with them (repeat). Films can be made at a low cost. I have been making low-cost films.... If you make low-cost films and if you can get to the larger minority audience scattered across the world. The larger minority audience... who would be seeing your film and that way I keep going. That is in spite of the fact that I am a popular failure at the box office, I keep going.

Sen and Arun Kaul of the Film Forum (Bombay) had come out with a *Manifesto for the New Indian Cinema*, when they collaborated for the film *Bhuvan Shome*, which is considered the first film that ushered in the New Wave in Hindi. The budget of the film, financed by the erstwhile FFC, was Rs 1.50 lakhs and was totally shot on location introducing actors, Utpal Dutt and Suhasini Mulay who later became popular in Hindi films.

The New Wave films challenged the approach of the popular filmmakers to the filmmaking itself and also brought about a change in the taste among the viewers. The impact was total. The studio-based films became a thing of the past, just as *New Wave* films, the good old Bollywood began to adapt outdoors to foreign locations and new technologies to recapture their pre-eminence. The FTII-trained actors, cinematographers, audiographers and editors ventured into Bollywood giving popular films a fresh look in approach, content, technology and even financing. Shyam Bengal got Gujarat Cooperative Milk Marketing Federation, known by its brand Amul, to fund a feature film on the cooperative. By the 1990s, filmmaker SudhirMisra[35], son of a Lucknow film society activist, began to make films which are mainstream but totally different and still popular. FTII-trained actors like Jaya Bhaduri Bachchan,[36] Shatrughan Sinha,[37]

Naseeruddin Shah[38] and Om Puri[39] established themselves as mainline Hindi film actors, though most of them were introduced by the *New Wave* filmmakers. While the New Wave filmmakers and actors got into the mainstream film circuits, the film society films were still out of the normal film screening circuit.

**Alternate Networks of Film Screening**

I visited *Bharat Bhavan* in Kolkata to see what was left of the CFS and met the president Pradipta Shanker Sen in 2012. The one hour I spent at the CFS office, under the gaze of a huge portrait of Satyajit Ray, gave me an idea about the present state of affairs of CFS and many existing film societies across India.

Most films are now on DVDs and a projection system makes it possible to hold a film screening in a house. This is the transition of not just CFS but most existing film societies, from the regular 35 mm cinema houses, 16 mm projectors now to the digital projectors. The *Bharat Bhavan* building has been taken over by its owners and the CFS office has moved out as the rental became unaffordable.

In Kozhikode, Kerala, I was told the oldest *Aswini* Film Society, frequented by filmmakers G Aravindan and John Abraham, survives on a gift of a digital projector by some well-wishers from the Gulf countries. The majority of the film societies turned to digital projections and only booked theatres if they had a film festival, that too supported by local governments or similar agencies with huge funds.

Very few film societies have a screening theatre and cultural complex of their own like *Suchitra* in Bangalore, *Ritwik Sadan* of the Berhampore Film Society, Midnapore Film Society in West Bengal and the Karimnagar Film Society owned *Film Bhavan* in Andhra Pradesh. All of them had come up on government-allotted land.

The *Suchitra* Film Society promoted the *Suchitra* Cinema Academy Trust, the first of its kind in India, and the construction of auditorium was inaugurated by Satyajit Ray on January 8, 1980. The first phase of the project was completed in September 1981 and the second phase in August 1986.

In Kolkata, *Nandan*[40] Film and Cultural Complex built by the then Left Front government was the byproduct of the fledgling Film Society Movement of the city. In Thiruvananthapuram, two cinema houses *Kairali and Kala Bhavan* were also established by the state government, catering to the film society culture of the city. The Kerala Government has taken its role in promoting alternate films further by building over 15 cinema houses across the state under its Kerala Film Development Corporation (KSFDC), though they have now become centres of popular film releases.[41]

Over the years, film societies were using small halls or academic institutions and their 16 mm projectors for their screenings. In Delhi, since the Central government was involved in the movement, the auditoriums of the films division, *Sapru House* and Ministry of Education were made available for screening for the Delhi Film Society. In Kolkata, the *Sarala Mandir* School and other halls were the favourite screening places of the film societies. In Mumbai, the hall of the National Centre for Performing Arts was the hot favourite of the film societies. In Thiruvananthapuram, a supportive Chief Minister C Achutha Menon, in the 1970s, asked the public relations department to install a 35 mm projector at the Tagore Centenary Hall to promote screenings by the film societies. The former chief minister was in the audience many times, says *Chitralekha*'s Managing Director Kulathoor Bhaskaran Nair. For 16 mm shows, the Museum Hall and Engineers Hall in the heart of the city were also available to the film societies.

The largest bill for any film society screening was the hall hiring charges, and hence with the fragile economics of the societies, most opted for 16 mm screenings at the local friendly educational institutions, with a 16 mm projector to screen the film loaned from NFAI or other sources. The archive had a good library of 16 mm films.

As the 16 mm projector and its musical sound vanished from the background of the film society screenings, film society activist K. R. Manoj made a film, in video, on the projector and its role to popularise the film society culture in Kerala. Such was the emotional association of the 16 mm film format and the projector itself for the film societies. In the early days of *Chitralekha,* Adoor Gopalakrishnan himself operated the 16 mm projector to avoid confusion in loading the reels of the film. Today, all the surviving film societies have shifted to the digital projection of films.

In 1983, reviewing the Film Society Movement, Chidananda Das Gupta noted:

> Paris has some 50 art house theatres, constantly showing film classics from all over the world. India has 216 film societies, but no art theatres. If 150, even 50, art theatres are established in the major cities in India and if censorship standards are somewhat relaxed, will the film societies survive?[42]

Clearly, despite Indira Gandhi's (as information minister of India) indulgence in giving instruction to the state government to provide government land for art house theatres across India, very few film societies could ever afford to utilise it effectively.

## Academics and Professionals as Audience

Who were the people out to make a difference in the film culture of India? Dr Pathy, the noted documentary filmmaker, D. Jefferies, A.Q. Jairazbhoy and A. Padamsee were among those who founded India's first film society, 'the Amateur Cine Society of India', Bombay, in the late 1930s, according to Chidananda Das Gupta. The CFS was started by Das Gupta, Satyajit Ray and his friends who had a deep interest in films. Later, Calcutta University Vice Chancellor became the president of CFS, attracting the cream of intellectuals and artists to the movement. Patna Film Society was formed by educationist Vijaya Mulay and her friends. Lucknow Film Society was the pioneering contribution of Professor Kailas Nath Kaul of Lucknow Botanical Gardens and the father of Gautam Kaul, the FFSI president in 2015.

The DFS was formed more or less by the officers associated with the ministry of education. The *Celluloid* Film Society of Delhi was started by two Delhi University students, who went on to make their own contributions in the field of technology.

Roorkee Film Society was of course formed by the academics of the town, particularly the Central Road Transport Research Organisation. In Bangalore, the film societies were flagged off in various public sector units and Indian Institute of Science. In Madras. it was more of an offshoot of an involvement of the upper strata of society and the cultural centers of consulates of countries like USA and Canada, with local politician Ammu Swaminadhan leading the torch of Film Society Movement in the already film-crazy city.

In Thiruvananthapuram, it was Adoor Gopalakrishnan, an FTII graduate, and his theatre and literary friends who formed the film society. They could carry the entire literary and academic crowd of the city. Later, professionals from Indian Space Research Organisation (ISRO), in the outskirts of the city, started a second unit. In Chandigarh, the PGIMER witnessed the formation of the film society. In Bhopal, it was again the students, with the help of their teachers, who formed the International Film Society.

In her document recommending the formation of FFSI, Marie Seton wrote in 1957:

> An incomplete survey of the film societies in India shows that there is a spasmodically active society in Bombay. In Calcutta, a film society has been inaugurated as a result of my six-day seminar in that city. In Madras, the British Council has been running an excellent film society, which will become independent as soon as there is a reasonable possibility of it being able to survive on its own. In Bangalore, the Indian Institute of Sciences has been running a Scientific Film Society. In Hyderabad, the Central Laboratories are planning to form a film society, while various people in Ahmadabad and Delhi hope to create their societies in the near future.[43]

Noting the enthusiasm of the academics to take film appreciation in India to a different level, Marie Seton along with Children's Film Society of India had proposed that the UGC organise university film clubs, which could have led to a long term development of the Film Society Movement. University Film Council was inaugurated with much fanfare in 1960, but it got caught in the heavy bureaucratic setup of UGC, which scuttled the move. Sashidharan, the NFAI Director, who succeeded P. K. Nair, remembers a Delhi University lecturer being posted at NFAI to work out the programme for university film clubs. Vijaya Mulay too remembers her consultancy arrangement with UGC on this project. However, today the NFAI has no such coordination with UGC, though many universities have started film studies in their mass communication curriculum across India.

## Film Appreciation as an Act of Connoisseurs

The British Raj, along with many of its positive and negative contributions, also gave India a much-needed modern education. Many bright young Indian minds gained an English education, and many in India found English education to be a window to the world, opening up new possibilities of the industrialized and fast-changing world outside India.

Vijaya Mulay wrote about her entry into film society[44] as follows:

> I learnt about language and grammar of cinema when as a student I joined the University of Leeds in UK in 1946 and after a steady diet of good cinema, found it difficult to digest the stuff that was then being shown in commercial cinemas (back home).

She along with like-minded people went on to form the Patna Film Society on her return to India.

Commenting on the growth of the DFS, eminent film critic Amita Malik, wrote; "Its membership was initially confined to civil servants, people involved in cultural activity, people from universities, both academics and students and the usual sprinkling of upper classes in search of culture."[45] A look at the other early film societies also points to this fact of the "aspirational class" of Independent India, out to prove a point with films. CFS was full of educationists who were film enthusiasts just as at Bombay Film Society, Lucknow Film Society, Roorkee Film Society or Patna Film Society.

With the ministry of education and Marie Seton playing a lead role, many educational institutions jumped on the bandwagon of film societies progressively. "Enthusiasm for cinema became respectable, and a wide range of people rushed to film societies," summed up Chidananda Das Gupta, in the introduction to his book.[46]

Commenting on the art of film appreciation, the first professor of Film Appreciation at FTII, Professor Satish Bahadur said in an interview:

> Cinema being the product of the 20th century has always been popular entertainment. Out of 100 films, maybe one or two could be put in the criteria of a good book being made.

The professor had made a 15-part television series under the UGC's country-wide classroom series on how to appreciate films.[47]

The professionals working in public sector units and scientific establishments in Bangalore pioneered the Film Society Movement and in many non-metro cities, the academia and literary crowd joined the movement. In Mumbai, the film technicians and filmmakers like K. A. Abbas carried the torch. In the state of Kerala, the Library Movement and the Little Magazine Movement of the 1960s and 1970s added to the interest in film societies, leading to its spread across the state, many of which are still continuing in various forms and shapes. The political support from the Left parties ensured that wherever they had a foothold, they looked upon film societies as part of their cultural sensitisation. The regional branch of FFSI in Kerala is run by the activists associated with Communist Party of India (Marxist). So are those associated with the societies in Kolkata.

In 1966, the government's decision to exempt film society films from censorship brought yet another kind of members into the movement. Those days, the European films itself reflected the sexual permissiveness of the continent and nudity of female characters was part of films, be it from France, Sweden or Eastern bloc. Till the time of 'video revolution', the lure of uncensored films also brought in a set of people into the film societies.

P. K. Nair observed as follows[49]:

> By the seventies, societies had sprung up in every nook and corner of the country, even in some remote places one

> never heard of before. The misguided proliferation brought all sorts of people to the movement. People who had never heard of Flaherty or Ozu,[48] or could distinguish between Einstein and Eisenstein, emerged as the new breed of film society organisers. Presumably, their only aim was to climb up the social bandwagon or getting invited to an Embassy cocktail party. The craze for watching uncensored films gave a membership boost to number of societies and even some of the organizers went out of the way to schedule such films in their programmes and take pride in the fact they have the largest viewership, using the same yardsticks as that of a commercial exhibitor, equating the two and thereby defeating the very purpose of a film society.

From finding out a new meaning and giving class dimension to the films and its appreciation and also a route for uncensored films, the Film Society Movement began to redefine the way Indians looked at films. The FFSI, NFAI and diplomatic missions never allowed themselves to be vehicles of crass films and only class films were allowed in the Film Society Movement, making it yet another class act of the aspirational society of a young independent nation. With active patronage of the government, Indian academia and professionals moved their films away from clutches of Hollywood and began to experiment with its own film aesthetics, some inspired by European, Latin American and Japanese films, which were freely available in the film society network.

## Reference

1. http://cherianwrites.blogspot.in/2016/02/from-nfai-collection-national-cinema.html
2. R. M. Ray, ed., *Indian Cinema in Retrospect: Speeches of the 1955 Seminar* (SangeetNatak Academy).
3. Marie Seton, *Portrait of a Director* (New Delhi: Penguin, 2003), p.58.
4. https://mib.gov.in/sites/default/files/Annual%20Report%202020-21.pdf p.95
5. https://en.wikipedia.org/wiki/Bollywood
6. Ibid.3.

7. Ibid.4.
8. http://cherianwrites.blogspot.in/2016/02/from-nfai-collection-national-cinema.html
9. https://censusofindia2021.com/literacy-rate-of-india-2021/
10. Ibid.2, p.29.
11. Ibid.2, p. 29
12. NFAI librarynotes.
13. Marie Seton,*Booklet on Film Appreciation* (New Delhi: NCERT, 1956).
14. Chidananda Das Gupta,*Cinema of Satyajit Ray*(Viking, 1980).
15. H. N. Nara HariRao, ed., *The Film Society Movement In India* (Mumbai: Asian Film Foundation, 2009),p.71.
16. https://en.wikipedia.org/wiki/Odessa
17. Chidananda Das Gupta, *Seeing is Believing* (Viking, 2008),p.85.
18. https://en.wikipedia.org/wiki/Samik_Bandyopadhyay
19. Mari Seton, *Article in Indian Film Quarterly*1956.
20. H. N. Narahari Rao, ed., *The Film Society Movement In India* (Mumbai: Asian Film Foundation, 2009). p.21.
21. Ibid., p. .35
22. Ibid., p. 73.
23. IFSON, 1981, NFAI library.
24. RTI reply from NFAI.
25. https://en.wikipedia.org/wiki/Jean-Luc_Godard
26. https://en.wikipedia.org/wiki/Werner_Herzog
27. https://en.wikipedia.org/wiki/Federico_Fellini
28. https://en.wikipedia.org/wiki/Ingmar_Bergman
29. https://en.wikipedia.org/wiki/Mikl%C3%B3s_Jancs%C3%B3
30. https://en.wikipedia.org/wiki/Krzysztof_Zanussi
31. https://en.wikipedia.org/wiki/Akira_Kurosawa
32. http://cherianwrites.blogspot.in/2016/02/soruce-of-films-and-film-programs-of.html
33. Interaction with Adoor Gopalakrishnan.
34. http://vkcherian.blogspot.in/2012/06/mrinal-sen-at-90-riding-wave-of.html
35. https://en.wikipedia.org/wiki/Sudhir_Mishra
36. https://en.wikipedia.org/wiki/Jaya_Bachchan

37. https://en.wikipedia.org/wiki/Shatrughan_Sinha
38. https://en.wikipedia.org/wiki/Naseeruddin_Shah
39. https://en.wikipedia.org/wiki/Om_Puri
40. https://en.wikipedia.org/wiki/Nandan_(Kolkata)
41. http://www.ksfdc.in/html/cinematheatres.php
42. Ibid.17. p.99
43. http://cherianwrites.blogspot.in/2016/02/marie-seton-from-cfs-published-in.html
44. Ibid. 17.
45. http://cherianwrites.blogspot.in/2016/03/the-role-of-film-societies-by-amita.html
46. Chidananda Das Gupta,Introduction of *Cinema of Satyajit Ray*(Viking, 1980).
47. https://en.wikipedia.org/wiki/Satish_Bahadur
48. https://en.wikipedia.org/wiki/Yasujir%C5%8D_Ozu
49. http://cherianwrites.blogspot.in/2016/02/havefilm-societies-lost-their-relevance.html

# 5
# The Film Society Movement: As a New Window on the World for Film People

## The Film Society: A Personal Account

Looking back, as a degree student, I ask myself what made me join the *Chitralekha* and *Chalachithra* film societies in Thiruvananthapuram in 1976. Clearly, my interest in literature and arts pushed me to the film societies. The fact that one could see films from various countries of the world, just as one could read books from various countries in a library, drove me to the film societies. The library movement that had taken root in almost all the villages in Kerala, had already put me onto the library circuit as a high school student. For me, it was a natural progression to move from books to films.

There was no television in Kerala's capital in those days, and films were the only medium of mass entertainment. Slowly, I found myself among various groups of people discussing literature, films, art and politics. I also found myself in the esteemed company of writers, theatre personalities and filmmakers. One of the most rewarding memories of those days was being in a queue at the city's Sreekumar Cinema house, where the English film, *One Flew Over the Cuckoo's Nest* by Czech filmmaker Milos Forman, who migrated to Hollywood, was being shown. I found myself standing and waiting behind legendary filmmaker Adoor

Gopalakrishnan and his wife, Sunanda, in the queue. After his first two films, Adoor had already become a celebrity in Kerala.

When I was in the second year of my degree course, I began to spot filmmaker G. Aravindan, writer Padmarajan, who entered into filmmaking later, theatre activist Professor Narendra Prasad, (later he became a popular film actor), among the film society crowd at the Tagore Centenary Hall. That was where I also met my lifelong friends like film writer M.F. Thomas, who was the general secretary of *Chitralekha* and Vijayakrishnan, the film critic and an entire group of students from the Trivandrum Fine Arts School. I was happy to hang out with them.

## The Beginnings

Adoor, recounting the formation of the *Chitralekha* Film Society in 1965, said[1]:

> I am an academically and professionally trained filmmaker. I have studied cinema at the Film Institute in Pune (second batch). I was very clear about what I wanted to do. In fact, I went on to initiate the Film Society Movement in Kerala, because, first, I wanted the intelligentsia in Kerala to become aware of a cinema of high calibre that existed in the world outside. Also, I wanted to continue watching international cinema after leaving the Film Institute. The Film Society Movement is not a mass movement. It is aimed at a small, niche and discreet audience, good critics and passionate film lovers.

*Chitralekha* was inaugurated by the then governor of Kerala, Bhagwan Sahay, in July 1965, with the city's literary figures in attendance and was organised by Adoor and his friends from theatre and literary fields.

The film society crowd was a mix of literary people, students like me, state and central government officials, college lecturers and bank employees, officials from the Indian Space Research Organisation (ISRO) and Keltron, the fledgling public sector electronic company of Kerala of the 1970s and 1980s. I recall the presence of Keltron's first chairman, the legendary K.P.P. Nambiar, who rose to become secretary of the Central Electronics Department, as a member of the *Chitralekha*. Nambiar used to come with his wife to the screenings. K.N. Raj, a former Delhi University Vice Chancellor, who had established the Centre for Development Studies (CDS) near the *Chitralekha* film co-operative complex, was another celebrity member. The membership was coveted those days, with the elite from all circles of the city vying for it, recalled M.F. Thomas, who was the secretary in the 1970s.

Thiruvananthapuram, being the capital of Kerala, was not just the seat of the state's political power but was also the favourite centre of academic and literary figures, as well as many Left-leaning institutions. *Malayalees* had come to accept films as a serious art form, with filmmakers Adoor and Aravindan winning the National Awards. Film societies began to be seen as a charmed circle of cultural, political activists and intellectuals, who thronged there in numbers in the 1970s and 1980s.

"After the screenings, we used to walk to the bus stop and discuss the film as a routine act, till we got our respective buses home," recalled Vijayakrishnan, the noted Malayalam film critic.[2] The, "we" he described, were Gopi, who later bagged the *Bharat* award for the best actor of the year 1972 for his performance in Adoor's film, *Kodiyettam,* and MF Thomas. The who's who of Malayalam media, literature and films become connoisseurs of cinema as an art form through the screenings of *Chitralekha* from 1965—85.

Watching films from various countries made me curious about publications like the British Film Institute's journal *Sight and Sound* which was available along with various British newspapers at the local British Council Library. They helped me track the developments happening in international cinema. I also found American film publications, like UCLA's *Film Quarterly*, in the university library and books like *Films As An Art.*

### Defining Film Societies and Cinephiles

There were many like me, in other cities, getting initiated into the world of films; the usual cinema houses did not attract us like the film society did. T.V. Chandran, the National Award-winning Malayalam filmmaker recalled his days with the film society: "I used to jump the gates of USIS in Bangalore and later in Chennai to see films. I kept detailed notes of each film." Just like the film societies, the screenings at the United States Information Service (USIS), Alliance Francaise and Max Muller Bhavan in metro cities had also become the favourite haunts of film buffs in the 1980s and 1990s and continue to be so even now.

Abhija Ghosh, a JNU scholar, noted[3]:

> Film societies signified different initiatives in different locales and among different groups, ranging from selective and alternative cultural groups, cooperative communities to powerful pedagogical and political forces, generating discourses on cinema. Among other things, the movement witnessed productive collaborations, long-lasting friendships, debates on cinema, censorship and membership, internal fissures, and problems of sustenance. However, these aspects involving the members of the societies and *cinephiles* have been overwhelmed by institutional discourses on good cinema and auteur studies of preferred filmmakers.

The brain behind the movement, Chidananda Das Gupta, too, defines the Film Society Movement as "homogeneous groups which attracted people with certain common cultural backgrounds". It is well known that Das Gupta's CFS drew a huge crowd from academia. Calcutta University Vice Chancellor Nirmal Kumar Siddhanto was its president when CFS restarted in 1956.

Pradipta Sen, who was a member from those days, recollected the golden days of CFS, as follows[4]:

> The membership grew from 250-300 to 2500. Apurva Kumar Chanda, DPIR, Education, of West Bengal, also got associated with CFS. BN Sircar of New Theatres and the Eastern India Motion Pictures Association was a patron of CFS. Prachi Cinema--all Bengali cinema houses--allowed free shows. "In the early 1960s, we organised an Eisenstein Film Festival at the Academy of Fine Arts, it opened to a full house, and, even Ray, who came to see the Russian maestro's film, had to sit on the stairs, such was the rush.

## A New World View Through Films

The act of seeing films was treated with such passion that even Ray could not resist creating his own compilation of music for *Battleship Potemkin* when he saw it for the 22nd time. "To the surprise of the visiting Eisenstein Archive curator from Moscow, Ray described the incident," recalled Samik Bandyopadhyay[5], formerly of Seagull Books. Ray was playing the long-playing records (LPs) of music he compiled at the show but did not keep that particular music track to be shared with the excited curator.

MRINAL SEN WITH CFS MEMBERS AT THE INAUGURAL SHOW OF 'CALCUTTA 71'

**Figure 5.1.** Mrinal Sen at a CFS Screening

*Battleship* was the prized procession of CFS in the late 1940s itself and that 16 mm print continued to be the very first film of pre-*Pather Panchali* days of most film societies and remains one of the most screened films of most societies even today.

The DFS's biggest draw was the vice-president of FFSI, Indira Gandhi, who rose to become the I&B minister in Lal Bahadur Shastri's cabinet and later prime minister. In 1964, Gandhi, as I&B minister, had to sit in a room adjacent to the projection room at the Sapru House Hall, where Ingmar Bergman's *Wild Strawberries* was shown. Freedom fighter Aruna Asaf Ali and the then defence minister, V. K. Krishna Menon, were patrons of DFS, apart from the officials of various ministries, academia from Delhi University and the city's elite. *Akka* (Vijaya Mulay) recalls Krishna Menon rushing in to see Satyajit Ray's film *Devi*, which was previewed at DFS. I. K. Gujral, who succeeded Gandhi, as I&B minister, was a treasurer of FFSI during the 1960s.

It seems that the BFS was the most elite of the lot. Led by R.E. Hawkins, the general manager of the Oxford University Press (OUP), BFS had S.T. Berkeley Hill, V.M. Vijakar, V.N. Raiji, Padma Raiji, M.P. Strimpel, J. Farbtein, A. Bhaskara Rao and K.L. Khandapur of the Film Division. By 1962, Jag Mohan and M.V. Krishnaswamy were also on the committee. The BFS was closed in 1962 and its funds amounting to Rs 1,500 were transferred to the Film Forum, the film society pioneered by K. A. Abbas.

According to a note by R.E. Hawkins, "The first Indian film to be screened by the society was *Uljhan*, produced and directed by N.R. Acharya. The director and cameraman were present during the discussions (which followed). In the same year, Chetan Anand's *Neecha Ghar* and *Ishara* were shown."[6]

Adoor recalled the initial growth of the movement in Kerala[7] as follows:

> *Chitralekha* was not only the first film society to be formed, (at Thiruvananthapuram) but it served as the nucleus of the movement. We were promoting and supporting enthusiasts in each town to form societies, we shared the films we sourced for screenings, and supplied relevant literature with them to be distributed to their members. We became a virtual voluntary agency to coordinate the film societies in Kerala, much before FFSI actively began to undertake it. We also motivated the University Students Unions to conduct film appreciation camps and enlightened them on the new culture of cinema.

In Mumbai and Bangalore, the professionals of various public sector units, like the Bhabha Atomic Research Council (BARC), Bharat Electronics, and ISRO, found the booming Film Society Movement an attractive place to groom their interests in films. "The scientists from BARC were regulars at our screenings, "said V. Sasikumar, a film society activist who was then working at the Department of Telecommunications in Mumbai.

In Bangalore, Nara Hari Rao, an engineer with Bharat Electronics, started the *Suchitra* Film Society and later became the FFSI president. In Thiruvananthapuram, Chalachithra was floated by the engineers of ISRO. George Mathew of *Chalachithra* and V. K. Joseph, who was the secretary of Kerala FFSI in2015 were employees of ISRO. Soorya Krishnamoorthy, who, later, parted with Chalachithra to begin his own cultural outfit, *Soorya,* was also from ISRO.

## Towards a New Idiom in Indian Films

While individual film societies were blooming in the metro cities, the government of the young nation too woke up to the immense possibilities that films as a medium had thrown up. Setting the agenda for the 1955 *Sangeet Natak Akademi* seminar on films, its chairman, Dr Rajamannar, said, "The film should also be judged by the standards which we employ to judge any other work of art. The film is a new art form, which is in a continuous state of development... India must and will make its distinctive contribution to the film art of the world and I am confident it will."[8]

The seminar directors were Prithviraj Kapoor and Devika Rani, and it was attended by the vice-president of India, S. Radhakrishnan, and Indira Gandhi, along with a host of filmmakers from across India. Admitting that the influence of films in India was greater than newspapers and books (due to literacy levels in 1955), Nehru, in his inaugural speech, went on to say that films have to be "treated realistically as something of the highest importance in the life of a country". Nehru ruled out the government setting the agenda for the film industry but went on to say that negative tendencies like warmongering through films will be stopped and the government itself will produce films for children and other films without competing with the industry.[9]

Indira Gandhi emphasised the quality of art and cinema in her speech, presenting the National Awards of 1966. "Quality comes from intellect, technical mastery, and the determination to be honest. Above all, quality comes from courage, courage to be different, to be non-conformist," the later Prime Minister pointed out.[10]

Both Jawaharlal Nehru and Indira Gandhi had clearly set their agenda for films, extending official patronage to cinema as an art form and also for the development of an audience for it. Indira Gandhi, even after relinquishing her post as the vice-president of FFSI, lent her social secretary, Usha Bhagat, as its joint secretary, thus keeping a close eye on the Film Society Movement.

### The Political Patronage

Jawaharlal Nehru, the Oxford-educated scholar statesman, had clear plans for a mass medium like cinema. In 1950, he formed an expert committee of films for a new policy regime on films under S. K. Patil, and they made recommendations which were far-reaching. In 1951, he appointed a French Indian, Jean Bhownagary, as the advisor to the information and broadcasting ministry for flagging off the first International Film Festival of India. He also invited Marie Seton from the British Film Institute to evangelise films for educational purposes across India and to precipitate the budding film societies into an organised movement across the country. A fact confirmed by Shyam Benegal, a veteran filmmaker of the new cinema of India, who became the president of FFSI in 2009.

When India became Independent in 1947, the leadership of the time felt that cinema had a role to play in the development of the country. People like Jawaharlal Nehru and others felt that cinema, an important component of popular culture, had great potential in terms of supporting the development of the country... In addition to this, they set up a high-level committee under S. K. Patil in 1951-52 to look into the problems of the film industry itself. This resulted in the formulating of a film policy that included:

(a) A Film Finance Corporation for financing of feature films.

(b) A film school to train filmmakers in all disciplines.

(c) A children's film society to encourage the making of films for children.

(d) Re-organisation of the film certification policy (which, until then, followed the British Censor Code).[11]

However, since a policy on films was implemented later, Adoor Gopalakrishnan, Benegal's contemporary, does not give full credit to Nehru for that. He prefers to give credit to Indira Gandhi for bringing Marie Seton to spread the Film Society Movement. Answering the same question, whether the movement and new cinema were a result of the Nehruvian policy initiative, Adoor said; "I can't say if it was a planned initiative by the Nehruvians. But the S. K. Patil Committee appointed by the Nehru government had recommended many measures to improve the standards of the Indian film industry, such as setting up a film institute, institution of National Awards, a film financing institution and the National Film Archive."[12]

The sequence of activities by the government indicates that without the political and personal patronage of Nehru, there was little scope for an early Film Society Movement in India. Nehru and his trusted aide, V. K. Krishna Menon, brought in Marie Seton to advise the government on how to promote films as an educational tool. After her lecture tour in India, she wrote a booklet named *Film Appreciation,* which was published by the Ministry of Education. A few other monographs on film appreciation written by Marie were also published by NCERT during those days.

**Figure 5.2.** Marie Seton with Satyajit Ray

The formation of FFSI was in 1959 following a report by Marie Seton to the Ministry of Education after her lecture tour of various Indian cities. The government allowed FFSI to import 16 films for circulation from its affiliated members. It also provided an exemption from censorship for FFSI-circulated films. States were asked to provide entertainment tax exemption for screening by the film societies and allot land for screening halls for alternate films.

Indira Gandhi intervened personally from time to time with state chief ministers to ensure the exemption of taxes was not a deterrent for the smooth running of the film societies. The only other film expert committee constituted by the government, after the committee of 1951-52, was in 1980, when Indira Gandhi was the prime minister, though the committee was initiated during the regime of Morarji Desai as prime minister. The committee was headed by Dr. K. Shivarama Karanth, an eminent Kannada literary figure. No other prime minister, after Gandhi, showed any particular interest in films and the film field was left to fend for itself. The political leaders were content with being seen with celebrity film stars and film personalities at India's International Film Festivals and National Film Award functions, over the years.

In his first review of the FFSI in 1965, Das Gupta wrote:

> The union minister for information and broadcasting has requested all state governments to exempt all member societies of the federation from entertainment taxes and other levies. The federation has so far received a total of Rs 10,000 from the union government, Rs 5,000 from *Sangeet Natak Akademi* and Rs 3,000 from *Sangeet Natak Sangam*, Madras, as grant-in-aid.[13]

The central government's grant for FFSI continued till 2014 and the last annual grant amount was Rs 6 lakh.[14]

## Creating *Rasiks* Out of Cinephiles

For any work of art to flourish, it needs appreciation and criticism; appreciation to encourage the artist, and criticism to look at the form and structure of the work of art. Film appreciation was seen as more of a star-gazing activity by the writers in the pre-film society era and there was hardly any film criticism as a genre in the 1950s to 1960s.

Though the likes of K. A. Abbas started off as a film critic during the 1930s itself, the genre was full of stories about films and actors, bereft of any analysis with technical and aesthetic tools. One of the reasons was that films were not yet accepted as a mainline art, like writing, theatre, painting or music, though cinema had all of these in it. The absence of literature on films, their technicalities and their developing aesthetics, added to the problem in the 1940s and 1950s. That is why, Vijaya Mulay talked about creating *rasiks* through film societies and the late K. Bikram Singh,[15] erstwhile bureaucrat and filmmaker, talked about the need to have a classic approach in appreciating films. "Classic", he defined it as in music or painting.

Chidananda Das Gupta wrote over 24 pages explaining the concept of *Margi* and *Desi*, the traditional 'classical and folk' divide in his last book. He went on to defend this classification and pointed out that, "One advantage of accepting the age-old division between *Margi and Desi* or classical and folk (more correctly pop in the urban context) is that neither category can then demand the non-existence of the other." All of them were emphasising the need for the classic approach to film as an art, which the film societies promoted through their screenings, publications and discussions.[16]

**Figure 5.3.** Indian Film Quarterly

The *Film Quarterly* of CFS, in 1956, emphasised the need to bring in the *Margi* aspect to Indian films through informed criticism and literature on films. "As a journal of the Calcutta Film Society, it represents and becomes an instrument of a new movement to promote the growth of a better cinema and better audience. Its objectives are to develop the two elements which are so lacking in our cinema and film criticism; thought and sensitivity," said its first editorial.

In her memorandum to the government for the formation of FFSI, Marie Seton addressed the issue of film appreciation and criticism. "In order fora film society should be dynamic and serve its fullest purpose, it is essential to have discussions and lead the members into its fullest participation. Further, it is essential that any central film institute keeps in constant dynamic contact with film societies and the real desires of the public so that both can grow." Seton was equally keen that India promote university film clubs to enlist a new generation to the Film Society Movement.[17]

## The University Film Council

The suggestion for a University Film Council found an immediate welcome at the UGC headed by C.D. Deshmukh (1896–1982), a distinguished civil servant who had resigned from Nehru's cabinet as finance minister and was appointed UGC chairman for five years (1956–61). Deshmukh, who was the first chairman of the Reserve Bank of India and had held other important positions, appeared to be an enthusiastic votary of the Film Society Movement, as he established a University Film Council, headed by a former I&B minister in Nehru's cabinet, R.R. Diwakar (1894–1990), another politician scholar from Karnataka.

On New Year's Eve (1959–60), the Film Council was inaugurated by the UGC chairman. Inaugurating the first meeting, Deshmukh said, 'The Film Society Movement in the universities and colleges would definitely bring about a healthy trend in the production of feature films. The film medium could be utilised to act as a positive and corrective force in shaping a balanced view of life among the youth."[18]

The UGC had approved the scheme to start film clubs in affiliated campuses and 14 universities had approved the proposal. The UGC appointed Marie Seton as the technical advisor and instituted a grant of Rs 5,001 for those institutions to form film clubs.

In his inaugural speech, Diwakar said that the council would make available 16 outstanding films of the times, both Indian and foreign to the clubs. The films were those that the students did not have a chance to see at commercial theatres. Mahendra Nath, member secretary of the Film Council, said that the British Film Institute had promised to support the initiative.

*The Times of India* reported as follows[19]:

> As things are today, the students have no opportunity to see any of the avant-garde films or experimental films or documentaries. The result is that most of them have never seen a picture from countries like Japan, France, Italy and Poland, which have produced some of the most expressive films in the last fifteen years.

This was the period that recorded the emergence of Akira Kurosawa in Japan, Vittorio De Sica in Italy, Godard and Truffaut in France and Andrzej Wajda in Poland. "All that a university has to do is to buy a projector, reserve a large hall in one of its buildings for the showing of films in the evenings, and appoint a person for correspondence and other work," the report pointed out.[20]

In a letter to *The Times of India*, published on Christmas day, 1959, Marie Seton wrote: "The idea of film societies in the universities was brought to the University Grants Commission by the Children's Film Society and it is the Children's Film Society which suggested my name for nine months to commence this valuable scheme." Marie also mentioned that FFSI was formed with six film societies earlier in December 1959, noting the "ever-growing interest in better films".[21]

## FTII-NFAI Summer Residency Churning Out *Rasiks*

Vijaya Mulay lamented that the University Film Council got entangled in the bureaucratic web of UGC and did not finally take off. Indeed, it was a big loss to the Film Society Movement. However, in1967, the National Film Archive, established in 1964, initiated an annual summer film appreciation course which was to be organised with FTII for selected academics and film buffs across India. The summer course found instant acceptance among University teachers and students and film society workers, as it promised them a feast of great films across the world and interactions with filmmakers and film theoreticians across India.

**Figure 5.4.** Mari Seton and Satish Bahadur at FTII-NFAI Film Appreciation Course

The credit of starting and maintaining this summer residency goes to Marie Seton, Professor Satish Bahadur, who started one of the first University Film Clubs at Agra University, and P. K. Nair, the director of NFAI. Nair and Bahadur defined film appreciation, formulated the curricula and conducted the course, setting the basis for film studies in India as a serious vocation. The summer residency remains a much-awaited annual event for film buffs so far. The last available announcement for the summer course was in 2020, that too online due to the pandemic season health protocols.

Together with Bahadur at FTII, Nair created an army of film *rasiks* across the country, over the years. "Looking back, Prof Bahadur and Nair created and nurtured a new regime of film appreciation, across the country through these summer courses," Anil Srivastava, their contemporary, recalled. From government servants to university lecturers, film society members and journalists rushed to Pune for the summer course.

**Figure 5.5.1.** John Dayal

**Figure 5.5.2.** Sudhir Nandgaonkar

**Figure 5.5.3.** Rashmi Doraiswamy

**Figure 5.5.4.** M. F. Thomas

The Film Society Movement, along with the appreciation courses, threw up a generation of film critics and new cinema writers across India in all languages. Several important critics, journalists and intellectuals joined this movement: Amita Malik, who criticised DFS for limiting its membership to 250 and forced them to raise it to 500, Hamimuddin Mohammed, who joined the Film Festival Directorate, Vasant Sathe, Muriel Wasi, Jag Mohan, Iqbal Masood, Khalid Mohammed, John Dayal, Anil Saari, Deepak Roy, Shanta P. Coudhary, Sadanand Menon, Ravi Vasudevan, Ashish Rajadhyaksha (Author: *Indian Cinema in the Time of Celluloid*), Rashmi Doraiaswamy and my friends from Thiruvananthapuram, M.F. Thomas and Vijayakrishnan, who taught me the basics of film aesthetics.

There is a special set of film writers like Das Gupta and Sudhir Nandgaonkar, who were also full-time film society activists. Chidu *da* held the CFS flag high from the word go. Sudhir*ji* was a man for film societies in Mumbai, and the rest of Maharashtra, till his death in 2022.

"*Prabhat Chitra Mandal* was established in 1968 by a group of five film critics. Vasant Sathe, an English writer on cinema, was its president and Sudhir Nandgaonkar, the general secretary. All the film critics with Sathe-Sudhirji's team were professional writers and regulars with various Marathi newspapers. The society was named 'Prabhat' to cherish the memory of Prabhat Film Co. lead by V. Shantaram in the early 1930s and 40s," said Sudhirji, in an interview.[22]

The names are endless if you compute all regional language writers. The list of National Award winners in the category, with books on films and writers on films, includes most of these names. They exhorted the readers into a new culture of films as art with their writing, helping a generation to see films in a more aesthetic manner.

Film critic-turned-filmmaker, Khalid Mohammed[23], remembers seeing Godard's *Breathless* at the Film Forum in the 1960s. "It changed my outlook towards films," he said. No wonder the period made the JNU scholar Abhija Ghosh write:

> The trajectory of the Film Society Movement was affected by a period of *cinephilia* that was sincerely invested in the aesthetic possibilities of cinema, and was equally informed by the celluloid materiality of the form they engaged with... And, on the other hand, the rare opportunities of watching international and art cinema, combined with the consciousness of the transitory nature of the celluloid image, significantly transformed the viewer/member's temporal and spatial relationship to cinema.[24]

Indeed, it was the combined assault of the political leadership, the government of the day, filmmakers, cultural icons, academia and media on the prevailing, rather crass, cinematic sensibilities, through the Film Society Movement, which triggered far-reaching positive changes in the genre of popular cinema as well.

## Uncensored Films as a Pull Factor

In the 1960s, Europe, after the Second World War, was undergoing what is now called a sexual revolution. Naturally, their films too reflected the new sexual culture, discarding the Victorian morality about sex. Nudity of characters and sexual acts in films were no longer a taboo. "The sexual revolution, also known as the *sexual liberation*, was a social movement that challenged traditional codes of behaviour related to sexuality and interpersonal relationships throughout the Western world from the 1960s to the 1970s", Allyn David was quoted in his book.[25]

India, not just in the 1960s, but even in 2023, has not come out of the Victorian morality and nudity in films continues to be a big no! As the film societies began to flourish with films from Europe, censorship of these films became an issue, as they had nudity and sexual acts, which was shocking for the Indian conservative society. European diplomatic missions, who gave these films free to the FFSI network, insisted that the censor's conservative cuts would not be allowed for these films. The FFSI was stuck with these tempting offers to screen high-quality films, but there was no way they could show them without censorship.

Satyajit Ray, as FFSI president, wrote to Indira Gandhi, on the issue. Gandhi, the then I&B minister, who conceded to the request for an exception of censorship for FFSI screenings, ensured a steady source of films from both Eastern and Western blocks of Europe. The period was 1964–66; much before the video and digital revolution; in a bold decision, she exempted the FFSI films from censorship. The official argument was that the film society members were cultured adults and connoisseurs of art who were used to exposure to nudity etc.

The final official order came out in 1966. The order empowered an FFSI committee to preview films and recommend to the government for censorship exemption for screening in FFSI-affiliated film societies for three years.

The step facilitated the rush of non-English films, from Europe and Latin America to the FFSI network of societies, many of which had explicit female nudity, which made film societies attractive to a new group of people, who were not necessarily connoisseurs of cinema or attracted to films with aesthetic content. This was the period when uncensored films were strictly illegal in India and sex in films was a taboo, not to speak of nudity per se. Naturally, there was a rush to join film societies in the 1970s and 1980s, till the arrival of video, DVDs and the Internet, by certain middle-class lumpens.

I remember the DFS in the 1980s, overflowing with such members and locking its membership. From 500, DFS reached 1500, and a new set of members, other than the *margis*, as Chidu *da* described, entered the circuit. The phenomenon spread to all the urban centres where film society membership had become a status symbol by the 1970s; the centres began to be filled with dubious characters, so much so, that these viewers would leave the hall immediately after a sexual act or a nude scene in a film.

**Figure 5.6.** A still from Polanski's *Knife in the Water*

The craze for watching uncensored films gave a membership boost to the number of societies in the 1980s till the arrival of videos, DVDs and Internet porn. Some of the film societies scheduled such films in their effort to increase the membership, using the same yardsticks as that of a commercial exhibitor, thereby bringing undesirable elements to the network, defeating the very purpose of film society screenings.

"No wonder such gatecrashers could not thrive for long. They had to have their natural exit," pointed out P. K. Nair, in an article in 2004.[26] This, unfortunately, turned the societies into a totally male-dominated movement and women kept off from the crowd which were rather crudely "enjoying uncensored films."

In his review of the Film Society Movement, in 1983, Chidu *da* too noticed this populist trend in the movement which he had originally heralded. He noted that it was a deliberate decision of FFSI to go all out and expand membership on a large scale, a decision made by the All-India Conference of Film Societies in Calcutta in 1967, to address the issue of economic liabilities of individual societies.

Chidu *da* observed as follows:

> The harm done should not be measured in terms of the shows of films with nudity and sex, because the notion that they are a corrupt adult audience is in itself highly questionable. What was lost in the process was the interest in good cinema on the part of the large majority of the film society members.[27]

The new kind of members had choked the film societies across the country, a fact I personally found out in Delhi in 1981. This may have put off many young entrants in the 1980s and contributed to their lack of interest when the movement was in serious crisis by the end of the decade. The crisis was mainly due to the advent of national television, video and DVD, making the film society circuit less attractive as uncensored films. This made the movement fall back on its original supporters in various other streams like academics and literature and the film industry itself.

## Influence of Other Movements: Literary, Library and Leftist

Out of the 293 film societies affiliated to FFSI in 2014, (as submitted to the I&B ministry), 118 are in Kerala alone. Kerala has been unique in the spread of film societies since the 1970s. The reasons for this unique phenomenon are manifold. However, one of the most compelling reasons can be the other parallel movements which were already there; the Library Movement of the 1950s and 1970s along with the little magazine groups which sprang up across Kerala.

When the Library Movement celebrated its silver jubilee in 1971, the Film Society Movement was taking off in Kerala. It had 4,000libraries spread across the state and half of them had their own buildings, with good reading halls. The libraries had a membership base of 650,000 and stocks of over 7 million books. (*Kerala Library Movement–Silver Jubilee Souviner-1971*). Just like the Film Society Movement, the Library Movement in Kerala had its own crisis following the arrival of multi-channel television which beamed captivating tear-jerkers. Unlike the little magazine groups, which were more of a Leftist cultural renaissance, the Library Movement ran parallel to the freedom movement and was led by a visionary activist, P.N. Panicker.[28]

"Read to Grow", was the motto of the Library Movement. When the Kerala Film Society movement celebrated 50 years of its existence in 2015, marking the 50th anniversary of the *Chitralekha* Film Society, formed in July 1965, the founder of the society attributed the spread of the movement to a festival they had organised for the all-India literary festival at *Aluva*, near Kochi, in January 1966.

Gautaman Bhaskaran described the emergence of the Film Society Movement, parallel to the literary one, in the authorized biography of Adoor Gopalakrishnan, as follows:[29]

> The fifth All India Writers Conference at *Aluva*, Kerala, in January 1966, provided a wonderful opportunity off the ground. They organised screenings of 15 world classics—to coincide with the conference—in the state's nine districts as well as in bordering Nagarcoil in Tamil Nadu. Vans carrying prints (of films) criss-crossed the region pushing and promoting a novel cinema culture and arousing public interest in different genres,.

The collection of films included Ray's *Devi* and Ritwik Ghatak's *Mege Dhaka Tara* along with Russian, Polish, French and Hungarian films. Adoor strongly believes that the film festival of 1966 made a deep impression on the viewers across Kerala, that films were an aesthetic art object, and created a hunger for such films in a population who were already exposed to quality literature through the Library Movement. The libraries also organised discussions on new books and held at least one annual function with a writer participating in it. This was the pattern in which film societies organised festivals of films with screenings and discussions with filmmakers in the days to come.

The period also saw the Kerala People's Arts Club (KPAC),[30] promoted by the Communist Party of India (CPI), successfully staging its production—*You Made Me a Communist*—throughout the state. The KPAC was an affiliate of the Indian People's Theatre Association (IPTA), which had already produced films with K. A. Abbas. Within a decade, Kerala had the largest number of film societies in the southern region, with over 100 units spread across the state.

"Each town had a film society and they not just screened the films, but organised serious film discussions," recalled Vijayakrishnan, one of the early film society evangelists. Vijayakrishnan travelled across the state introducing a new kind of cinema and wrote extensively on films in Malayalam journals. He was the first to be given the National Award in 1983 for the best book on cinema, for *Chalachitra Sameekha*, published by Current Books, a popular Malayalam publishing house.[31]

Though the Left Front governments in Kerala and West Bengal have been supporting the Film Society Movements, and they even established centres like *Nandan, Kariali* and *Kalabhavan* art house theatres to screen quality films, there was never a full-throttled and direct support to the culture of new cinema. In West Bengal, information minister Budhadeb Bhattacharya, who later became chief minister, was the force behind *Nandan*, the film and cultural complex, whose logo was designed by Satyajit Ray. His department also promoted many young filmmakers and is credited with the promotion of Ritwik Ghatak's film packages across India. They organised a Ritwik film festival in 1981, with a workshop with the late filmmaker's celebrated students like Kumar Shahani and Mani Kaul, when the late Safdar Hashmi was head of the Information Office of the West Bengal government in New Delhi.

Professor Mihir Bhattacharya, who introduced film studies as a postgraduate course at Jadavpur University (the first in any university in India) in Kolkata, listed the contribution of the Left in films and culture in those glorious days of IPTA.

> If you look back on the years marked by the vital presence of the Indian People's Theatre Association in Bengal – the 1940s and 50s, in particular, though the movement started earlier and lasted longer – you may find that the mental map of culture you have prepared needs considerable revision... Therefore, what looms

> large in my mapping happens to be *Nabanna* of Bijan Bhattacharya, *Raktakarabi* of Shombhu Mitra, *Angar and Tiner Talwar* of Utpal Dutt, *Ebang Indrajit* of Badal Sircar, the novels of Manik Bandyopadhyay, Satinath Bhaduri, Samaresh Basu, Sulekha Sanyal and Nani Bhowmik, the poetry of Bishnu Dey, Arun Mitra, Samar Sen, Subhash Mukhopadhyay and Sukanto Bhattacharya, the music of Ravi Shankar, Jyotirindra Maitra, Hemango Biswas, Binay Ray and Salil Chowdhury—and the incomparable Harindranath Chattopadhyay who composed largely in Hindi—the choreography of Uday Shankar, Shanti Bardhan and Shombhu Bhattacharya, the paintings and sketches of Somenath Hore, Jainul Abedin and Chitta Prasad, the photography of Sunil Jana, the graphics of Khaled Chowdhury, the cinema of Nimai Ghosh, Satyajit Ray, Ritwik Ghatak and Mrinal Sen, and the like. Much of what I have listed has endured and a good many of the texts have achieved the status of modern classics.
>
> The ideological projection of my mapping is obvious; most of the texts had deep links with the organized cultural movement, inspired, aided and propagated by the Communist Party of India.

The professor, who is associated with the Left in West Bengal, pointed out that "there are some exceptions, though. *Raktakarabi* and *Ebang Indrajit,* and *Pather Panchali* and a few others, had no manifest links with the party or the movement."[32]

In Kerala, the CPI(M) had floated its own film production unit named *Janashakthi Films* and even co-produced one of John Abraham's films, *Cheriyachante Kroora Krithangal* (Cruel Deeds of Cherian), in the 1970s. They have been openly supporting the Film Society Movement and their local units have been the strongest supporters behind Kerala FFSI's regional activities. The Left and Democratic Front government in 2010 allotted Rs 50 lakhs for the film societies as a one-time grant for the FFSI Kerala unit. Though there are occasional allegations of partisan attitude in the activity of the Kerala FFSI unit, the Left parties must be given full credit for sustaining as many as 119 film society units across the state and even celebrating 50 years of the Kerala Film Society Movement in July 2015.

"In Kerala, unlike earlier days, when the entire movement was identified with few film societies, FFSI remains a strong entity, engaged in spreading a better film culture," FFSI Keralam's general secretary (2012), VK Joseph, a former ISRO employee, explained. FFSI Kerala actively supports the International Film Festival of Kerala with its Open Forum and also organises a short film festival, Signs, every year.[33]

Despite their steady and visionary involvement, the Left has always been caught between the mass and aesthetic appeals in cinema. In a note sent to the then chief minister and Polit Bureau member of the CPI(M) Budhadev Bhattacharya, veteran actor and theatre activist, Utpal Dutt, explained the predicament of the Left parties on cinema, art and the Film Society Movement. He pointed out:

> At present, the so-called 'good films' are totally alienated from the masses. They are explicitly directed at the petty-bourgeois elite and these elitist directors proudly proclaim that the masses are too backward to understand their masterpieces... Typical of this is these elitist directors' demand for 'alternate channels' of release, a cowardly admission that they do not even dare to challenge the commercial cinema in its own circuit.[34]

Gautam Kaul, president of FFSI in 2015, acknowledged the support by the Leftists to the Film Society Movement, over the years. According to him, the Left's support to the movement stemmed from former Soviet leader V.I. Lenin's identification of cinema as a medium of great influence on the masses, as far as back in the 1920s. Socialist realism was the keyword for the Left in culture, which both Kerala People's Arts Club (KPAC) and IPTA upheld. The films from the Eastern Bloc and Latin America too upheld Leftist thought in films till 1991.

"Until the middle of 1990s, the Film Society Movement in Kerala was kept completely free of any political colour or character even as we were regularly screening films from countries like the Soviet Union, Czechoslovakia, Hungary, Poland, Cuba, etc," said Adoor. Just as in Kolkata, the Left, especially the CPI(M), appeared to push its people to capture leadership roles in the FFSI in Kerala as well. Capturing and usurping the movement was the key to a section of the Left leadership and their followers in arts, culture and cinema.

Till the 1980s, mainstream cinema was treated as 'not so cultural' and viewed as an essentially 'black money laundering' investment by dubious businessmen. However, with a series of government interventions through institutions like the FFC, FTII, NFAI and with the support of the Film Society Movement, the sector became respectable. The national and international awards, the celebrity status of filmmakers and artists made it glamorous, though money laundering, big money and 100-crore-plus budgets continue to plague mainstream cinema. Many national and international corporates and media houses, with their film companies, were producing and distributing films by 2000.

### Film Societies as an Urban Act

The Film Society Movement did create much excitement in the urban centres of India, though in certain places, where the parallel literary and political movements existed, they took the movement seriously. It got the official patronage of the government, and the National Film Awards to many of its patrons encouraged the movement, giving it a larger-than-life image.

Chidananda Das Gupta observed, as follows[35]:

> The movement (FS) has an impact far in excess of its size. It prepared the foundation for India International Film Festivals and built an audience for the new cinema. At its peak in the late 1960s and early 1970s, the FFSI had about 300 film societies affiliated to it. Many societies had as many as 2000 members.

Clearly, the Film Society Movement was the need of the times, a yearning of the new republic to look for a place for its own, indigenous and original films in the world map of great cinema, while providing credibility and respectability to the evolving art form, along with other traditional arts, and enriching the national cultural space.

The official FFSI website claims that one of the significant achievements of the Film Society Movement is perhaps the great opportunity it provided to millions of cinema lovers to watch and appreciate non-Hollywood world cinema. Without the tireless efforts of FFSI, classics of great masters like D.W. Griffith, Sergei Eisenstein, Vittorio De Sica, Roberto Rossellini, Federico Fellini, Jean Renoir, Francois Truffaut, Jean Luc Godard, Ingmar Bergman, Satyajit Ray and Akira Kurosawa would have remained inaccessible to the cineastes in India.

The FFSI accessed and circulated films from most of the film-producing countries in Asia, Africa, Latin America and Europe. Promoted by the FFSI, the Film Society Movement inspired generations of Indian filmmakers to create a cinema with a different texture, originality, narrative and feel, in contrast to the mainstream cinema in India.

Starting with Satyajit Ray and Mrinal Sen, filmmakers like K. A. Abbas, Ritwik Ghatak, Shyam Benegal, Basu Chatterjee, Basu Bhattacharya, Govind Nihalani, Adoor Gopalakrishnan, G. Aravindan, Aparna Sen, Girish Kasaravalli, Amol Palekar, B. Narsing Rao, Ketan Mehta and many others are products of the Film Society Movement, though some were trained at FTII. The movement also succeeded in bringing about a qualitative change in the style of film criticism in India; it brought a greater analytical depth to film criticism. It also worked as the basic inspiration to include film studies in the curricula of several universities," the FFSI website has noted.[36]

In its report, the Film Enquiry Committee headed by Dr. Shivarama Karanth, in 1980, took stock of the role of the Film Society Movement:

> While the Film Society Movement has made a distinct contribution to the propagation of film consciousness, the movement has remained largely confined to major urban centres. Its expansion has been handicapped on account of non-availability of exhibition facilities and lack of awareness on the part of the government to appreciate the crucial role which this movement can play in creating an audience for good cinema by changing audience tastes

through regular exposure to good films to a cross-section of people.

The report stated that in 30 years the movement only had 200 societies with about 75,000 members, though it acknowledged that 300 other societies had applied for affiliation with FFSI.[37]

In 2015 too, the number of FFSI-affiliated film societies remained almost the same with 293 of them affiliated to FFSI. It did not have a larger-than-life image or a credible pull among the target audience and was limited to the film academia and students. Since government funding stopped in2014, there has been no official documentation of the number of film societies since then, though the FFSI website carries its own claim of its members, many of which are defunct or only on paper.

Indeed, even in its reduced profile, the Film Society Movement supplies the largest resource pool of film academia in India. Clearly, the movement, over the years, attracted a spectrum of people with great brilliance, vision and aesthetic talent, and serious academic minds and scholars, who chose to examine the aesthetics of cinema and its impact on society, through complex and lucid exposition and analysis of the best of films from India and the world.

## Reference


1. http://cherianwrites.blogspot.in/2016/02/adoorgopalakrishnan-on-film-society.html
2. https://en.wikipedia.org/wiki/Vijayakrishnan
3. Abhija Ghosh, *Celluloid in Transit: Film Society Cultures in India,*, M Phil ThesisJNU.
4. Interview with Pradipta Sen.
5. https://en.wikipedia.org/wiki/Samik_Bandyopadhyay
6. H. N. Narahari Rao, ed., *The Film Society Movement In* (Mumbai: Asian Film Foundation, 2009), p.26.
7. http://cherianwrites.blogspot.in/2016/02/adoorgopalakrishnan-on-film-society.html
8. R. M. Ray, ed., *Indian Cinema in Retrospect:Speeches of the 1955 Seminar*(Sangeet Natak Academy), p. 23.
9. Ibid. 8, pp.28-29.

10. *Selected speeches of Indira Gandhi* (New Delhi: Publications Division, Ministry of Information and Broadcasting, GOI)p.279.
11. https://cherianwrites.blogspot.in/2016/02/interview-with-benegal.html
12. http://cherianwrites.blogspot.in/2016/02/adoorgopalakrishnan-on-film-society.html
13. Ibid. 6, p. 73
14. http://cherianwrites.blogspot.in/2016/02/reply-from-ministry-of-i-ffsi-funding.html
15. https://en.wikipedia.org/wiki/K._Bikram_Singh
16. Chidananda Das Gupta, *Seeing is Believing.*
17. shttps://cherianwrites.blogspot.in/2016/02/marie-seton-from-cfs-published-in.html
18. https://cherianwrites.blogspot.in/2016/02/press-report-of-film-council.html
19. Ibid.
20. Ibid.
21. https://cherianwrites.blogspot.in/2016/02/typical-film-appreciation-course-by.html
22. https://cherianwrites.blogspot.in/2016/02/interviewwith-sudhir-nandgoanker.html
23. https://en.wikipedia.org/wiki/Khalid_Mohamed
24. Ibid.
25. David Allyn *Make Love, Not War: The Sexual Revolution* (Little, Brown and Company, 2000), pp. 4–5.
26. https://cherianwrites.blogspot.in/2016/02/havefilm-societies-lost-their-relevance.html
27. Ibid.
28. http://www.pnpanicker.org/aboutpnp.html
29. Gautam Bhaskaran, *Adoor Gopalakrishnan* (Penguin–Viking-2010), p.66.
30. https://en.wikipedia.org/wiki/Kerala_People%27s_Arts_Club
31. https://en.wikipedia.org/wiki/Vijayakrishnan
32. http://cherianwrites.blogspot.in/2016/03/cinema-and-bad-new-times.html
33. https://www.facebook.com/public/Ffsi-Keralam
34. *Utpal Dutt on Cinema* (Kolkata: Segull, 2009), p. 149.

35. Ibid.
36. https://en.wikipedia.org/wiki/Federation_of_Film_Societies_of_India
37. Ministry of I&B, *Report of the Working Group on National Film Policy* (New Delhi: Ministry of I&B, GOI, 1980), p. 13.3.23.

# 6
# The Great Fall and Changing Viewing Habits in the Digital Era

In 1980, as a student at the Indian Institute of Mass Communications (IIMC)[1] in New Delhi, I tried to become a member of the DFS. As a member of '*Chitralekha*' and '*Chalachithra*', I thought it would be easy to get into DFS. I still remember the huge crowds at the FICCI auditorium, at Mandi House, where the screenings were held. I was new to the city with no friends in the DFS. Many discouraged me from joining DFS, saying "It was full of people who just wanted to see uncensored films."

They, instead, advised me to attend the screenings at the cultural diplomatic centres like the Soviet Cultural Centre, Hungarian Information Centre, Max Muller Bhavan and the USIS to keep my appetite for good films going. I became friends with many of the organisers at these diplomatic mission centres as a student of IIMC, and the Hungarian Information Centre even invited me to join them as the editor of their journal *News from Hungary,* helping me stay put in the capital. Graduates from IIMC were welcomed in most newspapers then, as the Institute had a good reputation in media circles in the 1980s.

The IIMC too had a good collection of documentaries. I remember seeing most of the Dutch documentary films by Bert Haanstra at the Institute. I was the only student in my batch who had already seen *Battleship Potemkin.* Professor D.N. Choudhary, son of the famous writer Nirad C. Choudhary and

Professor Viswanathan, from the Tamil film industry, encouraged me to undertake a diploma project on video, while most of my colleagues had written projects. My diploma project was a documentary on O.V. Vijayan's cartoons, with an interview with the cartoonist at our studio.

I had invited filmmaker Kumar Shahani to a lecture at the Institute after I met him at one of the seminars in Delhi, and that could have prompted my professors to push me to make a video project. The writer in me was active with occasional dispatches for *Kalakaumudi* publications on films and film seminars, back home in Trivandrum (now Thiruvananthapuram). By the end of the decade, my occasional writings in English publications in Delhi and Malayalam publications got me into the hallowed circles of film critics and the film festival circuit of Delhi. I was mighty pleased when Anil Saari, the eminent film critic, asked me to write an obituary on filmmaker John Abraham for *The Hindustan Times* in 1987.[2]

After joining the Hungarian Information Centre in April 1981, I found myself among the organisers of the evening film screenings, getting many friends to fill in the empty seats at the last minute. I had not joined the DFS, whose reputation had begun to decline considerably as the membership was overwhelmed by the middle-class lumpens rushing for 'uncensored' films to gaze at female nudity. At the Hungarian Centre screenings too, I found a group of middle-aged people walking out after a scene with nude women or a sex act in the film. It took some time to dawn on me that DFS was going down, and it finally shut down in 2006. Though I heard about 'Celluloid,' the film society of Delhi University, it was impossible for me to attend its screenings at the North Campus considering the city's transport facility in those days.

### Pioneers in Urban Centres Leave FSM

A similar fate was being faced by film societies in other metro cities too. During the 1970s, Bombay (now Mumbai) had 18 film societies. 'Film Forum' was the strongest with 1,500 members. However, after the departure of Basu Chatterjee and Arun Kaul, its membership started dwindling.

Amrit Gangar, Regional Secretary of FFSI, to *The Times of India*, reacting to an article on the plight of film societies of the city by Khalid Mohammed, wrote:[3]

> The Film Society Movement in Bombay has lost the kind of hold it had a few years ago. It has now to find a way out of the problems that keep mounting, rising costs, dearth of theatres, and as Khalid Mohammed has observed in his assessment, the general apathy of the people towards better cinema.

However, there was at least one society which was taking shape even in those days. "We started our full-fledged office so that we could serve our members better. This resulted in getting more members. Of course, in strong programming and participation in film festivals, '*Prabhat*' stood first," recalled Sudhir Nandgaonkar of *Prabhat Chitra Mandal*, and the FFSI former Secretary who had kept the movement alive in Maharashtra during the difficult times.[4]

Pradipta Sen of CFS, who also saw this period, confirmed the fall. By the early 1960s, CFS had over 2,500 members on its rolls but sadly today it has been reduced to a mere 250. "The success of CFS made others too venture into organising film societies. Three other film societies sprang up in Calcutta, Cine Club, Cine Central and Cine Institute, Sen pointed out.[5] Over the years, Ray and the pioneers of CFS lost interest in the functioning of the society. Though Ray previewed his film *Devi* in New Delhi at DFS, no such privilege was given to CFS in Kolkata. "The uncensored films had brought in such an undesirable crowd to the film society circuit that even Ray distanced himself from the Movement he pioneered," noted the Kolkata-based film writer Abhijit Ghosh Dastidar.[6]

In many cities, the pioneering societies were seen as elite zones and getting a membership was difficult; however, it was easy to get a membership in the new ones. That explains why many film clubs sprang up in most urban centres. Cine Central, established in 1965, organised a children's film festival and an annual festival at 'Nandan', the cultural centre, in association with UNICEF and the West Bengal Government till the 2010s.

It still participates in the annual Kolkata Book Fair and sells DVDs and scripts of famous films, through its stall. By 2023, the Kolkata International Film Festival had become a State Government affair.

**Figure 6.1.** A screening at CFS in the 1960s

## *Chitralekha*: The Best Experiment of the Film Society Movement Fails

In Trivandrum too, *Chitralekha's* screenings came to a halt by 1985. *Chitralekha* had an impressive membership over the years, but it was perceived as too exclusive, with high-profile film and literary figures in it. The waning interest of Adoor, *Chitralekha's* founder, in the regular activities of the society, as he was busy with his film productions, and his growing differences with the Film Cooperative's Managing Director Kulathoor Bhaskaran Nair, added to the society's woes. The cooperative and the film society had an umbilical cord connection and trouble in its leadership broke this unseen cord, leading to the collapse of both the pioneering organisations.

The success of the Film Cooperative, which was a unique experiment of its kind, led to the government taking over the land and the buildings. Though the success lasted only for over a decade, *Chitralekha* Film Cooperative remains the best highlight of the New Indian Cinema, as well as the Film Society Movement of India; an experiment, which will remain a milestone in the history of world art house cinema.

**Figure 6.2.1.** Chitralekha film complex

**Figure 6.2.2.** Kulathoor Bhaskaran Nair

The Film Cooperative, which started with a loan of Rs 15 lakh, from the state government in the 1960s, has repaid the amount to the exchequer, after a negotiated settlement with Kerala Financial Corporation. *Chitralekha* Film Cooperative produced three feature films *Swayamvaram, Kodiyettam* and *Prathisandhi*, a commissioned film on family planning for the Government of India, all directed by Adoor.

"We also produced 25 documentaries for various organisations from 1965 to the early 1980s. *Swayamvaram* was made for a small budget of Rs 2.5 lakh and it earned a revenue of Rs 5-8 lakhs. *Kodiyettam* was even more successful. We had planned not just the Film Studio at Aakulam, in the outskirts of Thiruvananthapuram, but an entire artistes' village, where cultural icons from various fields could live together," Kulathoor Bhaskaran Nair, who was the Managing Director of the 'paper organisation' recalled the golden decade of the cooperative.[7] Nair passed away in 2020.

Adoor's biographer Gautaman Bhaskaran wrote as follows:[8]

> The Chitralekha Film Cooperative, which built a full-fledged studio including a recording theatre, a processing laboratory and editing facilities, helped produce the cinema of artistic content. Gopalakrishnan's first two works *Swayamvaram* and *Kodiyettam,* and several documentaries were made by the *Chitralekha* film unit. Aravindan's debut work *Uttarayanam* and many other movies of many FTII graduates in the 1970s, emerged from the studio or with the help of its equipment.

Adoor jocularly describes the complex as their unit's gift to the Government of India. The erstwhile *Chitralekha* Film Studio Complex is now the headquarters of Southern Air Force Command. The Studio complex, which ran into financial troubles, was taken over by the government and given to the Indian Air Force to house its Southern Air Command. The picturesque complex, designed by the British-born Laurie Baker[9], the famous architect-low cost builder, who was a resident of Thiruvananthapuram, is still known as the Chitralekha complex.

"Sadly, the Chitralekha Film Society and Film Cooperative faded into oblivion by 1985, following Adoor Gopalakrishnan's disassociation from both. His differences primarily with Mr. Nair (Kulathoor Bhaskaran Nair), led to Gopalakrishnan's exit, and like many other film institutions in India which wind up after that one key man bids adieu, *Chitralekha* too floundered after its very spirit and soul left," Adoor's biographer described the failure of the experiment that was once watched with envy by filmmakers across India and the world.[10]

Together, with the other Laurie Baker-designed institution, Dr. K N Raj promoted the Centre for Development Studies (CDS).[11] *Chitralekha* Film Studio Complex, built in 1975, remains an important landmark of the capital of Kerala. Filmmaker Adoor, the spirit behind the film cooperative and society, has a house built in traditional Kerala architecture, a *nalukettu*, like his character in *Elipathayam*, near one of the gates of the complex, from where he has made 10 more films, which put him on the global film map.

## Emergence of National and Satellite TV Channels

I remember seeing Godard's film, *Week End*,[12] on the impact of live TV on people, much before TV as a live medium arrived in India. It was like a fairytale spectacle in the 1970s for India. But looking at the infiltration of television as a medium in all spheres of life with their 'breaking news,' live coverage and sting operations, one can easily say that we are more in an Orwellian (George Orwell-British Novelist) world. Big Brother is watching you, commenting on and sometimes interfering in your life too on a 24-hour basis. Films, which re-create the world in time and space, have no chance in all these live shows. Films help you only to reflect on the past, if you still find the time to do so, in the present, TV has taken over the mind space of the people over and above space for films.

The growth of television in India was in a controlled fashion by the government till 1991. India got into the television age with an experimental television service in Delhi in September 1959 and was boosted with the introduction of colour television in 1982, when the Asian Games were held in New Delhi. The National Network of terrestrial channels in the metros and a few capital cities had the newscast in the evening from the Asiad days. By 1984, most state capital TV stations were connected to Delhi and thus national programming started with news, current affairs and serials.

*Hum Log,* depicting Delhi's middle-class life, became a pioneer among Television serials and was soon taken over by *Ramayana* and *Mahabharata* mythological serials in the latter part of the 1980s. This situation continued till 1991 when the Gulf War brought satellite television channels to India. The 1990s saw national and international satellite television channels getting launched in India. An early private Indian channel like Sun TV started its programming with telecasting films in 1992. They showed Tamil films continuously, mesmerising the already film-crazy population of the province. Weekend films and weekly musical shows such as *Chitrahar* aired on *Doordarshan,* the national television owned by the government, had made a huge impact on television viewers deflecting their attention from cinema houses. Evenings were no longer the exclusive arena of films or theatre in India.

In 2015, the government statistics show that *Doordarshan* operated 33 satellite channels, with a vast network of 67 Studios and 1,416 transmitters of varying powers and provided TV coverage to about 92 per cent population of the country. By 2023, the *Doordarshan* had been relegated to a government mouthpiece and lost its market position badly to private satellite channels. "As of February 2022, DD Free Dish hosted 164 channels including 91 *Doordarshan* channels (comprising 51 educational channels launched during the pandemic) and 73 private channels," the Federation of Indian Chamber of Commerce and Industry's (FICCI) annual report of 2022 revealed. The cable and satellite television market in India emerged in the early 1990s, spurred by major international events like the Gulf War and the growth of homegrown media companies. Overall TV connections will keep growing at a healthy pace of over five per cent a year to cross 67 per cent of Indian households by 2025.[13]

The world has also been undergoing major changes during the 1980s and 1990s. The authors David Page and William Crawley wrote:[14]

> Three important developments underpin the media revolution, which has changed the way South Asians see the world—the demise of Communism, the increasing integration of world markets, and very rapid advances in communication technology. In the aftermath of the collapse of the Soviet bloc, free trade and the free flow of information became dominant philosophies of the late 20th century, with the United States the chief protagonist of both.

## Fall of the Soviet Union and Eastern Bloc

The period also saw the inflow of films from Soviet bloc countries dry up with the fall of the Soviet and the entire Eastern bloc countries. *Perestroika* (restructuring) and *glasnost* (openness) of the Soviet Union headed by Mikhail Gorbachev, led to the slow dismantling of the Communist Party-ruled regime in the Soviet Union and Eastern bloc countries, and many independent and non-Communist States sprang up. The state-owned system of filmmaking came to a halt in these countries. The Cold War climate had made Eastern and Western blocs compete to supply films to the FFSI network of film societies in their bid to influence the urban educated in India with their respective ideologies. With the fall of the Eastern bloc and less active cultural diplomacy from the Western bloc, the biggest source of contemporary films from Europe dried up for the film societies. Filmmakers who enjoyed state patronage for their creative activities were left to fend for themselves in the Eastern Bloc. It took another decade for films to re-emerge from these countries. The economies of these countries dipped, and the cultural field was thrown open to market forces. The Russians shut down their huge network of information and cultural centres across India. In Delhi, the Soviet Information Centre at Connaught Place was closed, and the property was sold to a corporate house. The bubbling Soviet Cultural House, which was a hub of Soviet culture, began to be known as a beer guzzler's paradise with a pub coming up there. The Soviet cultural centres in other cities also faced closure, though some have been re-established in the 2000s.

For the film society movement, these developments had a double whammy effect: the onslaught of television taking away its audience and the fall of the Soviet bloc drying up the free and easy flow of films to screen. I cannot help but describe an incident involving the Soviet Cultural Centre and parallel cinema here. Kerala's Left ideologue Chintha Raveendran's film *Ore Thooval Pakshikal (Birds of the same feather)* was being screened at the Soviet Cultural Centre. The CPI(M)'s then General Secretary EMS Nampoodiripad, attended it and the entire senior Soviet Diplomats associated with the Centre lined up at the entrance to receive EMS. For them, a Communist Party secretary is like their prime minister. That was the protocol many of these institutions gave to even a film viewer leader. Raveendran's film was nominated for the Moscow International Film Festival that year. The *Gorky Sadan* at Kolkata, the cultural centre of the Soviets, was also the patron of the film society screenings of the city, indicating the broad support the Eastern bloc gave to such cultural movements.

### Film Society Movement at Crossroads

All these political and media developments happened from 1984 to 2000, when the fledgling Film Society Movement was undergoing a crisis due to the new-found media grabbing the attention of Indians. The sudden spurt of visual entertainment through television took away a major chunk of the film society members, who were mostly middle-class professionals. The national network of *Doordarshan* showed almost all FFC-financed films and commissioned films with Satyajit Ray, Mrinal

Sen, Adoor Gopalakrishnan and Shyam Benegal for the national network. Most of these films, even of the old maestros, were telecast on the national television network, including several national award-winning films. *Doordarshan* itself began to patronise such films, along with popular Hindi and regional films in regional language channels. I remember viewing a Ritwik Ghatak film festival in early 1989 on *Doordarshan* National channel, aired with subtitles. *Doordarshan*, during that period, became another arm of the Film Society Movement by airing New Wave and award-winning films on Sunday afternoons and late nights, though its main forte was the popular Bollywood films and serials like *Ramayana* and *Mahabharata*.

The period also saw many international film festivals springing up in cities like New Delhi, Kolkata, Bangalore, Mumbai and Thiruvananthapuram. These festivals were organised by the leading film societies of the region in collaboration or directly by the state governments. These festivals were in addition to the India International Film Festival, which was anchored at Goa by 2000. Thus, the exclusivity of the Indian Film Society as a sole avenue for new cinema and uncensored foreign films, especially from non-English speaking countries, was seriously challenged.

## The Format Changes: Video, DVD and Internet

The early 1990s saw new information technologies and mobile phones arriving in India. First, it was video technology as television networks had a huge appetite for it. Films began to be converted into video format to be played on TV sets. The urban middle class began to patronise video libraries which mushroomed across urban centres to see films at home. Video films substantially reduced the cost of making films and hence most documentaries took to that format. Television channels had a huge demand for various programmes to fill their 24-hour telecast slot, leading to a spurt in video production, akin to a cottage industry, in urban centres across India. The only video production house in Delhi in the 1980s, CENDIT, established by Rajiv Jain of *Celluloid* and Anil Srivastava of Lucknow film societies, became a centre of attraction. "My working life has been spent with CENDIT, involved with activist and developmental videos," Jain recalled the CENDIT days.[15] Video studios mushroomed in urban centres in India by the 1990s. Private viewing of even feature films through video format and television became the order of the day.

The worst was yet to happen to the traditional film formats. There were global developments in information technology and India became a major back-end service point–the IT outsourcing capital of the world. This led to changes in video and digital film formats reaching India almost at the same time as it did in Western countries. This eliminated pre-90s analogue formats of films and everything went digital. There is a massive digitization programme at the film archive of the country—NFAI—to make its collection accessible to interested people. Films are made and screened only in digital formats and every 10 years the digital formats are upgraded. The popular 4K resolution video of 2023 is expected to get an upgrade to 8K soon.

This made tectonic changes in the traditional film backend technological industry. The world leader in celluloid film technology, Kodak closed shop in 2012. They have Kodak home theatre TV screens and cameras for popular use.

Kumar Shahani, the eminent filmmaker, observed:[16]

> The world of films will be different now, with each image being captured and seen through the aesthetics of the person who shoots it. A photograph can never be the reflection of reality as such, as it can be modified in umpteen numbers of ways through digital technology.

Kumar, who refused to work in digital format and preferred his old 35 mm analogue film format found himself outdated, and he stopped making films. He continued as a film theoretician though.

A look at the number of films censored by the Censor Board of India reveals it all. In 2014, the annual report of the Information and Broadcasting Ministry documented that it censored a total of 12,977 films for viewing in India. Out of the total number of films censored, those in celluloid format numbered just 74, but in video format, there were 5,098 films and the digital format dominated with 7,805 films.[17] In 2021, there is hardly any format other than digital among the 12,144 films censored by the Central Board of Film Certification of India.

The emergence of video and digital formats also impacted the Film Society screenings as they had to do away with the 16 mm and 35 mm film prints and adopt new technologies. In early 2010, when Cine Central got a film from the Swedish Film Institute for their annual festival in Kolkata in the old format, they found themselves spending a huge amount of money to courier the prints, upsetting their fragile budget. Obviously, they could not incur such huge expenditure in any future festivals, as DVD and Blue Ray and now DCP format can be transported across the globe with minimal charges.

The years 1984 to 2000 will be documented as the worst period in the history of the film society movement in India. During those years of terrestrial and satellite television channels spurt in India, numerous films were being beamed on a daily basis. Every major network had a few movie channels. By 2020, during the COVID pandemic, exclusive OTT (Over the Top Technology) channels proliferated, making film viewing an entirely personal affair, be it on mobiles, laptops or home theatre screens. Filmmakers have found a new revenue model in selling their film's television and OTT rights, over and above the conventional screens and television channels. Most countryside cinemas have shut shop as they all were banned from screening films for two years leading to the collapse of their business. The industrial body FICCI, which conducts an annual media and film industry meet in Mumbai, commissioned a study by the global consultants KPMG year after year to give an overview of the entertainment industry. The last published study observed:

Television is the largest medium for media delivery in India in terms of revenue, representing around 45 per cent of the total media industry. The TV Industry continues to have headroom for further growth as television penetration in India is still around 60 per cent of total households and increasing to 161 million in 2013. The number of Cable & Satellite (C&S) subscribers increased by nine million in 2013 and touched 139 million. Excluding DD Direct, the number of paid C&S subscribers is estimated to be 130 million. This C&S subscriber base is expected to grow to 181 million by 2018, representing 95 percent of TV households. Of this, the paid C&S base is expected to be 171 million in 2013, representing 90 percent of TV households.[17]

But by 2020 the trends have changed, and TV registered a 13 percent negative growth and OTT channels began to replace them. "2020 also saw 28 million Indians (up from 10.5 million in 2019) paying for 53 million OTT subscriptions leading to a 49 per cent growth in digital subscription revenues, thus clearly indicating that subscription fared better than advertising revenues," stated the FICCI report of 2020.[18]

Raman Raju, who was the FFSI secretary from 1988–92 gave an overview of the period of transition of the media habits of Kolkata those days. "Film societies were a male-dominated arena and few of them were for uncensored films. But with the arrival of video, there was a power play too, as new technology was looked down upon by most Kolkatans who were averse to the change in technology and wanted to retain their old film habits. We screened *Umatic* formatted films in Alliance française, Max Muller Bhavan and Gorky Sadan were showing 35mm films," Raju recalled.

Television's popularity and reach sparked off a video revolution. Satellite and cable television added to the spurt in video programmes. The late-night television films and shows opened up an entirely new legal avenue for Indian viewers to access soft porn without conventional censorship, just like the uncensored films of the film society circuit. There were a few channels known more for their late-night films than any other programmes, till the Indian government came down heavily on them with conservative guidelines. The immediate impact on the Film Society Movement was that those in its circuit, relishing uncensored films, lost interest in the membership of the societies and moved on with the videos.

Following the economic reforms in 1991, the Indian film industry emerged as the world's largest, despite Hollywood's glamour, fame and financial muscle. The nickname 'Bollywood' for the Indian film industry may be a misnomer, but it reveals the association of the city of Bombay with the film world, as it produces the largest number of films in Hindi.

In 2012, Bollywood produced 1,602 films, compared to a mere 476 from Hollywood. India also beats Hollywood hands down in ticket sales. For instance, in 2012, Bollywood transacted an impressive 2.6 billion in ticket sales as against the United States, whose number was 1.36 billion. However, Hollywood does have more financial clout and leads the way in terms of box office revenue. American films grossed $10.8 billion in 2012. Even though India produced more films, the Indian film industry could only manage $1.6 billion.[19]

Pointing out the post-pandemic recovery scene of the film industry, the FICCI report stated[20]:

> A total of 757 films made it to the theatres in 2021 across languages. The highest number of films was released in Telugu (204) and Tamil (152) and only 84 films were released in Hindi language. However, the screen count was estimated at 9,423, a marginal decline over 2020.

The impressive growth of the film industry did not find a parallel in the Film Society Movement during the period. Until the arrival of DVDs, now Blu-Ray and OTT, the digital format together with television led to the closure of almost half of the 300 film societies. The changing media formats and the flood of television channels and digital media took away people's attention span too, leaving the film societies to the more serious film buffs.

Opender, a Western region FFSI activist, aptly spells out several issues that led to the slide of film societies in the late 80s and early 90s. The biggest problem was finding a theatre for the screening of 35 mm films, as 16 mm had become obsolete. The absence of a cheaper and handy format was yet to arrive (the DVDs had not arrived then). The lack of a credible second line of leadership was also becoming an issue. Foreign films got undue importance in matters of film appreciation, as against Indian films among film societies.[21] International directors Ingmar Bergman, Federico Fellini, Akira Kurosawa, Krzysztof Zanussi, Jiri Menzel, Miklós Jancsó became more popular than Indians like Girish Kasaravalli, Adoor Gopalakrishnan, Mani Kaul or the maestros from Bengal in the film society circuit. The elitist nature of the film societies of big cities and their lack of effective positioning with the new middle class that emerged following the 1991 economic reforms, took away the glamour and status quotient from the movement. Above all, the failure to take the movement to the universities affected its sustainability in the long term.

Though the decade marked a crisis period for the movement, it was during this period that *Suchitra* Film Society built and inaugurated its complex in Bangalore. *Prabhat* in Mumbai,

Madras Film Society continued to organize its activities. The star societies at the height of the movement like CFS, DFS, Film Forum and *Chitralekha* were sinking.

This was also the period when the veterans of the Film Society Movement were passing the baton to new leadership, as they themselves were overwhelmed by the fast-paced changes such as video, television and the fall of the Eastern bloc and economic reforms.

Chidananda Das Gupta observed[22]:

> It has become necessary now to treat the FFSI as a major instrument of the development of film appreciation, professionalise its management and cleanse it of the elements that have drifted into it for doubtful pleasures of purveying uncensored films or finding their way into diplomatic cocktail parties.

"The new formats increased the acceptability and transportability of films. But the Kolkata film societies have to cater to the old clientele. What they have done is to club the screenings of various groups together," pointed out Raman Raju, FFSI secretary in the 80s and now leading the Chidananda Das Gupta Foundation at Kolkata.

Recording the crisis in the Film Society Movement, U Radhakrishnan, the FFSI, Northern region secretary wrote:

> The decade of 1984-1994 was the period during which the Film Society Movement in India, in all the regions,

with no exception, suffered a severe setback and activities almost came to a standstill. The number of Societies in the Southern region reduced from 140 to 70, Northern region came down from 41 to 18, Western zone which was the worst hit, suffered a big slide from 25 to 10 and the Eastern region, though there was no reduction in the number, the activities slumped to the lowest level.[23]

**Figure 6.3.** Vijaya Mulay with U. Radhakrishnan

A list of film societies in different regions over the years clearly shows the rise and decline of the movement. The FFSI started with six film societies in 1959 and had impressive growth for the next two decades. By 1964, there were 23 film societies; by 1967 the number grew to 108 film societies affiliated with FFSI. The eastern zone dominated the activity with 63 film societies. In 1971, the FFSI had 111 units across India. By 1980, when the Film Society Movement peaked across India, there were a total of 216 film societies with FFSI, and the southern region dominated with 95 units.

The crisis period 1984–94 brought the FFSI units down to 98 in 1994. But again by 2014, the count had improved to 292 units, with more than half in the southern region. Kerala led the pack with 113 units (compilation from FFSI documents).

By 2023, the northern region had very few film societies. While the eastern, western and southern regions were holding on to the numbers they had, very few of them appeared to be active.

**Advent of the Internet: Online Dating to Pornography**

By 1995, India also allowed the entry of the Internet into the public arena, and by 2000 various Indian and foreign websites began to open new vistas for the urban Indian population. The 'dotcom boom' changed the media industry landscape, including that of films. There was a dotcom for everything, be it films, or people involved in films. The Amazons of the world began to sell films from all over the world, online. Slowly, some of these films began to be uploaded on the internet for free downloads, though the quality of such films was not good by any standards.

The internet always had a driver in the carnal feelings of humans. Dating, sex chats and porn sites were all part of it. Interpersonal relationships went global, and the much-cherished privacy went for a toss. Nudity is no longer a taboo, with internet access providing a gateway to the underbelly of human culture as never before. Over the years, there has been a replication of everything human on the internet. It was during the same period that the advent of new technologies arrived in India. First, video technology as television networks demanded it. Films began to be converted into video films to be played on TV sets. But the worst was yet to happen to the traditional film formats. There were global developments in information technology and India became a major back-end service point–IT outsourcing capital of the world. This ensured the film formats changed at a fast pace. Today, there are no films as they existed in pre-1990s formats; everything is digital. There is a massive digitization programme even in NFAI and films are made and screened only in digital formats and every 10 years the digital formats get upgraded.

> The period of 1984–2000 was the worst for film societies across India. The period witnessed tremendous growth of satellite and television channels, beaming numerous films daily. Every major network had a few movie channels and the COVID year of 2020 saw exclusive OTT channels proliferating, making film viewing an entirely personal

> affair. Filmmakers have found a new revenue model in selling their film's television and OTT rights, over and above the conventional screens, which have become part of major malls in urban centres. According to a FICCI-commissioned study by the global consultants KPMG: "Television is the largest medium for media delivery in India in terms of revenue, representing around 45 per cent of the total media industry. The TV Industry continues to have headroom for further growth as television penetration in India is still around 60 per cent of total households and increasing to 161 million in 2013. The number of Cable & Satellite (C&S) subscribers increased by nine million in 2013 and touched 139 million. Excluding DD Direct, the number of paid C&S subscribers is estimated to be 130 million. This C&S subscriber base is expected to grow to 181 million by 2018, representing 95 percent of TV households. Of this, paid C&S base is expected to be 171 million in 2013, representing 90 percent of TV households.[24]

In Delhi, during the 1980s, Central Delhi's Maharashtra Rangayan was the Delhi Malayalee Film Societie's (DMFS) favourite screening theatre for Malayalam films, and the Sunday evening shows were a packed family affair, recalls a member. But today, even the most famous Malayalam director's film screening needs the backing of a cultural organisation as there is hardly any film-crazy public as in the 1980s. DMFS used to organise receptions for National Award-winning Malayalam films in Delhi with the filmmaker, as there were always a couple of awards for Malayalam films and technicians. The last time such an event happened was sometime in early 2000. In short, it is difficult to get an audience for such events and screenings even for ethnic population-based film societies.

Television's spread brought a video revolution. Satellite and cable television were added to the video programmes. The late-night television films, and shows, opened up an entirely new legal avenue for Indian viewers to access soft porn without conventional censorship, just like the uncensored films of the film society circuit. There were a few channels known more for their late-night films than any other programmes, till the government came down heavily on them with conservative guidelines. The immediate impact on the Film Society Movement was that those who were there for uncensored films lost interest in the membership of the societies.

By 2000, with the emergence of regional film festivals organised by the state governments, the FFSI and its units lost its prime position as the exclusive venue of 'uncensored' films, which it had from 1966. There was squabbling by the FFSI leadership about giving free censorship to individual societies and their festivals and many complained to the central government. The government appointed a committee headed by filmmaker Shyam Benegal to examine the issue. The committee favoured a one-time grant of exemption to any registered body with the government to screen uncensored films, as against the three-year grant for uncensored films in the FFSI circuit. This effectively ended the prime status of FFSI being the exclusive channel of 'uncut' films in India and also the status of a second censor board of India.

## Arrival of OTT Platforms for Films

The pandemic of 2020-21 saw OTT and video platforms like YouTube proliferating in India, replacing theatre viewing with home theatre screens. The FICCI media report of 2022 revealed:[25]

> Video viewers increased by 10 per cent (47 million) in 2021 to reach 497 million, which is around 94 per cent of smartphone owners and wired broadband subscribers. We estimate video viewers will cross 600 million by 2024. We estimate that an all-time high of 100+ films released on streaming platforms directly, without a theatrical release. During the pandemic, consumers have started to get into the habit of watching new films online, and we believe this trend is here to stay.

In 2023, all DTH and digital media entities entered the OTT channel era, increasing the competition in the sector. Airtel, Jio telecom operators and multinationals like Amazon, Netflix, Hotstar, Disney Channel and a host of Indian media houses launched their own OTT film channels, which have become the flavour of the home theatre-viewing middle class.

This effectively transitioned film viewing from a communal to an entirely personal affair.

Adding the booking of online film sources was specialised by channels like *Criterion* and *BFI player*, which catered to film connoisseurs across the world with a varied collection of old and new classics; some are pay channels and some sell films on various easy-to-personalise formats.

## Film Societies Enter the Digital Era

Together, digital technologies, VCD, DVD and OTT have created a revolution of sorts across the world of films. The viewer has the option to see the films on his/her laptop computer, in full-screen mode today. From huge boxes of celluloid films, the delivery mode of the films has now been converted to one or two CD-boxed sets which could be easily transported, through post or courier, crossing all international borders, cutting across all complex tax and import duties. Online booksellers like Amazon, began to include DVD films on their virtual shelves. The films of the world are getting digitised and reduced to compact discs, which are available readily across the globe.

However, digital technology has its own issues. The VCD and DVD disc contents could be easily copied, and this technological aspect paved the way for everyone to copy films, making the traditional distribution systems obsolete and copyright go haywire. Adding to the agony of the filmmakers, who invested deeply into the medium, was the arrival of the internet as a medium with huge storage, as well as downloading capacities. Though there are anti-piracy laws to protect the copyrights of filmmakers across the world, pirated copies of popular as well as classic films are available at throwaway prices. I was surprised to see a list of all the classics I wanted to see all my life as a film society member in the 1970s, 1980s and 1990s, available for Rs 5,000, in a corner of Thiruvananthapuram in 2000. Each city in India has its share of these grey markets. In Delhi, Palika Bazar can provide film buffs with the best of classics, and in Kolkata, street vendors cater to this market. In each city, there is an informal circuit to quench the new generation's thirst for the latest and best of world cinema.

Digital technology always expands like an amoeba and finds its own solution to the issues its development creates. Together with strict copyright laws and now OTT formats, illegal copying has become a thing of the past.

However, the official FFSI history of the Film Society Movement records that the availability of films in DVD format by 2000 had become a boon for the surviving film societies. Most of the classics too were available on DVD, and FFSI officially promoted the use of DVD format and projections for screenings, as it eliminated the cumbersome process of transporting films across the country.

The FFSI may not have promoted the digital formats officially, but there were film enthusiasts like C. Saratchandran in Kerala and Anil Srivastava, who established CENDIT in New Delhi with friends like Rajeev Jain and Aveek Ghosh of Celluloid Film Society, to popularise new technologies through their interventions, much before FFSI stepped in with new formats.

"Our credo was democratisation of communications. New Technologies have made it possible and CENDIT became redundant," said Rajiv Jain, of Delhi University and later CENDIT.[26]

Saratchandran, who worked with Malayalam filmmakers G. Aravindan and John Abraham and had also worked with the British Council of Saudi Arabia in the 1980s took upon himself the onus to make video and digital technologies popular among the alternate film circles in Kerala, much before the format became acceptable elsewhere. He was not just a film enthusiast, but a product of the little magazines wave of the 1970s and 1980s in Kerala and was also exposed to the changing technologies at the British Council, where he worked as a consultant. He carried back a huge DVD library of world films when he returned to Kerala in the late 1990s and travelled from town to town screening those films, introducing the film society network to the digital world.

While Anil Srivastava was winding up CENDIT, which promoted video technology, in New Delhi; Sarat, as he is popularly called, went around with one of the few digital projectors in Kerala and screened DVD films, including his film on John Abraham, giving a new life to the sagging morale of the Film Society Movement hit by Television, video and DVDs.

"He was a one-man army in popularising the digital format. He also made a two-hour film on John Abraham. He went around Kerala showing his film and other films in digital format, through the projection system brought from Saudi Arabia," recalled K.N. Shaji, Editor of *Samkramanam and Niyogam,* the little magazines in Malayalam of the 1970s and 1980s. Sarat was the co-founder and active organiser of the 'Vibgyor' film festival. He was also a prominent supporter of 'Vikalp', a platform to defend freedom of expression, and resist censorship. At the time of his demise, he was working on documentaries on industrial pollution due to a gelatin factory near Thrissur, and a film on the state of the Chaliyar River. He had an untimely death on April 1, 2010, when he fell out of a running train.

### Regional Responses to Crisis

The crisis period did not end well for many regions, especially the Eastern and Northern regions. In Kolkata, film societies did not find the transition to digital technology easy. In fact, the city's film societies began to jointly organise film screenings to overcome the crisis when memberships dropped and funds were not easy to come. Though the joint screenings affected the individuality of the film societies, they helped the city continue its pioneering role among the film societies. When the FFSI celebrated its Golden Jubilee in 2009, the Eastern region had only 70 survivors, and only 25 of them had been operating for more than 25 years. The number further dipped to 65 in 2015. The worst affected was the Northern region. Pioneers like the Delhi Film Society stopped screenings in 2006, following the detection of financial fraud. After Indira Gandhi's death in 1984, government patronage slowly waned.

The flood of videos and TV channels took away members of most film societies. Unlike in other regions, the shift to a digital format did not evoke new enthusiasm among the potential members in the Northern region. In 2009, there were only 10 film societies in the region and only four were found active, while the rest were trying to keep afloat. For serious filmgoers in New Delhi, screenings at India International Centre, India Habitat Centre and the cultural centres of the diplomatic missions of Germany, Italy, Spain, France and Hungary catered to the rich traditions of film appreciation in the city. The Delhi Malayalee Film Society has its own audience, and the Malayalam filmmakers look to the society and its main organiser U. Radhakrishnan for the screenings of quality films. Many other regional groupings like Bangiya Samaj and Kannada Society also occasionally organise screenings of regional films. Various screenings of the Directorate of Film Festival and the now redundant *Osian* Film Festival continued with the city's annual film screening traditions. The number of film societies in the Northern region was 11 in 2015 and most of them are now defunct. "There was a film society at Jodhpur, Rajasthan, running till 2010, but with the death of its founder, that too closed down," says Punkaj Butalia, a former secretary of FFSI Northern region.

Interestingly, the Western and Southern regions have seen a growth in film societies after the crisis. This can be attributed to the emergence of second-level leadership and the smooth adoption of digital technologies in West and South India. The Western region has seen a growth of almost 20 film societies in the decade after the crisis and the introduction of digital technologies. From a mere 13 societies, the number went up to 32, and there were 8,300 film society members across the region by 2009. Continuing growth saw the number of film societies reach 45 by 2015.

In the Southern region, barring Kerala, the number of film societies went up by 13, taking the tally from 40 to 53 in 2015.

Kerala may be the only state which has its own FFSI region, after a court battle in 1985 with the parent body. The region which was formed officially in 2000 had 70 film societies attached to it and by 2015 it had grown to 118 units though very few are active on a monthly basis. The crisis and the recovery period also saw the FFSI headquarters moving out of Kolkata's Bharat Bhavan. It first moved to Mumbai from Kolkata in 2006, with the election of Sudhir Nandgaonkar as the secretary of FFSI.

Nandgaonkar procured a permanent office for the FFSI and its regional outfits in Mumbai from the state government and restarted its monthly newsletter. Later, when Narahari Rao became the FFSI president, Bangalore became the headquarters. The FFSI changed its rules to ensure that the secretary and treasurer of the organisation are from the same region/city and that its national office works from that city/region. This change was made to ensure effective coordination between regions and to help the regional leadership to get a chance to be elected for national posts.

In 2015, with Premendra Majumdar becoming the FFSI secretary, the national office shifted back to Kolkata's Bharat Bhavan, where it was based from 1959 to 2006. In 2023, Amitav Ghosh as secretary and Premendra Majumdar as vice president held the FFSI Kolkata office.

## Uncertain Future

The COVID pandemic of 2020-21saw OTT and other online formats arriving on the media scene. It has paved the way for online film societies, which schedule films every week and then discuss them over online platforms. *Talking Films Online* (TFO) with membership across India, including film studies people and a few others is an online film society, which may be working outside FFSI and other formal affiliations. One can also see a big spurt of various online interest groups among film buffs, who are eager to find their own peers across the networked universe through the internet. It is time that FFSI looked up newer formats to cope with changing technological formats and film viewing habits. As of now, there is no future for the old analogue format film societies, given the technological revolutions and changing viewing habits of people.

## Reference


1. http://www.iimc.nic.in/
2. https://www.facebook.com/johnabrahamdirector/photos/pb.198076013566188.-2207520000.1456938066./ 856293871077729/?type=3&theater
3. https://cherianwrites.blogspot.in/2016/03/amrit-gangars-letter-to-editor-times-of.html

4. https://cherianwrites.blogspot.in/2016/02/interviewwith-sudhir-nandgaonkar.html
5. https://cherianwrites.blogspot.in/2016/03/cfs-cine-central-interviews.html
6. https://cherianwrites.blogspot.in/2016/02/soruce-of-films-and-film-programs-of.html
7. Interview with Kulathoor Bhaskaran Nair, MD Chitralekha Film Co-operative.http://www.prd.kerala.gov.in/towardsmorevisual.htm
8. GautamanBhaskaran,Adoor: A Life in Cinema (Penguin–Viking, 2010), pp.70-71
9. https://en.wikipedia.org/wiki/Laurie_Baker
10. Ibid. 8, p.73
11. http://www.cds.edu/
12. https://en.wikipedia.org/wiki/Weekend_(1967_film)
13. https://assets.ey.com/content/dam/ey-sites/ey-com/en_in/topics/media-and-entertainment/2022/ey-ficci-m-and-e-report-tuning-into-consumer_v3.pdf P. 35
14. David Page and William Crawley, *Satellites Over South Asia*(Sage, 2001), p. 21.
15. https://cherianwrites.blogspot.com/2023/04/note-from-rajiv-jain-founder-celluloid.html
16. https://en.wikipedia.org/wiki/Kumar_Shahani
17. http://cbfcindia.gov.in/html/uniquepage.aspx?unique_page_id=20...
18. https://www.kpmg.com/IN/en/IssuesAndInsights/Articles Publications/Documents/FICCI-KPMG_2015.pdf
19. Ibid. 13, p. 148
20. Ibid.
21. H. N. Narahari Rao, ed., *The Film Society Movement in India* (Mumbai: Asian Film Foundation, 2009), p.119.
22. http://cherianwrites.blogspot.in/2016/03/the-das-gupta-article-on-fsm-89.html
23. Ibid. 19, p.112.
24. Ibid. 13, p.36
25. Ibid. 13, p. 63
26. https://cherianwrites.blogspot.com/2023/04/note-from-rajiv-jain-founder-celluloid.html

# 7
# The Star Film Societies and Survivors

The Film Society Movement of India has seen many bright sparks among its member units during the last 75 years, contributing immensely to the development of film as an art and its appreciation. They were spread across the country from North-East to South and from Chandigarh in the North to Thiruvananthapuram in the South. In 2023, the spread of surviving film societies are limited to East, West and South.

Profiling some of those film societies that survived the onslaught of the digital revolution and even reinvented themselves to be up and running deserve to be featured along with the few surviving old ones. Some have re-formatted themselves for the new audience and in some cases, a new enlightened leadership has emerged giving a contemporary look to the Movement itself. Few older ones are surviving in most regions by associating with regional film festivals, mostly supported by the state governments of the region. The emergence of online film societies is indeed a new phenomenon and new packages catering to film buffs, and new filmmakers are another interesting development which is propelling the old movement.

But FFSI, the 64-year-old apex body, has little to contribute in all this, as its leadership, just like the organisation, is a legacy in 2023 and threatened by a breakaway group of film societies in Kolkata itself. Forum for Film Studies and Allied Arts, headed by filmmaker Goutam Ghose and veteran film and theatre critic,

Samik Bandyopadhyay as its vice president, is clearly taking away the *crème de la crème* of the city's film connoisseurs, going by their programme sheet. Political patronage by certain groups and its sectarian approach seems to be the issue in Bengal and in Kerala, going by the parallel, dissident activities of FFSI in both states.

### The Calcutta Film Society

In March of 2023, Calcutta Film Society (CFS) treasurer Asoke Bhattacharya, a retired professor from Jadavpur University sent me the latest issue of CFS Bulletin and a photograph of its release at the Kolkata Press Club. "After we lost the Bharat Bhavan office space and post-COVID pandemic, we are still trying to reorganise and be up and running," stated Asoke Bhattacharya of CFS, describing the present status of oldest film society, asking me to mention it in the popular online forums of film writers.

**Figure 7.1.** Pradipta Sen and Dr. Santanu Bandhopadhyay at CFS during the release of the Ray Bulletin, 2023

The history of Indian film societies cannot be written without featuring the CFS. Though it is not the first film society in India, it was the first to make a difference in the Indian film world, with just two individual contributions. The first was Satyajit Ray, the filmmaker, and the second was Chidananda Das Gupta, the film writer. Both Ray and Das Gupta are colossuses in their fields and have become part of Indian film history. India is yet to witness a film like *Pather Panchali*, which excited the world, changing the path Indian films were taking till then. August 26,

1955, the day *Pather Panchali* was released, will remain etched in golden letters in the history of Indian films.

Das Gupta described the CFS, the Film Society Movement[1] as follows:

> In October 1947, Satyajit Ray, and a group of like-minded enthusiasts, anxious to open a window on world cinema, so tightly shut during British rule, started the Calcutta Film Society. In no time, it turned into a movement, which spread all over the country, providing a new impetus to film viewing, film criticism and eventually to filmmaking. Among the filmmakers directly or indirectly thrown up by the movement, were, apart from Satyajit Ray himself, Ritwik Ghatak, Mrinal Sen, Shyam Benegal, Adoor Gopalakrishnan and many others.

The CFS was the first film society to import a film, *Battleship Potemkin*, in 1948, and had to dodge the police in its initial screenings. The film went on to become the first film among many film societies in India, and the box carrying the print of the Russian classic crisscrossed the country. Apart from Jean Renoir, Roberto Rossellini, John Huston, Frank Capra, Vesvold Pudovkin and Nikolai Cherkassov, the filmmakers were guests at CFS in those early days before *Pather Panchali*.

Chidananda Das Gupta recollected in a video interview:[2]

> Calcutta Film Society remained active up to about 1952. It never went above 50people as its membership. We were very snobbish about it; we thought everyone may not become members of the society. Only people who were really interested, only people who had dreams of making films one day, writing about films and becoming film critics, that kind of person must join the film society. Quite snobbish in our attitude! So, our membership did not increase very much.

Though, there was a period of lull following the International Film Festival (IFFI) of 1952, the release of Ray's first film and Marie Seton's frequent visits to Calcutta revived CFS in 1956, that too with a journal, *Indian Film Quarterly*. CFS president,

Pradipta Shanker Sen, a 92-year-old retired journalist, who had seen the revival recalled those days nostalgically:

> The CFS restarted in 1956 with the active participation of Marie Seton, who began to frequent the city to meet Satyajit Ray, who was making waves with his first film. There was already excitement about the success of *Pather Panchali* in Calcutta. The CFS was revived with Chidananda Das Gupta as secretary and filmmaker Purnendu Patri was also there. The annual fee those days was Rs 30.[3]

**Figure 7.2.** Pradipta Sen and others at the CFS office in Bharat Bhavan, 2012

The revival witnessed about 300 members joining the CFS and in six years the membership increased to 3,000. The huge number remained on its rolls, till other film societies like Cine Club, Cine Central and Cine Institute came up, according to Sen. In the 1960s and 1970s, Nirmal Kumar Siddhanto, Vice Chancellor of Calcutta University, Apurva Kumar Chanda, DPIR Education of West Bengal, BN Sircar of New Theatres and DIP Pramanick of Eastern India Motion Pictures Association were associated with CFS. Prachi Cinema, an all-Bengali cinema house in the city, allowed free screenings, waiving off the Rs 15,000 rent for a film. At a retrospective of Sergei Eisenstein's films at the Academy of Fine Arts, "the crowd was so much that CFS founder Ray was seen sitting on the stairs and watching the films. That was in the early 60s," Sen recollected the golden days of CFS.

*The Statesman*, the city's premier daily newspaper, carried reviews of the films screened by CFS, exciting the city's cultural elite. These films were sourced from diplomatic missions of most countries and FFSI sources. The annual fee went up to Rs 100 from Rs 30 and the life membership from Rs 3,000 to Rs 25,000. Nandan's 16 mm and 35 mm screening facilities and digital projection at their office were the order of the day pre-COVID for CFS. The CFS religiously observes the release of *Pather Panchali*, with an annual function in the last week of August, with film and cultural personalities of the city, to ruminate on the golden years of the CFS and Film Society Movement.

## Cine Central and Cine Club of Calcutta

There are a few film societies across the country, which came after the formation of FFSI, and Indian urbanites considered being a part of the movement as a status symbol in the 1960s. Cine Central of Kolkata was one such society established in 1965 and continues its activities through milestone annual events. A Children's Film Festival in collaboration with UNICEF from 2006 and the Calcutta International Film Festival in 1986 have now been taken over by the state government. The Cine Central website states that the first show of the society was held at Tiger Cinema on October 31, 1965, with the screening of *The Road to Life*, and very soon the society became an established name in the Indian film cultural arena.

The society regularly organised country, theme and director-specific film sessions and festivals. They also screened retrospectives of both young and veteran film directors. Cine Central has been organising successive International Children's Film Festival and Fair at Kolkata *Maidan* opposite Birla Planetarium, with generous support and cooperation from the state government, UNICEF and various corporate houses. Since 2006, they have made the Children's Film Festival an annual event. International Children's Film Festival has become an important program of society's activity. Cine Central Calcutta also introduced Calcutta International Film Festival in 1986, the first-ever independent international film festival in India, which is now the Kolkata International Film Festival organised by the Government of West Bengal.[4]

The Cine Club of Calcutta, established in 1961, also had an impressive beginning, with over 1,200 members enlisting in a year. The *Cine Club* used to offer its films to other societies, after their screenings. Ram Haldar, its founder, was a bookstore owner who was also a member of the CFS. Haldar was the first to introduce books like *Film Forum*, and *Film Sense* by Eisenstein, *Film Technique* by Pudovkin, *Reflections of Cinema* by Rene Clair, *The Art of Film* by Lindgren, and *Sight and Sound* magazine of British Film Institute to Calcutta.

*Cine Club* rode on the high point of the Film Society Movement and Haldar steered its growth till 1968. The Club also published two journals, *Kino* in English and *Chitrakalpa* in Bangla, to which the stalwarts of cinema and the Film Society Movement in Kolkata contributed regularly. In 1974, they added *Cine News* to the publications. The Club became a member of the British Federation of Film Societies and instituted the Film Appreciation Award in 1974-75 for encouraging the production of quality films in the Eastern region. In 1977, the Club hosted a three-day film appreciation workshop in which 40 students participated. It also instituted the annual Ritwik Memorial lecture in 1979, delivered by eminent film personalities.

### Forum for Film Studies and Allied Arts

Kolkata may have been the headquarters of FFSI for long years, but it has its share of dissidents and the Forum of Film Studies and Allied Arts—FORUM—is one such parallel platform of film societies. FORUM was set up through the cooperation of like-minded people, to make a concerted effort to re-define, disseminate, and nurture the film society ethos and allied arts in 2008. The FORUM has dedicated itself to organising activities and programmes in association with interested film societies, film students and cultural bodies to develop a better understanding of cinema and allied arts, and build public opinion to develop more facilities for film viewing and film studies, as well as promotion of allied arts, says the leaflet announcing a contemporary

Venezuelan film festival at Nandan–the art complex–in the 2nd week of April 2023.

"We are an apex body of 17 like-minded film societies, just as FFSI," said the FORUM's president and eminent filmmaker, Goutam Ghose.

Ghose further pointed out:

> We cannot get back the golden age of film societies, but the response was good; mostly from middle and older age groups, not so much young people. The idea was to show films, organise discussions and annual lectures. With new technologies, the perceptions change, perceptions of filmmakers and audience change...with the cellphones the attitude also completely changes... a few assemble, 20 or 30 people, and watch a film on YouTube...we are working hard to connect to people and arrange films and get them to view it collectively and discuss it. These days' people don't discuss it collectively, they tweet or write in social media.

The FORUM is planning regional film packages too, apart from films from various countries. In April 2023, the FORUM had a festival of Venezuelan films at Nandan and Robin Mukherjee, the secretary, said that over 200 people attended its inauguration in a hall with 160 seating capacity. According to him, the FORUM came into existence as he, as an activist of Cine Academy, the film society of the city and also secretary of the Eastern region of FFSI found that people of the then ruling political party–CPI(M)–with no links to films were coming into leadership positions in FFSI.

Mukherjee said:

> I resigned from FFSI and was working with Gorky Sadan to mount screenings of Cine Academy from 1990, but in 2008 with the blessings of Samik Bandyopadhyay and Goutam Ghosh formally launched the FORUM as an alternate body. In Kolkata alone, they have four film societies attached to them. They are Cine Academy, Cine Institute, People's Cine Society and Film Club.

FFSI activities, he said, are not regular and they wanted to avoid that and bring in monthly screenings of films. He admitted the average age of the members was 60 and above as they were not able to attract young people. "But we have a lot of joint programmes with Satyajit Ray Film and Television Institute (SRFTI) and that fills the gap of youngsters," he added.

Mukherjee, now in his 70s and retired from a shipping company, has been active with film societies since the 1960s. The FORUM also conducts an annual lecture in memory of Kalyan Mitra, one of their vice presidents who passed away in 2010. Nine lectures that were held have been compiled into three books. They also hosted the Carlos Saura Film Festival and discussions about the work of the Spanish filmmaker, who passed away in February 2013, in association with SRFTI.[5]

### The Delhi Film Society

The Delhi Film Society (DFS) was the most privileged of the film societies across India. The membership and the leadership were the who's who of the nation's capital in the 1960s and 1970s. Diplomatic missions vied with each other to patronise the DFS by offering their films and bringing in filmmakers from their respective countries to meet Delhi's film buffs. The Cold War era made sure DFS got plenty of films from both the Eastern and Western Blocs.

Former Resident Editor at the *Financial Express*, newspaper, Dr. Y. C. Halan, who was a member of DFS from the 1960s, gave an overview of DFS as follows:[6]

> I have been a member of DFS since the mid-sixties. I will continue to be its member as I am a life-member. I was told that the best films, particularly non-commercial, and non-English speaking countries were not shown in India. Those were the days when foreign films were not freely allowed. Such films were brought in by the embassies and were routed through film societies. The Film Society Movement was at its peak as persons like Usha Bhagat, Social Secretary to Prime Minister Indira Gandhi were associated with it. Serious film buffs were interested in watching such films. The best films by the best of directors

> were brought in by embassies and shown to society members, as it had the who's who of the city as members.

He went on to become a member of the executive committee, treasurer, secretary and president during the 1970s and 1980s. Dr. Halan recounted his DFS experience:

> It was the period during which Gautam Kaul joined DFS, when he was transferred to Delhi. John Joshua was the secretary and Gopal the president. There was intense politics between the two groups of Vinod Mehra and John Joshua. Vinod was the protégée of Vijaya Mulay and was able to dislodge John and hold control of it. The DFS was at its peak during the 80s and the frequency of films shown was almost five to seven in a month. Slowly, a message went around that uncensored films were shown and this attracted a large riff-raff to the film society. This was the beginning of the decline of DFS. Later in the 90s, the Film Society Movement became dormant because of two reasons: The advent of TV and liberal import of films. The censoring policy also became liberal.

"The membership of DFS was a status symbol in the 70s and 80s," pointed out another life member of DFS, filmmaker and writer late Deepak Roy in 2014 before his demise.[7]

The DFS obviously was a privileged society to have the *crème de la crème* of the capital city of India and was also a recipient of all government patronage as far as its screenings and special occasions were concerned. Hence, the admission was not automatic, but after an interview.

Dr. Halan pointed out as follows:

> The uniqueness of DFS was its elitist membership. People serious about films, particularly the appreciation part, were members. Many of them became filmmakers like Pankaj Butalia, Gopi Gajwani and Bikram Singh. Many were politically and culturally powerful like Vijaya Mulay, Bhagat and Gautam Kaul. These people ensured that only serious members joined DFS. This helped to build up quality membership. It deteriorated fast as these persons left DFS.

There is an unconfirmed story that Rajiv Gandhi, then an Indian Airlines pilot, who later succeeded his mother Indira Gandhi as Prime Minister, was not admitted to DFS. "I do not remember why the membership was rejected. I only saw his name in the register of applicants. At that time the membership was after an in-person interview. He may not have come for the interview," said Dr. Halan, when asked about the incident. Despite the best patronage, Dr. Halan finds the DFS' impact to be marginal.

> It did make an impact, but in a limited way. The fact that many of the members produced films, Gopi Gajwani, Pankaj Butalia and Bikram Singh directed and produced feature and documentary films, adds to its impact.

The crowd at DFS became increasingly mixed in the 1980s, as those looking out for 'uncensored' films began to dominate it. There was an incident involving a French filmmaker who addressed DFS members after the screening of his film. One of the members said he found the film "sadistic" much to the surprise and shock of the filmmaker. "The member put his feelings about the film so rudely that the filmmaker had to be admitted to the hospital after the screening," recalled Partha Chatterjee[8], a film scholar who was present at the screening. Deepak Roy recalled an occasion when DFS had to stop the screening of Italian filmmaker Pasolini's, *The Gospel According to St. Matthew*, as the film had no subtitles. "It was a mixed crowd," recalled N.K. Sharma of *Sahmat*.[9]

The abrupt end of DFS came in 2006, when Gautam Kaul[10], its last president, found that the treasurer had withdrawn a fixed deposit without authorisation. The incident, which became a police case, led to the end of screenings at DFS. There are societies like *Tasveer* five cultural centres of the diplomatic missions, India International Centre and India Habitat Centre and regional film clubs, like *Delhi Malayalee Film Society*[11], which have divided the dwindling number of serious film viewers in the city making a DFS revival impossible.

**Celluloid: The Film Society of Delhi University**

Though the University Film Council movement of UGC flagged off in 1960, it did not take off. However, two Delhi University students Rajeev Jain and Avik Ghosh, together with a group of film buffs, started a film club '*Celluloid*' in the mid-sixties and ran it successfully for over two decades. "The primary movers were Deepak Nayyar (later VC of DU), Avik Ghosh and myself. John Joshua of DFS encouraged and supported us. We were essentially a university society; however, a major French Film Festival took place which was only open to members, but so many University members also joined," recalled Rajeev Jain.[12]

*Celluloid* started off in 1967 and Pankaj Butalia, who ran the film society from the 1970s and became FFSI Northern region secretary, was a student who attended the inaugural function of the society. In the initial stage, a lot of other students and teachers of Delhi University joined them. The films were shown at the same hall where DFS screened the films, the auditorium of the Centre for Educational Technology (CET)at IP Estate. East Germans, Russians and other diplomatic missions gave films which were in 35 mm format and the screenings had to be at the CET. By the 1970s, the founders left the university and a teacher of Khalsa College, Bikash Roy Choudhary, took over the running of *Celluloid*.

Pankaj, a documentary filmmaker who worked in Delhi University colleges as a lecturer, recalled:

> By 1975, I took over from Bikash and I ran it for the next eight to nine years. I tried to involve PG students and some teachers and they would come, join, and then leave and it went on for 10 years and then I got completely disinterested. By 1986, I left *Celluloid*, but I was secretary of FFSI in the early 80s after I had passed on the leadership to Mihir Pandey of Ramjas College. By then Celluloid had become immensely popular with members other than students of Delhi University.

Pankaj Butalia narrated the almost 35-year-old history of the first major University film society of Delhi and India:

> In the early 70s we had a film festival with the Indian *New Wave* films. I remember watching Kumar Shahani's *Maya Darpan*, Mani Kaul's *Duvida*, Adoor's *Swayamvaram*, Shyam Benegal's *Ankur* and Ritwik Ghatak's *Jukti Takko Aar Gappo*. Kumar Shahani came and gave a lecture. Next five to eight years Celluloid was bursting with energy. It was one of the most active film societies of Delhi and we had around 350 members. Membership was Rs 40-50 a year. More people joined and we shifted the screenings to the University's Tagore Hall. By then we had a 16 mm projector gifted by the American Centre. We also got another projector to replace the old one from the Australian High Commission. Max Muller Bhavan also gave one later. We maintained it ourselves. It went on till the early 80s up to the 90s when it died down. It was revived again by Bikash Roy, the first screening at Miranda House, but by then video had come in and others like India International Centre had started showing films and slowly the screenings got subsided. But Bikash again revived at Khalsa College in the late 90s with students and teachers of the college. Bikash died in early 2000 and the society also died along with him.

Looking back, Pankaj described *Celluloid* and India International Centre screenings with the most serious viewers of serious cinema. Celluloid had a membership of around 300, but every screening had about 100-odd viewers. He credits this to the late Sudhanshu and his brother Sudhir Mishra, who became filmmakers, and Ravi Vasudevan of CSDS, Madan Gopal Singh and Rashmi Doraiswamy with Jamia University, film scholars and Professor Ira Bhaskar, head of Jawaharlal Nehru University School of Arts and Aesthetics, from Lady Sriram College Film Society. Rajit Kapur, the Hindi film actor, was a member of *Celluloid*. "There were serious discussions on films with these people after the screenings," recalled Pankaj Butalia.[13]

### Film Forum, Bombay

*Film Forum* Bombay will be known as the filmmaker's film society; going to the filmmakers it has contributed to Indian cinema. The *Forum* was formed in 1964 by the trade unions of the then-Bombay film industry. The country's first film society, the Amateur Film Society of India, merged with Film Forum. The Forum itself was the creation of the filmmaker K. A. Abbas, the critic-turned-political activist-filmmaker. Other illustrious names from the *Film Forum's* table included Basu Chatterjee, Govind Nihalani, Bikram Singh, the film writer, and Khalid Mohammed. Mrinal Sen's landmark Hindi film *Bhuvan Shome*, which kicked off the New Cinema movement in Hindi, was produced by Arun Kaul from the *Film Forum*. Both Mrinal Sen and Arun Kaul had also published a 'manifesto' for New Cinema those days.

**Figure 7.3.** Arun Kaul with Mrinal Sen

Filmmaker-critic Khalid Mohammed[14] entered the film field through *Close Up*, the magazine of *Film Forum*, brought out by Basu Chatterjee, and K. A. Abbas. "I joined the magazine to write and learn," said Khalid, who went on to become the film critic of *Times of India*, Mumbai, and later editor of Filmfare, recounting his days with *Film Forum*. He remembers seeing young Mani Kaul and Kumar Shahani at the screenings. "Films of Godard, Ozu, *Battleship Potemkin*, *Rashomon* of Kurosawa were all big draws," added Khalid, who feasted on the experimental films which were aplenty. He attributed the idealist leadership of people like Abbas, Basu Chatterjee, and later Gopal Doothia, to be the force behind the success of the *Film Forum*, which had over 2,000 members by 1969. "Basu Chatterjee maintained a library of film books. The leadership inducted potential film buffs and provided them constant education through films and discussions on films," recalled Khalid, who turned filmmaker through the film *Fiza*.

"If the young generation is inducted, the Film Society Movement can exist," he pointed out, adding that the society itself had changed, "There is no pure love, things have become commercial." The period of selfless, idealist leaders is over, and the Film Society Movement has to acknowledge that and go about it.[15]

*Film Forum* undoubtedly carried the flag of the Indian Film Society Movement with its galaxy of filmmakers and film critics. Apart from the filmmakers, critics like V.P. Sathe and Jagmohan were also associated with the Forum. It also had affiliations and collaborations with the British Film Institute, Cine academies of the USSR, France, Poland, Czechoslovakia, Japan, and Sri Lanka (then Ceylon). The *Forum* organised a retrospective of Indian Cinema in Paris in collaboration with *Cinematheque Francaise* in March 1967. The best film magazine of the FFSI also was brought out by *Film Forum*. The magazine called *Close Up* had an editorial board consisting of Dr. Gopal Dutt, Basu Chatterjee, Arun Kaul, K. A. Abbas, Bikram Singh, V.P. Sathe, Jagmohan, Ram Maheshwari, Mrinal Sen, Arun Kaul, Vikas Desai, to name a few. The *Film Forum* was among the few film societies which had a vast library of books on films. The Film Society was the first to introduce an award in the name of D.G. Phalke for the Filmmaker of the Year from any of the Indian languages. However, after the departure of Basu Chatterjee and Arun Kaul, *Film Forum* started dwindling, leading to its collapse in the early 1990s.

### *Prabhat Chitra Mandal*, Mumbai

While *Film Forum* has become a star of the past, it is *Prabhat Chitra Mandal* (PCM), which is carrying the flag of the Film Society Movement in Mumbai today. According to Sudhir Nandgaonkar, a Marathi film critic and one of the founders of *Prabhat Chitra Mandal*, the society was established in 1968 by a group of five film critics. Vasant P Sathe, an English writer on cinema, was the president, and Sudhir Nandgaonkar its general secretary. All the critics were professionals involved in writing for various Marathi newspapers. The name of the Film Society *Prabhat* was given to cherish the memory of Prabhat Film Co. Led by V. Shantaram in the early 1930s and 1940s.

Nandgaonkar, who died in 2022, described the early days of PCM in an interview in 2012 as follows:[16]

> Prabhat started initially with 30 members but within three months, its membership reached 200. The membership fee was Rs 36/- per annum. Slowly, we gained ground and the members' confidence, due to our programming and selection of foreign films. We celebrated our first anniversary with the festival of Prabhat Films and V Shantaram inaugurated it. Our programming was so strong that we were choosing new films to celebrate anniversary day. The films got released after our show. Since the founders were journalists; we got good support from newspapers in Mumbai and we celebrated our 10th anniversary with a package of top-10 films from the *Sight & Sound* magazine. Then I&B Minister LK Advani inaugurated the festival with a seminar on censorship. Many stalwarts from the film industry such as Raj Kapoor, Shyam Benegal, BR Chopra and others participated in the seminar which was a grand success.

The 1960s were the days of the *Film Forum*, but PCM found its own channels to sustain itself, with a Marathi flavour adding to its activities. "During the 70s Mumbai had 18 film societies, the Film

*Forum* was the strongest with 1,500 members. We started our full-fledged office to serve our members better. This resulted in getting more members. Of course, in strong programming and organising of film festivals, Prabhat stood first," the late Nandgaonkar explained in an interview in 2012.

It surpassed the other film societies in 1992 by organising 27 films of Satyajit Ray to mark his Oscar Award. It got financial support from the Government of Maharashtra for the Ray Film Festival.

PCM was screening films at Mini Chitra, a cinema hall where the capacity was 80 seats. So, for two shows it could have 250 members and could not enrol members beyond that. There was a waiting list for membership.

However, after the advent of colour TV in 1984, the audience for commercial cinema dwindled and the membership of film society also went down. "Slowly, the craze for TV died down, with the advent of the global economy and more channels. At this juncture, PCM organised the Ray festival and enrolled 700 members. The venue was YB Chavan Centre Auditorium with a 625 seating capacity. PCM initially had a membership of 250 members and during the crisis period (1984 – 90) it went down to 150 members, then after an impressive growth to 700 in 1992, the membership has now stabilised to around 500", PCM's founder-leader, Nandgaonkar who served as FFSI secretary along with filmmaker Shyam Benegal as president, described the ups and downs of his film society. PCM was fuelling the growth of film societies in the Western region with language-specific festivals and appreciation courses.

PCM has three screenings a month, all in DVD and digital projection, till the pandemic. Every six months the society conducts a festival and a one-day appreciation course, apart from the monthly study group and book releases on cinema. Prabhat has published a monthly magazine called *Vastav Roopwani* for the past 20 years. The magazine has subscribers from all over Maharashtra besides the society's own members. Prabhat is credited with restoring Phalke's *Raja Harishchandra*, the movie, which was screened all over India. They restored and donated the film to the National Film Archive and also celebrated the birth centenary of the father of Indian cinema with the state government's support. Prabhat also faced the threat of a ban for using a commercial theatre for its screenings by an overzealous Police Commissioner. It took two years of a PIL in the Bombay High Court to overrule the ban during which they shifted the screenings to North Bombay.

Prabhat also started The Third Eye Asian Film Festival in 2002 in Mumbai, though it is now organised by a sister body, the Asian Film Foundation. The festival helps Prabhat increase its membership year after year. The results are there for everyone to see, as Marathi cinema is making waves at the National Awards. Just like the films from Bengal, Karnataka and Kerala, there appears to be a craving among people for better films in Marathi too.

## Suchitra Film Society, Bangalore

If there is any film society in India which has fulfilled the dreams of the pioneers and is still flourishing, it is the *Suchitra* Film Society of Bangalore. *Suchitra* has its own cultural complex in Bangalore with films as the focus area. The complex is not managed by the founders of the film society but by a second generation of leadership. "I resigned from *Suchitra* in 2003, so that the new generation can manage the affairs," H.N. Narahari Rao,[17] *Suchitra's* founder and former FFSI president, and a retired engineer from Bharat Electronic Ltd, a public sector corporation at Bangalore, pointed out. The foundation stone for the *Suchitra* Cinema and Cultural Trust complex, promoted by the Film Society, was laid by none other than Satyajit Ray, in 1980. "We need art theatres to find an outlet for good films. This is happening here for the first time in India," Ray said at the function in 1980.

**Figure 7.4.** *Suchitra* Complex, Bangalore

*Suchitra* was established in 1971, with the patronage of veteran filmmaker M.V. Krishnaswamy and with the active involvement of engineers from Bharat Electronics Ltd, Indian Telephone Industries Ltd., Hindustan Aeronautics Ltd. and bank employee unions of Bangalore. There were 11 film societies those days and all of them had a waiting list for membership," Rao recalled in a written reply in 2012.

After the COVID pandemic, *Suchitra* is active again with weekly screenings, said Harish, one of the office bearers. He talked about German films and specially curated film festivals and films from the Bangalore International Film Festival being screened at the film society. *Suchitra* Cine Academy and *Suchitra* Film Society conducted a two-day Film Appreciation Course on February 23 and 24, 2023, its premises. On both days, the course started with the screening of selected World Classics followed by a discussion. A Facebook post of *Suchitra* on February 20, 2023, announced the continuing activities of India's most robust film society in Bengaluru.[18]

With the active support of public sector professionals from the science city of India and the excitement created by the films of Pattabhirama Reddy, Girish Karnad and B.V. Karanth, *Suchitra* had to close its membership by the end of the 1970s as they already had over 1,000 members. By 1979, journalist Subba Rao, who had enormous clout with the state government, became the president of the society. He got the Bangalore Development Authority (BDA) and the then Chief Minister Ramakrishna Hegde, to allot land for a cultural complex in South Bangalore. By 1980, the foundation stone was laid. By 1983, the trust managed to get state government funding, and by August 1986, the *Suchitra* cultural complex was inaugurated.

"The initial purpose of the complex was for film screenings. Slowly, the centre got into other areas of culture, starting a children's wing, *Kalakendra*, a film school, and a centre for drama. The state government and voluntary donations keep the centre going," Rao said. "We may be among the few film societies who offer short-term courses on filmmaking, apart from appreciation courses," Prakash Belawadi, a character actor in films, who was managing the complex, pointed out. The screening theatre has 16 mm, 35 mm and LCD projection systems with a seating capacity of 150. Despite the impressive facilities, filmmakers like Girish Kasaravalli didn't get a proper release of their films at *Suchitra,* as they are still in the old mould of screening for their members. Filmmakers felt it has become yet another cultural complex, not an outlet to promote regional films through the release of such films.

*Suchitra* Film Society has at least five screenings every month. With 600 life members and 200 annual members, it has the patronage of film enthusiasts of the IT city. During the Bangalore International Film Festival, the society is actively associated with the *Chalachitra* Academy of Karnataka. A host of temporary members get added to the society during this period, as they have free entry at the Bangalore festival. Promoters see *Suchitra* as a cultural hub and assembly point of intellectuals and as a film school. The trust has already signed a memorandum of understanding with the Guttenberg University of Sweden for a film school. *Suchitra* is also a consultant to Karnataka's Chalachitra Academy for spreading film clubs across the state and receives an annual grant for that.

The first film screened by the society was the V. Shantaram movie, *Dr Kotnis Ki Amar Kahani.* The society became the star among film societies in the city, with the huge success of Ingmar Bergman festival in 1972 and the Indian 'new wave' films in 1973. The 1977 festival 'Nostalgia', where 80 films were screened in six theatres caught the attention of the entire Film Society Movement of the country. *Appreciation,* a monthly bulletin, has been published for the past 31 years. From 2006 onwards, *Suchitra* collaborated with the state government in organising the Bangalore International Film Festival and also hosted an All-India Film Societies conference.[19]

## *Chitralekha* Film Society, Thiruvananthapuram

In July 2015, the Kerala unit of FFSI organised a meeting of the film society activists and film buffs at the Hassan Marikkar Hall, Thiruvananthapuram. The assembly called *Experiences and Memories was* by the initiator of the Film Society Movement in

Kerala and Adoor Gopalakrishnan, the filmmaker. The event was celebrating 50 years of the formation of the first film society of Kerala, *Chitralekha,* by Adoor and his friends. "It was in 1965, July 3rd week, that *Chitralekha* Film Society was inaugurated by the then Kerala Governor Bhagwan Sahay." Apart from Adoor, G. Ramachandran (Gandhigram), K.P. Kumaran later filmmaker), theatre actors, Karamana Janardhanan Nair, Gopi and Adoor's *Gandhigram* colleague, Kulathoor Bhaskaran

Nair formed the initial team of the society," MF Thomas, the film writer, who was the general secretary of *Chitralekha*, recollected. *Chitralekha's* arrival on the cultural scene of Kerala's capital was welcomed by the media, as the film society was described as an avenue to see the best of world films.[20]

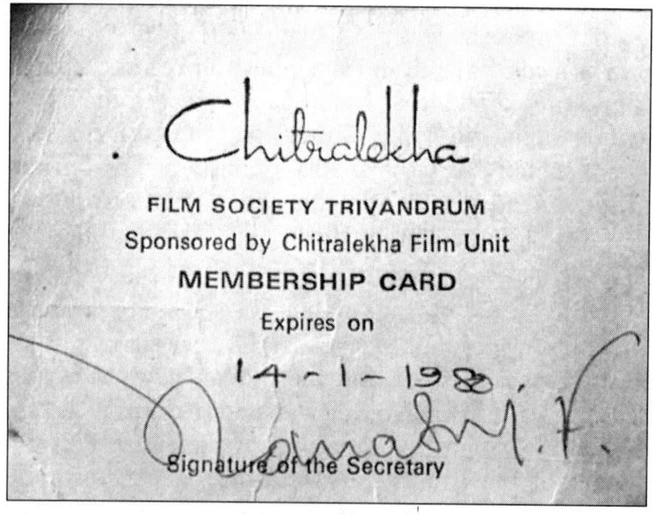
Chitralekha
FILM SOCIETY TRIVANDRUM
Sponsored by Chitralekha Film Unit
MEMBERSHIP CARD
Expires on
14-1-1980.
Signature of the Secretary

**Figure 7.5.** *Chitralekha* membership card

"The society had an initial membership of around 70. Adoor himself used to operate the 16 mm projector. There was one occasion when a Pasolini film, *Gospel According to St. Matthew* had only four members. However, the Cuban film package of Thomas Alea had a good audience. When the *Passion of Joan of Arc* was shown without subtitles, Adoor read the French translation. Prior to his first film, Adoor was involved in all aspects of the society. A souvenir with serious writings on films in Malayalam and a glossary of film terms were also published in the 1960s itself.

Gautam Bhaskaran recorded in his biography of Adoor:

> The society (*Chitralekha*) published thought-provoking literature on cinema. The first publication was planned and executed even when Gopalakrishnan was in Pune, and articles were on film technique, technological innovations, performances, direction, scripts and so on. The journal was the first of its kind in Malayalam and included writings by eminent personalities, such as Ray, Ghatak, Abbas, cinematographer Mankada Ravi Varma, actor Balraj Sahni, Das Gupta, veteran journalist BK Karanjia, writer Marie Seton and Professor Satish Bahadur. A photo feature on world classics and a glossary of technical terms added to its uniqueness.

M.F. Thomas, who retired as an Editor at Kerala *Bhasha* Institute, recounted the initial days:

> There was much commotion when the Chinese film *Road to Victory* was to be screened in 1972. It was screened at the Tagore Centenary Theatre with a police presence, as it was one of the first occasions where a Chinese film was screened after the Indo-Chinese War of 1962. The package of uncensored FFSI circuit films also became a big hit in *Chitralekha* too. Jiri Manzil's Czech film, *Closely Observed Trains* was one such hit, as was *A Blonde's Love* by Milos Forman. There was also a package of Indian 'New Wave' films from the then Film Finance Corporation. *Chitralekha* had an illustrious academic and public sector membership. Dr. KN Raj, a former Vice Chancellor of Delhi University, who was back in town to establish the Centre for Development Studies, Keltron Chairman KPP Nambiar and his wife Saroj Nambiar, novelist Padmarajan, theatre person and critic Narendra Prasad, G Aravindan, filmmaker, and the who's who of Kerala art and culture based in the capital city were members of *Chitralekha*. Anyone, who wanted to nurture a national and international outlook in arts and culture wanted to be part of the *Chitralekha*.

Recalling the initial days, Adoor said:

> Actually, the *Chitralekha* Film Society was a wing of the *Chitralekha* Film Cooperative, registered in 1965, soon after I passed out of Pune. It was established with the help of a large number of friends and well-wishers. Many contributed along with the Kerala Government, taking the shares of the cooperative. So, we had a paid-up share capital, meagre though it was.[22]

**Figure 7.6.** First film souvenir of *Chitralekha*, 1965

Gautaman Bhaskaran wrote about the formation of *Chitralekha*[23], "This was the first time a cooperative of this kind had been set up in the country to produce, distribute and exhibit pictures. The film society was a part of the exhibition and education process to spread a healthy culture by screening different kinds of celluloid fare and publishing serious literature on it."

The society had also laid the foundation for the spread of the Film Society Movement with just one act—organising screenings of 15 world classics to coincide with the fifth All India Writers

Conference at Aluva, near Kochi in 1966, across the State. The 15-film package was also shown in all the then-nine district headquarters and in Nagercoil, thereby exciting film buffs with a new genre of films.

Films like Roman Polanski's *Knife in Water, La Verite* of Henri-Georges Clouzot of France, *Devi* of Satyajit Ray and *Meghe Dhaka Tara* of Ritwik Ghatak paved the way for the Film Society Movement to spread across Kerala. In a decade after the creation of *Chitralekha*, Kerala had 42 film societies spread across its districts, the largest a single state had.[24] A host of National Awards for Adoor's first film *Swayamvaram*, in 1973, further excited the Film Society Movement spreading it to most small towns.

By the time I arrived in the city in 1976, a membership of *Chitralekha* had become a "status symbol" in Kerala's capital, and *Chalachitra*, promoted by the officers of ISRO, was the steppingstone for students like me to get into a film society. *Chitralekha* was also mentoring new film societies across the state, with its advisories for formation, as well as making films, available for the members along with the relevant literature. The film society could influence the universities in Kerala to conduct hugely successful film appreciation courses, making the Movement a "cool" event among the higher education circles.

By 1972, *Chitralekha* had become a huge establishment with its Film Studio coming up on the outskirts of the capital city. The Laurie Baker-designed studio complex, built with a generous loan of Rs 11 lakh from the cooperative department of the Government of Kerala under one of the most enlightened chief ministers, C. Achutha Menon, had become the pride of the cultural field of Kerala. The Film Complex remains one of the unique experiments, though short-lived in history. The first two feature films of Adoor and 25 documentaries were produced by the film cooperative. Adoor got busy with making his films and the film society activity was left to a new team, most of them were closely working with Adoor and the film cooperative's Managing Director Kulathoor Bhaskaran Nair.

"The main advantage of *Chitralekha* was that it was formed and manned by film professionals. And throughout its active life 1965 to 1980, never did we sever from our initial motive, that is to administer and propagate a film culture in its pure form," recalled Adoor.[24]

By the late 1970s and early 1980s, the growing differences between Nair and Adoor led to the collapse of *Chitralekha*. However, Nair had already done the groundwork for the formation of the Kerala unit of FFSI. Nair organised state film societies under the banner of the Association of Film Societies in FFSI 'Keralam.' The Association fought a legal battle with Central FFSI at Calcutta High Court for allowing a separate region for Keralam, forcing the FFSI into an out-of-court settlement.

In 1985, a local unit of FFSI namely FFSI Keralam, was formed, which also hosted the Silver Jubilee of FFSI in India, during the period. *Chitralekha* Film Society had its screenings till 1985 when an old member and bank employee C.G. Philip steered it from the period after Adoor stopped being active. After Philip got transferred out of Thiruvananthapuram, the working of the film society and later film cooperative also came to a halt, though it remained on paper. *Chitralekha's* contribution to the film culture and Film Society Movement for Kerala is unique and historic. In 2023, Kerala had the largest number of film societies in India with over 125 units functioning across the length and breadth of the state carrying on the legacy of the movement.

### *Chalachithra* and *Aswini* Film Society

*Chalachithra* Film Society, Thiruvananthapuram, has always had a special place in my heart. It was they who gave me the first entry to the wonderful world of meaningful films. Though I was not present for the inauguration of the Society on June 11, 1976, by the then Chief Minister of Kerala, late C. Achutha Menon, I was admitted as a member before the end of the year. *Chalachithra* was established by five ardent film lovers—N Krishna Murthy, George Mathew, S.B. Jayaram, K.N.G. Kaimal and M.N.D. Nair, all working in the prestigious Vikram Sarabhai Space Centre, the Thiruvananthapuram unit of the Bangalore-based Indian Space Research Organisation (ISRO).[25]

*Chalachithra* started with a membership fee of Rs 25 per year or Rs 7 for three months, and some open memberships (for festivals). It became popular with government officials; Kerala university crowd, bank employees and student film buffs like me. The initial membership drive in August 1976, with the inaugural programme of a week-long festival of *New Wave* Indian films of Mani Kaul, Satyajit Ray, Aravindan, Avtar Kaul, Mrinal Sen and Basu Chatterjee, pushed the membership to 1,400 in less than two years and that remained for a decade. *Chalachithra* remains alive in the capital city of Kerala with its annual 'Aravindan Puraskaram' awards instituted in the name of the filmmaker but without any regular screenings.[26]

***Aswini* Film Society** is the sister society of *Chitralekha* in the northern Malabar region of Kerala. Established in 1969, with the same by-laws as *Chitralekha*, it was established by the brother of Mankada Ravi Verma, cinematographer of Adoor Gopalakrishnan. *Aswini* was patronised by literary figures, including writer/Filmmaker M.T. Vasudevan Nair, former editor of the prestigious *Mathrubhoomi* Weekly and filmmaker G. Aravindan and his first producer Pattathuvila Karunakaran.

Chelavoor Venu, the society's leader from 1969, remains an enigma with his love for films and print media, as he always edits one specialised journal after another. *Aswini* started with Rs 50 as the annual fee. Contributions from its 300 members became instrumental in the completion of acclaimed filmmaker John Abraham's first movie *A Donkey in a Brahmin Village*, by funding it for post-production work. The film society was also the abode of writer-filmmaker Raveendran (Chinta Ravi).

*Aswini* has survived several ups and down. With the help of a digital projector, contributed by the friends of the society working in the Gulf countries, it is back on track with its monthly screenings. The Kozhikode-based society also played a leading role in the spread of the Film Society Movement of the Malabar region of Kerala, by sharing and organising films from embassies and NFAI with societies in nearby towns.[27]

With the founder Chelavoor Venu going through age-related issues, it needs to be seen how the new leadership will take over the legacy of the film society of the Malabar region of Kerala. FFSI Keralam made a film on Chelavoor Venu recently, as a tribute to his contributions to the movement.

**Banner Film Society: New Hope in Kerala**

If there is one film society in Kerala that is making a mark when others are going down, it is the *Banner* Film Society of Thiruvananthapuram. True to the *Chitralekha* legacy of the city, they have become a connoisseur's club, organising curated and well-planned film screenings, discussions and previews of films of new filmmakers.

**Figure 7.7.** Release of Banner-produced documentary on M.F. Thomas

Starting in 2004, *Banner's* vision was to have "a film society to create and sustain a filmy culture with social commitment as well as aesthetic taste." They appealed to the connoisseurs to dedicate a day to their specially curated film shows, every third Sunday of the month. With a 300-odd membership and viewership of an average of 70–100 on a given Sunday, they went on to showcase around four films a day starting from 9.30 A.M.. Members, depending on their daily schedule, can see any or all of the films screened. These films included theme-based ones, a selection of favourites of eminent directors and critics across India. They had curated screenings of World, Indian and Malayalam master directors, top films from international festivals, experimental films, and children's film festivals, apart from Malayalam top directors and critics' selections. Shyam

Benegal, Goutam Ghosh, Girish Kasaravalli and Aparna Sen's five favourite films were also showcased, giving the film society members a new experience of film aesthetics. *Chitralekha's* general secretary of the 1970s, M.F. Thomas, being their advisor, *Banner* paid tribute to him as an activist and critic by making a documentary on him and his work spanning five decades in promoting a new film culture. "Apart from screenings, we organise discussions on various issues of films, last being about Films and literature," R. Biju, *Banner's* secretary said.

While there are about 25 film societies registered with FFSI Keralam, in Thiruvananthapuram, *Banner* consistently stands out with its unique packages and innovative approach to sustain the film buffs 'interest. That makes it a true inheritor of the film society culture kicked off by the *Chitralekha* Film Society of Adoor and his friends in Kerala.[28]

## Guwahati Cine Club and North-East Film Societies

The eight-sister states of the North-East generally do not figure in mainline film activities, but with Assamese and Manipuri films making waves in National and International film festivals, one gets curious about the driving force behind such films. The Guwahati Cine Club (GCC), one of the oldest surviving film societies of India, pioneered by 'Bharat Ratna' (highest Indian civilian honour) Bhupen Hazarika in 1965, is one of the rare such groupings carrying on the legacy of the film societies and still holding the flag at Guwahati for North-East.

GCC celebrated its golden jubilee in 2015. Madhurima Sen Barua, secretary, of GCC, admitted that the Club's best days were from 1965–83, and they used to source films from FFSI, Cine Central, Kolkata, and a few diplomatic missions. Both the president of the club Absar Hazarika and secretary Barua are retired Assam Civil Service officials. GCC now hold regular screenings for its 84 life members and 70 general members.

"During the annual film festivals, the membership goes up, Barua said, admitting they receive a nominal grant of Rs 2.5 to 3 lakhs funding of the film festival. The Club remains non-political and groups of academics, students, film-related people and government servants patronise it. "We have informal discussions after the film screenings over a cup of team, mostly initiated by film persons in the audience," Barua stated. They used to have screenings at the Assam *Sahitya Sabha* Hall and film festivals are conducted at Rabindra Bhavan, with a seating capacity of 500. The students at Bhupen Hazarika Film Institute also participate in Club activities.

A few film personalities of Assam were also associated with GCC. Padum Baruah, a pioneer of Assamese Art films was the vice president during the 1960s. Dr Bhupen Hazarika was one of the founder members. Eminent film director, Dr. Bhabendra Nath Saikia Sur, was a past president. Manik Borah, an eminent documentary director, held the post of president as well as vice president. Ranjit Das, another award-winning director, was an executive committee member of GCC, Barua recalled the Club's glorious past.

Interestingly, Assam and Guwahati have many film societies including one in Guwahati University. There are film societies in Jorhat, Nowgong, Silchar, Karimganj and Tezpur towns in the state. As for other states, there was a unit in Shillong which was started in 1962. Manipur also has an old film club. No wonder, Assamese and Manipuri films make waves in the National Film Awards occasionally as there is an informed and aesthetically oriented audience, nurtured by film clubs of the area.

### Talking Films Online: The Emerging Future Format

The pandemic year of 2020-21 threw up various new digital formats in not just human interactions, but also in film viewing. Zoom, otherwise business meet video technology emerged as a major platform for meetings and discussions online. So has the new format of film viewing through OTT-Over the Top Technologies—through not just DTH television networks, but also on your mobile phones, creating a highly personalised film screening platform sourcing films from across the world, onto your big and small screens.

The popularity of YouTube and other video apps has increased multi-fold. Combining the new various digital platforms to see and discuss films is a new format of film society in India formatted by two women academics during the COVID pandemic.

Gita Viswanath, who taught for five years at Tolani College of Arts and Science, Adipur, Kutch, and three years at Maharaja Sayajirao University, Baroda, and Professor Nikhila H.S., Professor at the English and Foreign Language University (EFLU) can be truly credited for this new format of the film society, which is one of the first visible film clubs in the digital online world.

Gita Viswanath in an email interview said:

> TFO owes its genesis to the pandemic-induced lockdown during which we were watching a lot of movies as well as attending several online events through Zoom or Google Meet. A Facebook post by Nikhila H S, Prof. EFLU, Hyderabad, on film *Chola* (2019) by Malayalam filmmaker Sanal Kumar Sasidharan, generated a long discussion through comments. It was then that I sent a message to Nikhila saying that we should form an online group to discuss films. She responded immediately and set up a Zoom meeting for the coming Saturday (June 02, 2020) in which we discussed *Eeb Allay Ooo*. We decided on Saturday at 9 pm as our day and time. The pandemic gloom, we believe, was offset to an extent through film viewing and more importantly, getting together to discuss it.

I was introduced to TFO by Anil Srivastava, one of the pioneers of the Indian Film Society movement now settled in the USA, who is still looking at the changing digital formats of film screenings and film societies across the world. I joined them and found the format eminently suiting my time and interest in cutting through the clutter of good and not-so-good films. They select a film from various suggestions of members and share its online link, through WhatsApp and Facebook on a Monday. By Friday the Zoom link for the Saturday night discussion is also shared. I participated in a few discussions and found some well-informed and exposed academics of film studies departments across India and the USA participating in the discussions, which can be termed as truly academic and of high level.

Gita explained the new format of the film society and its growth. "As far as growth goes, well, we have around 320 members on Facebook; 155 on WhatsApp and growing. We have had some illustrious participants in our meetings such as Aparna Sen, Girish Kasarvalli, Adoor Gopalkrishnan, Prof Uma Chakravarti, Janaki Nair, filmmakers such as Balpreet Kaur, Rajeev Kumar, Abeer Khan, Shivendra Singh Dungarpur, Mamata Murthy, Hemant Chaturvedi, actors like Surinder Vicky, and several others. The month of June is celebrated as our anniversary month. We organise a Smartphone Short Film contest for students, which has proved to be a huge success. We also have a lecture series in collaboration with educational institutions. People have approached us to curate film festivals that we do on and off. We see this as a sign of our increased visibility."

TFO has not prescribed any criteria for members. As of now, we have teachers, researchers, filmmakers, students, and general film lovers as members of TFO. The current members have come through word of mouth and personal networks of the members. As for the selection of films, they follow an open process of curation. "TFO does not follow the orthodox method of curation in which the powers of selection and exhibition lie with an individual or small group of individuals. We follow an open-call structure. Anyone is free to suggest a film and lead the discussion on it. However, we need to pick films that are easily available online; they must have sub-titles; they must be accessed on free platforms such as YouTube and Telegram or should be made available by the discussant on a Google Drive link. The selection of films is thus equally based on such practicalities," Gita explained.

The membership is free and about 20–25 of the members participate in the discussion. I found the format of discussion very interesting as one discussant is asked to explain the film and members take turns to comment on it later, thus settling the yardstick and level of appreciation. There were participants from reputed academic institutions from India and abroad, ensuring the two-hour discussion was insightful.

One finds the format truly in tune with the digital lifestyle and screening formats, as the actual experience of the film is left to the viewer, but its appreciation is communal, helping it serve the functions of the good old film society online. The interesting aspect is that the group is not limited by ethnicity or even geographic boundaries of the countries. Truly united by digital technologies and meaningful films, such film groups link connoisseurs from across the world. It is indeed the format of the present and future, especially for film societies, struggling to cope with new viewing habits and technology.

TFO or such groups have no affiliations with FFSI or other legacy organisations. It is high time the old leadership of FFSI engages with such new formatted groups and re-invents itself to be relevant for the digital world.[29]

There are a few active film societies in North-East, Jamshedpur, Jaipur, Hyderabad and Pune. The Celluloid Chapter of Jamshedpur, established in 1985, is the leader in the region with its active film screenings, workshops, seminars, publications and festivals. The Imphal Film Society was set up in 1965. It is credited with the establishment of the Manipur film industry. The Society died a couple of decades ago, but the film industry survived. Aribam Siyam Sarma, the winner of many National film awards, is a product of this film society and the force behind new films in Manipur. The Shillong Film Club, which began in 1964, got wound up. The Jodhpur Film Society in Rajasthan, a pioneer under Professor Mohan Maheshwari, is now struggling to survive after his death. The lone film society in JK, Trikuta Film Society, was started in 1977 but closed abruptly in 1981 after its founder moved out of the State.

The choice of film societies in this chapter was to examine what had happened to the pioneers and highlight some successful and surviving ones. While searching for one of the oldest film societies at Faizabad in Uttar Pradesh, I found a new society functioning there, but without any FFSI affiliation. The word is out even in small towns that film societies/clubs are important for anyone who nurtures an ambition for a film career, and they organise clubs, with or without affiliation to FFSI. Such ambitions of youngsters have led to many successful rags-to-riches and success stories in Bollywood and other regional film industries. In the pursuit of a film career, many have understood that film societies/clubs are training grounds that will help them realise their dreams. And increasing number of regional film festivals across Indian big cities every year also adds allure to the film societies, as those getting hooked on to contemporary international films, find the film society circuit a suitable forum to satiate their appetite for quality films from across the world. The increasing number of film institutes and film studies departments in universities also add to the renewed interest in film appreciation and film societies across India, which is yet to be tapped by the FFSI, the official body of the legacy film movement.

## References

1. Seeing is Believing by Chidananda Das Gupta, Viking, 2008.
2. https://www.youtube.com/watch?v=QapaT0A-HMc
3. http://cherianwrites.blogspot.in/2016/03/cfs-cine-central-interviews.html
4. Ibid-3
5. https://cherianwrites.blogspot.com/2023/04/forum-for-film-studies-and-allied-arts.html
6. http://cherianwrites.blogspot.in/2016/02/interview-with-yc-halan-past-president.html
7. https://www.facebook.com/deepak.roy.148553
8. http://www.amazon.com/Hindi-Cinema-An-Insiders-View/dp/0195695844
9. NK Sharma is a former colleague of Safdar Hashmi of Jana Natya Manch and a theatre director. http://www.thehindu.com/features/friday-review/theatre/keeping-it-real/article4365920.ece
10. https://delhigovt.nic.in/dept/public/gkaul.htm
11. http://cherianwrites.blogspot.in/2016/03/delhi-malayalee-film-society-profile.html
12. https://cherianwrites.blogspot.com/2023/04/note-from-rajiv-jain-founder-celluloid.html
13. https://en.wikipedia.org/wiki/Pankaj_Butalia
14. https://en.wikipedia.org/wiki/Khalid_Mohammed
15. http://cherianwrites.blogspot.in/2016/03/notes-from-khalid-mohammed-interview.html

16. http://cherianwrites.blogspot.in/2016/02/interviewwith-sudhir-nandgaonkar.html
17. http://www.fipresci.org/people/h-n-narahari-rao
18. https://www.suchitrafilmsociety.com
19. https://cherianwrites.blogspot.in/2016/03/profile-of-bangalore-questions-1.html
20. https://cherianwrites.blogspot.in/2016/03/profile-of-chitralekha-with-mf-thomas.html
21. Adoor –A Life in Cinema by Gautaman Bhaskaran, Penguin –Viking-2010. P.68.
22. http://cherianwrites.blogspot.in/2016/02/adoorgopalakrishnan-on-film-society.html
23. Ibid- 21-P. 69
24. Ibid-22
25. http://www.isro.gov.in/
26. Notes: https://cherianwrites.blogspot.in/2016/03/profile-of-chalachitra-tvm.html
27. Notes. https://cherianwrites.blogspot.in/2016/03/notes-about-aswini-film-society.html
28. https://cherianwrites.blogspot.com/2023/04/banner-fs-profile.html
29. https://cherianwrites.blogspot.com/2023/04/tfo-gita-viswanath.html

# 8

# End of the Nehruvian Legacy in Indian Films

In April 2023, the government of the day merged all but one film-related institution established in the 1960s into the National Film Development Corporation (NFDC). These institutions included the National Film Archive of India, Films Division, Directorate of Film Festivals and Children's Film Society of India (CFSI). The decision followed a major policy shift through a cabinet decision of the central government.

"In December 2020, the Union cabinet had decided to merge four of its film media units, namely the Films Division, Directorate of Film Festivals, National Film Archive of India, and Children's Film Society, with the National Film Development Corporation Ltd. by expanding the Memorandum of Articles of Association of NFDC, which will then carry out all the activities hitherto performed by them with the objective of ensuring synergy, convergence of activities and better utilization of resources. The ministry had shared these major policy decisions in its interaction with the film industry held in Chennai and Mumbai earlier this month," an official press note said.[1]

## Major Policy Shift in Films

The decision followed a bureaucrat Bimal Julka-led expert committee report on the rationalisation of film media units to check the sagging fortunes of loss-making NFDC and Children's Film Society of India. Julka's LinkedIn profile said he is an experienced civil servant of 41 years with a demonstrated history of leading impactful projects across the Ministry of Defence, civil aviation, information and broadcasting, external affairs, finance, commerce and public relations in the government of India. The Expert Committee on Rationalisation/Closure/Merger of Film Media Units, also headed by Julka had Rahul Rawail, A. K. Bir, Shyama Prasad, T.S. Nagabharana, special secretary (I&B), director, NFAI, director, DFF, DG, Films Division and joint secretary (Films) as members.

The committee had a detailed mandate to examine the following. The Terms of Reference for the Expert Committee on Review of Autonomous Bodies were:

- Review of performance of Film and Television Institute of India (FTII), Satyajit Ray Film and Television Institute (SRFTI) and Children's Film Society of India (CSFI), as per the mandate under their Memorandum of Association. Whether objectives of these institutes have been achieved/ any shortcomings and reasons thereof.
- Review of the objectives of these institutes to ascertain if they are still relevant and continue to serve a "public purpose" and to examine whether the public purpose can be served in a more efficient manner by other entities in the government or the private sector. Whether the nature of the activities is such that these need to be performed only by an autonomous organisation. To suggest whether the government may consider corporatisation, merger, and disengagement by the government or closure of these institutes.
- Whether user charges are levied at appropriate rates and suggest measures for improvement of revenue generation to make the institution financially self-sufficient in the long run. Also, to suggest appropriate price indices for linking the user charges. Review the expenditure incurred by these institutes with a view to bringing the operation and cost efficiency in the working.
- Suggest a draft of the Memorandum of Understanding to be signed between the ministry and the institute on the same lines as done for CPSEs and laying down the

performance parameters and road map to carry out the intended course of action.

- Review of effectiveness and transparency in administration in FTII and SRFTI, transparency of procurement system, student grievance redressal mechanism and maintain proper discipline in the campus.

The Expert Committee on Rationalisation/Closure/Merger of Film Media Units had the following terms of reference:

- To review the functioning of NFDC and CFSI.
- To recommend whether to close NFDC and CFSI and explore any other alternatives, if required.
- To finalise the nature of the proposal Umbrella Organisation like a government body, a PSU or an autonomous organisation.
- To finalise the mandate of the proposed Umbrella Organisation after reviewing the mandate of all the constituent Media Units.
- To finalise the Organisational structure of the proposed umbrella organisation.[2]

The committee recommended that an Umbrella Organisation be set up with the following verticals:

- Film Production Cell-NFD, Films Division, CFSI.
- Film Festival Cell-DFF, FD,CFSI, NFDC
- Film Heritage Cell
- Film Knowledge Cell

The committee also recommended that the film units be merged under an umbrella organisation—National Film Development Corporation/Council/Corporation. The report put forth that the NFDC and CFSI's functions and FDs responsibilities –of production of documentary/PSA films—be put under the Film Production Cell of this umbrella body.[3]

Rahul Rawail, a member of the Julka committee in an article defending their decision for an umbrella organisation, observed:

> We all agreed that in the days gone by, these media units functioned in an exemplary manner and produced

> tremendous results, but over the last 10 years, they had all slid into a cesspool of muck due to inefficiency, over-staffing and corruption within each unit. The only unit that was devoid of corruption was the DFF though it was suffering due to the inefficiency of some employees, casual and permanent. .. NFDC, which pioneered a revolution in cinema, had in the last 10 years not contributed anything of quality and its workforce was having a ball at the expense of the exchequer. Films Division CFSI and NFAI were plagued with the same disease. Huge monies were being burnt and huge tracts of real estate were being wasted.

Adoor Gopalakrishan while replying to Rahul Rwail in the face of the article on the issue observed:[4]

> As a practitioner long associated with many of these institutes, I can say for certain that the merger is an ill-advised move made without any study or understanding of the functioning of these organisations. It looks like someone's weird, impulsive idea of bringing a comatose NFDC back to life. It is evident that the government has not gone into the simple exercise of studying why the NFDC has miserably failed in its assigned mission....
>
> One is at a loss to understand how the NFAI, which is the country's treasure trove of film heritage and culture, can be left to languish under a corporate body like the NFDC. It is one institution that has been performing exceedingly well from its inception.

The decision removed the film institutions which were directly under the I&B ministry into a public sector corporation, NFDC, which was facing deep financial trouble for decades. In short, the government withdrew direct patronage to the institutions mandated to create a new film culture and New Cinema, ending the Nehruvian era in films. The central government also stopped its annual grant to FFSI, the apex body of the film society movement, from 2014. National Film awards managed by professionals have been taken over by the I&B ministry, which in effect has become a political tool to curry favour in the film field. Thus, the government of India has totally changed its policy with regard to the promotion of good films and filmmaking.

Julka was neither a cultural figure like Dr. Shivarama Karanth, nor a politician like S. K. Patil, who was in the previous occasion in 1980 and 1951 mandated by the government of India to formulate policies for the film sector. While the committee has allowed FTII and SRFTI its original structure, it had added loss-making NFDC with new responsibilities of looking after not only the Film Division, which had a glorious history but, also, surprisingly, the National Film Archives. Contrary to the internationally accepted practice of keeping archives funded by the governments, those insensitive to film history decided to keep NFAI under a loss-making corporation, which can be wound up anytime in the future. The Children's Film Society of India has been given a quiet burial. Most of the government employees like the director of NFAI have gone back to the parental cadres, leaving this specialised archival body to greenhorns, who are mostly temporary employees of NFDC. It is widely known that the NFDC's main preoccupation is an event-management organisation for the government of the day, leaving its main focus on commissioning films to other groups, like the erstwhile Films Division. In effect, the BJP government at the Centre has completely changed the Nehruvian policy of films and left it to the whims and fancies of the officers deputed to the public sector corporation and their political bosses.

Adoor Gopalakrishnan pleaded for the film archive in a statement pointing out "Don't kill film institutions by merging them with a moribund body like the NFDC. Archive is a very expensive affair, which is the responsibility of the government, not any corporation... They were talking about institutions that were making losses as if this is a business."[5]

## Negation of Earlier Film Policies

The Julka committee totally negates the last of such committees under Indira Gandhi, on films, indicating a sharp change in political decision-making in the government. The last Film Enquiry Committee of the government in 1980, when Indira Gandhi returned as Prime Minister after a gap of three years, headed by the veteran cultural icon from Karnataka, Dr. Shivarama Karanth, stressed the need for a "National

Film Policy" and even suggested a *Chalachitra Akademi*. The *Akademi*, just like the *Sahitya*, *Sangeet Natak* and *Lalith Kala Akademies*, was meant to independently take care of the issues relating to the film field by the professionals themselves, in alliance with the government.

Justifying the new Akademi, the committee pointed out that: "Indian cinema has to be helped to evolve its own aesthetic values from our own cultural roots. This can only be done if cinema is given the full status of a cultural activity. We, therefore, recommend that a separate Akademi to be called *Chalachitra Akademi* should be set up exclusively with the object of promoting cinema as an art form, on the same lines as the other Akademies..."[6]

The committee wanted to amend the 1935 Cinematograph Act where the censorship of films remained with the Centre and exhibition was a concurrent subject. However, since the exhibition involved various taxes by the state government, the recommendation never crossed the hurdle of getting the state government's consent.

Earlier too, the government had withdrawn a bill from the Rajya Sabha in 1956, to take full control of the production side of the film industry as recommended by the 1951 Film Enquiry Committee headed by S. K. Patil. The committee had recommended that legislative action should be taken to declare the control of the production of films by the Union "expedient in public interest and thereby entrust the full responsibility for the production side of the industry to the central government". Patil had gone into the details of the nascent film industry of India in 1951 and projected a growth trajectory for the industry and strongly advocated a central intervention as they felt that the issues of the industry are "of a nature that can be comprehended only when viewed as a whole."[7]

The S. K. Patil committee's recommendation to establish a Film and TV training institute (FTII), Film Archive (NFAI) and Film Finance Corporation (FFC-NFDC) had indeed changed the course of Indian films. Looking back, the Patil Committee recommendations also laid the foundations for the development of the Indian film industry to reach the foremost position on the world film map by 2023.

With the Julka Committee, the government has shaken the foundations of the film sector built by Nehruvian policies and it needs to be seen what is in store for the future, for a sector which is only next to the mighty Hollywood of the USA.

## Big Void of Political Patronage

Indira Gandhi's assassination in 1984 left a big void in the film sector, especially in New Cinema and the Film Society Movement. No other prime minister gave such importance to films ever again. Neither did her son, Rajiv Gandhi, who succeeded her, nor the six others who succeeded her in the years to come, from 1984 to 2023. Though I. K. Gujral, a one-time treasurer of FFSI, as Prime Minister was expected to contribute to the sector, his short stint and political instability during the period, did not allow him to take any steps in a sector where he had deep personal interest.

"No Prime minister, other than Ms Gandhi, including her son, had any interest in films," said Gautam Kaul.[8] He, as FFSI president, was struggling to get the Rs 6 lakh annual sum allotted by the Planning Commission in 2009, which was granted to FFSI as an NGO. Kaul was not optimistic about getting the Rs 12 lakh which was still stuck in the files for the past two years (in 2015) as there is hardly any interest shown by the government. Post-2014, the FFSI has not received any grant in aid from the Central government, FFSI Secretary Amitabh Ghosh confirmed.

In 2013, a Right to Information plea on government funding to FFSI revealed that the I&B ministry had released a grant in aid to FFSI under the 10th plan scheme of Non-Government Organisations engaged in anti-piracy works/festivals and under the 11th plan scheme: "Export Promotion through Film Festivals in India & abroad". Under this scheme, the I&B ministry, from the financial year 2003-04 to 2006-07, granted Rs 4 lakh and in 2007-08, granted Rs 3 lakh, and thereafter doubled it to Rs 6 lakh from 2008-09.[9]

## Complete Abdication of Direct Government Patronage

The I&B ministry listed the following points to show their achievements in the film sector for the financial year 2014-15: "From April 1, 2014 to October 31, 2014, this Division has produced 35 documentary films. The Film Division has released 7786 prints of 39 approved films in Cinema Houses throughout the country. The Film Division has entered 47 films in 16 National/International Film Festivals. News Magazines on the 14th India Russia Summit-Moscow 2013, PM's visit to China 2013 and G-20 Summit Russia-2013 were completed. Eight films completed for Non-Theatrical release as outside production and 15 films as in-house production. Nine Films were completed for theatrical release as in-house production."[10]

However, by 2023, the ministry website has just one page under the category of films, giving links to its public sector and other divisions,[11] indicating that it has withdrawn its leading role in films.

The section of the annual report given by the Ministry on Film Development in 2015 read as follows:

> The National Film Development Corporation Ltd. was incorporated in the year 1975, with the primary objective of planning, promoting and organizing an integrated and efficient development of the Indian film industry in accordance with the national economic policy and objectives laid down by the Central Government from time to time. By merging the Film Finance Corporation (FFC) and Indian Motion Picture Export Corporation (IMPEC) with NFDC it was reincorporated in the year 1980. Since its inception, NFDC has funded/produced over 300 films in more than 21 regional languages, many of which have earned wide acclaim and won national/international awards. As a film development agency, NFDC is responsible for facilitating growth in areas/segments of the film industry that not only have a cultural bearing but also in areas which cannot be taken by private enterprises due to commercial exigencies thereby facilitating a balanced growth of the industry. However, even while its

role in the Indian film industry is largely developmental, as a public sector enterprise, NFDC also has a corporate mandate and is responsible for generating a healthy balance sheet. To its credit, NFDC was presented the Turnaround Award 2013 on November 1, 2013, by BRPSE (Board for Reconstruction of Public Sector Enterprises) along with three other Central Public Sector Enterprises (CPSEs), as all have posted profits for three consecutive financial years—2010-11, 2011- 12 and 2012-13. NFDC further enhanced its forte in production and distribution under the brand, 'Cinemas of India', production of advertisements, short and corporate films for various government agencies, film exhibitions, restoration, Film Bazaar, training in digital non-linear editing, cinematography, sub-titling etc."[12]

However, the main thrust of the ministry in the film sector appears to be the National Museum of Indian Cinema (NMIC). The annual report listed the objectives of NMIC as follows:

- To encapsulate the socio-cultural history of India as revealed through the evolution of its cinema.
- To develop as a research centre focusing on the effect cinema has on society.
- To exhibit the work of the noted filmmakers: directors, producers, institutions and others for the benefit of film enthusiasts and other visitors.
- To arrange seminars and workshops for filmmakers and film students.
- To generate and sustain interest in films and film movements amongst current and future generations.[13]

The National Film Heritage Mission (NFHM): "National Film Heritage Mission", a Rs. 597.41 crore project was approved by the I&B, Government of India in November 2014 through the Ministry of Finance for restoring and preserving the film heritage of India. This is a part of the 12th Five Year Plan, which will spill over to its 13th Five Year Plan as per the year-wise allocation of the Plan outlay. This new plan scheme has taken care of the digitisation/restoration of films available with NFAI, as well as other media units under the film wing of the

Ministry of Information and Broadcasting. The implementation of the planning scheme has been handed over to the National Film Archive of India, Pune, as described in the annual report of the NMIC project. In 2023 all these projects are under the NFDC, the umbrella organisation of the government for films.

### Film Societies disappear from Central Government Records

The FFSI, till 2015, got a mention in the ministry's report as a collaborator in organising a film festival in Delhi with the European Union. As a Non-Governmental Organisation (NGO) listed under the ministry, FFSI submits an annual report to the Ministry for grants-in-aid, there was no mention of FFSI or its activities in the annual report of the ministry, revealing the 'importance' that the government attaches to Film Societies. As an NGO, FFSI also supplies its army of film scholars and discerning selectors for various Indian film festivals, state governments' annual awards, and other film-related committees. The FFSI has been giving intellectual support to the government, and various other existing film promotional avenues, in identifying and promoting the quality of films in India, which can make the country proud at international film festivals; a contribution, which has been increasingly overlooked by the ministry over the years. But by 2023, FFSI will not exist for the government of India or its Ministry dealing with films, as there is no mention of it anywhere on its official websites.

"For the 2015 International Film Festivals, the Directorate of Film Festivals sent 15 names and gave the option of nominating five names to the Ministry. However, they have put the entire list on hold and asked for the profile of all 15, clearly indicating that the ministry is not going by the wisdom of the Directorate in this matter," pointed out Gautam Kaul.[12] Needless to say, such lists are normally filled with FFSI activists. By 2023, there are no such requests from the government to FFSI and the ministry and the political leadership decides on the jury of various national and international film festival selection associates.

### Legacy Institutions Face Uncertainty

In 2015, the government appointed an unpopular actor from Hindi television serials and film serials as the chairman of FTII.

The students went on a strike protesting against the appointment, as the actor had no stature, and his only qualification was that he belonged to the same ideological school as the political party ruling at the Centre. Commenting on the appointment of the actor as the Chairman, Adoor Gopalakrishnan, an alumnus, told *Hindustan Times*, "A premier institute such as this one has to be given its due respect. According to FTII Society rules, its members must be eminent people from the field of cinema, art, literature and theatre. This year that was not the case, barring a few eminent people who have resigned."[14]

The question is: how seriously have such institutions of national importance been treated by the government over a period of time? Already, the post of the Director of FTII has gone to serving civil servants, unlike in earlier years where eminent professionals like Girish Karnad and N. V. K. Murthy were the preferred choices for such a post. From imparting world-class training in filmmaking and television programming, the institute's leadership is trying to administer curricula set up by experts. The institute which produced almost all pioneers of the *New Wave* who have filled the National Awardees lists and have won several international honours including an Oscar is now reduced to yet another film training institute.

In 2011, the committee headed by P. K. Nair which went into the issues of the Institute recommended wide-ranging reforms including strengthening the infrastructure to cater to the increasing demands of the 11 courses it ran. In 2000, a committee had favoured handing over the Institute to the film industry and in 2010, Hewitt wanted the introduction of short-term courses at competitive rates to make FTII self-reliant. "Government should issue grants without interfering in administration. FTII should be permitted to raise funds from outside sources. We had suggested a raised fee of Rs 1 lakh per student across all courses. FTII could offer scholarships to those who cannot afford the fee," P. K. Nair had said then.[15]

Apart from administrative issues, the FTII appeared to be also suffering from an ideological positioning. Over the years, the FTII had produced left-liberal filmmakers, and, now, the obviously right-wing, Hindutva-leaning government insists on a change in the ideological moorings of the Institute. "No one can saffronise the technical aspects of film-making like lighting, camera, and sound. But the ideology can matter when it comes to the narrative," commented noted filmmaker, Shyam Benegal, on the change of guard and ideological leanings of the new FTII chairman.[16]

**Figure 8.1.** FTII Pune

The FTII which produced and supported better films and contributed to a new film culture was dependent on the Film Society Movement as a firm base of connoisseurs appreciating the films of young graduates of this institute. All major film societies from *Celluloid* of Delhi to *Chalachitra* of Thiruvananthapuram organised film festivals with the *New Wave* films in the 1970s itself, making those filmmakers stars of the sector. In his 1971 article on 'An Indian New Wave', Satyajit Ray wrote, "*Bhuvan Shome* may well define the kind of off-beat film most likely to succeed with our minority audience–the kind that *looks* a bit like their French counterpart, but it is essentially old fashioned and Indian beneath its trendy habit."[17]

Indeed, the maestro, like all other connoisseurs of arts, had taken note of the *New Wave* created by film society veterans like Mrinal Sen, Pattabhi Rama Reddy and FTII graduates like Mani Kaul and Adoor Gopalakrishnan.

The NFDC, which is the successor of the Film Finance Corporation (FFC), the institution which produced most of the new Indian Cinema is also in the doldrums. It still produces and coproduces documentary films under its guidelines for film production, but it only encourages debut filmmakers by undertaking 100% production of their first feature film. Unlike earlier years, it is no longer a production house sustaining new experiments in cinema, rather with the Film Division it caters to documentaries with a focus on North Eastern people etc.

By 2023, the newly empowered NFDC said its objective was to "develop talent and to facilitate the growth of Indian cinema in all languages through productions and co-productions, script development and need-based workshops," apart from promoting "Indian culture through cinema in India and overseas' while building 'a lean and flexible organization responsive to the needs of the Indian film industry."[18]

**Figure 8.2.** Film Appreciation Course, a group photo

The complete separation of FTII and NFAI, now as a wing of the corporation is the abrupt end of the Film Appreciation summer course, they used to organise together from 1967, which created a new stream of film academics and writers across India. The COVID season ensured the course became online and in

2023, the merged entity did not announce the new summer course.

A look at the earlier list of films honoured at the yearly National Film Festival conducted by the government also shows the declining number of the NFDC financed films in the list. In 1983-84, there were nine films including the Oscar award-winning film *Gandhi* in the award categories, as against just one film in 2011-12. Clearly, the NFDC is no longer the storehouse of quality, award-winning films.[19]

The NFAI has a 50-year-old legacy of archiving films and a collection of 18,878 films, reported as per the 2015 March annual report of the I&B ministry. In 2015-16, the ministry allocated Rs 7 crore as the annual budget for the archive which is the largest of the sort in the last decade. The reason is the ongoing digitization programme of old films and also the project on the National Museum of Indian Cinema (NMIC). However, the NFAI has continued to be leaderless for some time now. The director of NFAI had been in the acting capacity for years and the local senior Indian Information officer has been given the additional charge. This has put the Archive on auto-pilot mode.

My first visit to the archive in 2012 revealed that it was leaderless and I felt that the organisation was drifting. However, my second visit in 2014 showed marked improvement, maybe the director with additional charge was a person with some interest in the subject he/she was handling. Increasingly, film-related institutions are being handled by administrators from the I&B ministry and professionals in the field are not encouraged to take the reins in these organisations. With the merger of NFAI as a division of the NFDC, most government servants and old staff who built the organisation have either left or retired, putting the treasure house of films on an uncertain path.

All the institutions which the 1951 S. K. Patil committee flagged off appeared to be at a crossroads. These institutions are seen as a burden on the government exchequer putting its very existence into uncertainty. The Film Society Movement, which was the public arm of these institutions, is getting limited to pockets of influence and does not seem to have a role in influencing film policy or cultures anymore.

## Few State Governments Nurture Film Societies

Even as the central government's interest in films and the Film Society Movement was declining from the 1980s, the state governments have shown keen interest in their regional films and film culture. Many found the Film Society Movement to be a storehouse of experience in handling the policy on films.

**Figure 8.3.** Nandan Complex, Kolkata

Notable among the states, which have been coordinating with the Film Society Movement, are West Bengal, Karnataka, Kerala and Tamil Nadu. Kolkata, where the Film Society Movement was shaped into an all-India activity, also led the way in the new phenomenon. *Nandan,* the cultural complex in the middle of Kolkata, was the pet project of Buddhadeb Bhattacharya, who was the then information minister and even had a room there to meet his cultural activist friends, as long as he was in power. The foundation stone of *Nandan* was laid by Buddhadeb Bhattacharya in 1980 and it was inaugurated by Satyajit Ray in 1985, who designed the logo of the complex. The complex has been hosting various film screenings, and also the Kolkata Film Festival over the years. Even after the Left Front was voted out of power in 2011, the centre continues to be a cultural hub with films as the centre of the activity. In February 2013, the *Nandan* managing committee was headed by the Bengali film director, and Satyajit Ray's son, Sandip Ray, and the members included filmmaker Aparna Sen, daughter of the Film Society Movement pioneer Chidananda Das Gupta.

Around the time when Adoor Gopalakrishnan was winning the National Awards, Kerala woke up to an emerging new cinematic culture. In 1975, at the height of the Film Society Movement, the state government established the Kerala State Film Development Corporation Ltd (KSFDC), the first of its sort in any state. Then chief minister, C. Achutha Menon, from the Communist Party of India, was a film society admirer and even sanctioned a 35 mm projector at the Tagore Centenary Hall in the capital, where most of the 35 mm films were screened *by Chitralekha* and later *Chalachithra film* societies. KSFDC's mandate was to shift the Madras-centric Malayalam film-making in Kerala by giving incentives like production studios and facilities and also a subsidy.[20]

In the last 48 years, the KSFDC has met its purpose of shifting Malayalam film-making from Madras to Kerala. *Chitranjali* Studio Complex of KSFDC inaugurated in 1980, was truly a pioneer in introducing the latest film technology in South India, and it became the hub of award-winning filmmakers like Shaji N. Karun and K.R. Mohanan, two FTII graduates, who worked at KSFDC in senior positions. The Corporation also owns an exhibition network with 15 screens spread all over Kerala. The Thiruvananthapuram theatre complexes of KSFDC host the International Film Festival of Kerala (IFFK).

Following the recommendation of the Central Film Enquiry Committee in 1980, Kerala was also the first to establish its own *Chalachithra* Academy (Motion Picture Academy of the Kerala State) in 1998.[21]

The Academy is entrusted with the conduct of the popular International Film Festival of Kerala, the annual year-end film festival which attracts around 10,000 delegates in various categories. The FFSI *Keralam* is involved in conducting IFFK, as a partner to the Academy.

The FFSI Kerala chapter now has 113 film society units. The Left Front government sanctioned Rs 50 lakh to the FFSI Kerala unit to encourage film society activities in 2010 and they brought out a monthly journal named *Drishyathalam*. Just as in Kolkata, the Left parties dominate the FFSI Keralam and its critics say most of the film societies are with either the communist party unions or people affiliated with them.

It took another 11 years for the neighbouring state of Karnataka to have its own *Chalachithra* Academy in 2009. The Academy promotes film culture and conducts the Bangalore International Film Festival as a yearly feature since 2008, apart from conducting film appreciation courses in various parts of the state. The academy has also promoted the establishment of film societies in the state.[22]

Tamil Nadu, which is famous for its obsession with cinema and superstars, also has its own International Film Festival. From 2003 onward, the yearly event has been organised by a professional body called the International Cine Appreciation Foundation (ICAF), which works for the promotion of meaningful cinema in Chennai. The ICAF has more than 500 members, mostly film professionals and technicians. The Tamil Nadu government now patronises the Chennai International Film Festival, organised by the ICAF since 2008. Apart from the festivals, ICAF also has regular monthly screenings.[23]

Though the Centre abdicated its initial plan to mentor film appreciation as seen by the Film Society Movement and its pioneers, many state governments appeared to recognise such a civil society grouping when it comes to organising film festivals in their respective states.

## Absence of Political Patronage

The first major public consultation of films undertaken by Nehru's government in 1955 was to assign the responsibility of the film seminar to *Sangeet Natak Akademi*. The then Akademi Chairman, Dr. P.V. Rajamannar, identified its functions as "to set up high standards for this new art form without impairing its commercial value". Over the years, the academy did not find itself indulged in films leading the 1980 Film Enquiry Committee to recommend a *Chalachitra Akademi*, exclusively with the object of promoting cinema as an art form, on the same lines as the other Academies, i.e., *Sangeet Natak Akademi*, *Sahitya Akademi*, and *Lalit Kala Akademi*.

The functions of *Chalachitra Akademi* were listed in detail by the committee with a clear paragraph on the film society too. The academy was "to act as a centre for the propagation of film culture and film consciousness in the country by providing financial help and guidance for setting up Film Societies, film clubs and making film classics and artistic films available to these societies through the Film Lending Service".[24]

Explaining the role of the Film Society Movement in the proposed academy, the 1980 report wanted the film societies to be encouraged so that people, in general, can be initiated into "the art of cinema". The report went on to state that "it is obvious that the Film Society Movement has a very important role to play in "initiating" audience in the appreciation of good cinema. It is in this context that we have suggested that the Academy should be assigned the task of helping the growth of Film Society Movement".[25]

Indira Gandhi's last tenure as the Prime Minister was plagued by terrorism, a phenomenon new to India, thus occupying most of her time to handle the new situations, which ended her life itself. No other than Gandhi, the original supporter of the New Cinema/Film Society Movement could have initiated the formation of a *Chalachithra Akademi*. After her assassination in 1984, Rajiv Gandhi had too many legacy issues to handle and films were not his priority. A central *Chalachithra Akademi* remained buried in the files of the government of India.

The only recommendation of the committee in 1980, which the government accepted recently after the Indian film industry celebrated its 100 years, was the setting up of a National Film Museum.[26] However, at least two states went ahead and formed their own *Chalachithra Akademies* and many have their own art theatres in the state and district capitals.

*Nandan* in Kolkata, *Suchitra* centre at Bangalore and 15 Screens of Kerala's KSFDC remain as remnants of an unfinished plan across the country.

**Figure 8.4.** National Film Museum, Mumbai

The lack of political patronage to the Indian New Cinema and Film Society movement does not need further elaboration. According to Chidananda Das Gupta, from Nehru's regime to his grandson Rajiv Gandhi's period, the Film Society Movement and its leaders played an important role in the film policies of the government. It was Rajiv Gandhi who honoured the film society evangelist Marie Seton with the nation's third highest civilian honour, the *Padma Bhushan*.

Das Gupta observed:[27]

> Film Society activists were inducted into many Government committees and had a great deal of influence over India's third International Film Festival in 1965 (the second having taken place in 1961, nine years after the first in 1952). The fourth festival came up in 1969 and thereafter, under Ms Gandhi's Prime Ministership, a Directorate of Film Festivals was established under the Ministry of Information and Broadcasting in 1974 to hold an annual International film festival, as well as the annual National Film Festival at which president's awards were distributed. The 1960s thus laid the foundation for a government-supported serious cinema (or the 'art' film) which continued to develop through the 1970s.

The crisis of the 1980s and 1990s also saw a policy paralysis of the government-supported 'art' films. In his last book, Das Gupta, whose life was dedicated to this genre of films and the Film Society Movement, documented the decline of interest in the government. "In the 1980s, started the decline in the support systems for alternative cinema started. The governmental will to maintain the infrastructure in prime condition wavered. It relapsed into the common illusion of culture as a decoration to be worn on one's sleeve rather than an essential ingredient of national development, expandable whenever there was any pressure on resources. The International Film Festival of India, the National Film Development Corporation, the President's Awards, and the National Film Archive of India increasingly found their reason *d'être* coming into question. If they have not been abolished it has partly been due to inertia and partly the fear of alienating powerful sections of intelligentsia. They have therefore been allowed to continue listlessly, without positive faith in their necessity. This lackadaisical attitude has been further undermined by religious orthodoxies with their xenophobic compulsion."[28]

## Political Propaganda Through Films

In a way, Das Gupta could foresee the appointment of an actor known for his political contacts and mythological roles, as the chairman of FTII by a future regime; the NFDC going through restructuring as a sick public sector unit with the merger of the Films Division and Children's Film Society; the NFAI and the Directorate of Film Festival further making a big question mark on the future of these institutions. The government, which once toyed with the idea of taking effective control of film production to raise the level of film culture with the formation of a *Chalachitra Akademi*, have not only shelved such lofty plans but has also abdicated its plans to intervene in the film sector with its policy directions.

The current regime appears to have submitted itself to a box office-oriented dispensation, encouraging the propaganda genre of films while giving films such as *Kashmir Files*, tax exemptions. The Jury Chairman of the India International Film Festival, Israeli filmmaker Naved Lapid, had openly lamented about the inclusion of *Kashmir Files* in the competition, calling it a crass, propaganda film. "In his interview, Mr Lapid said that while he was watching the movie, he was shocked by the 'transparent combination between propaganda and fascism and vulgarity'".

"I couldn't help but imagine an Israeli film like this in another year and a half or two," he told *Ynet* a Hebrew media outlet.

What was more damaging was Naved's open criticism of the inclusion of the film and its promotion at IFFI 2022 by the government. "It's crazy, what's going on here. It's a government festival and it's the biggest in India. It's a film that the Indian government, even if it didn't actually make it, at least pushed it in an unusual way. It basically justifies the Indian policy in Kashmir, and it has fascist features," he said.[29]

The controversy followed marching orders for the chairman of the merged entity, NFDC, who was instrumental in the conduct of the IFFI.

However, those in the government appear to be happy clicking pictures with popular cine stars at film festivals whose presence has increased over the years.

If some films of international standards are still being made, it can only be due to the legacy, which films like *Pather Panchali* have built over the years with the so-called "minority audience". The National Film Awards and choice of films for international festivals from India are increasingly moving towards the so-called popular films made for mass consumption with an eye on the box office, dumping all pretensions of government as a connoisseur of art. Combined with this is the increasing trend of using and encouraging films for political propaganda and even encouraging such films through their placements in International Film Festivals and giving them awards in National Film Festivals. Sadly, in this policy regime, civil society movements like Film Societies find no place and are nowhere near the coveted public space they used to occupy before the digital revolution. If it survives in a few centres in India, it is just a legacy situation as Robin Banerjee, in his early 80s, running the film group *Forum* in Kolkata says.

> Most of our members are above 60 years of age and the young people come in when we collaborate with the Satyajit Ray Film Institute. The Film Society Movement for most young people appears to be a legacy one and interest among them is for those being trained to be in the film field or those academically engaged with the film

sector, as a host of universities have started film studies departments like the Jadavpur University in Kolkata in the 1980s.

Clearly, the Film Society Movement, which celebrated the *New Wave* in Indian films, leading to an attitudinal shift of common people with regard to films find itself has not been able to find its new path among the digital generation and waiting for new discoveries in format and approach to film appreciation and approach to films itself.

Adding to the movement's issues is the total lack of government and institutional support and a sudden scrapping of the Nehruvian policy of the country's patronage to such civil society groups, however small it was. Just as the film institutions created in the 1960s by the government the Film Society Movement too contributed to a major shift in appreciation and attitude of the people towards films heralding a shift from crass to class in the film sector itself.

## References


1. https://pib.gov.in/PressReleaseIframePage.aspx?PRID=1811671#:~:text=In%20December%2C%202020%2C%20the%20Union%20Cabinet%20had%20decided,convergence%20of%20activities%20%26%20better%20utilization%20of%20resources.
2. https://pib.gov.in/PressReleaseIframePage.aspx?PRID=1628752#:~:text=The%20Expert%20Committee%20on%20Rationalisation%2FClosure%2FMerger%20of%20Film%20Media,Films%20Division%20and%20Joint%20Secretary%20%28Films%29%20as%20members.
3. https://www.thequint.com/explainers/why-have-all-film-bodies-been-merged-with-nfdc#read-more
4. Times of India Jan.7/22
5. https://indianexpress.com/article/explained/explained-india-several-film-bodies-part-of-nfdc-7848252/
6. Report of the Working Group on National Film Policy, Ministry of I&B, GOI, May 1980. P.10.Para-3.8 &3.10
7. S. K. Patil Committee report, 1951.quoted in Ibid 1. P.4-para2.7
8. Interview with Gautam Kaul.
9. RTI on grants to FFSI by I&B Ministry.:http://cherianwrites.blogspot.in/2016/02/reply-from-ministry-of-i-ffsi-funding.html

10. http://mib.nic.in/
11. https://www.mib.gov.in/about-film-wing/films-wing
12. Ibid.10
13. Ibid.10
14. Ibid.8.
15. PK Nair –HT- http://www.hindustantimes.com/india/ftii-chairman-s-new-battle-students-strike-sceptical-film-fraternity/story-Y5qPb0zCtka1Tu0546ZpQJ.html
16. ShyamBenegal-HT http://www.hindustantimes.com/india/ftii-chairman-s-new-battle-students-strike-sceptical-film-fraternity/story-Y5qPb0zCtka1Tu0546ZpQJ.html
17. Our FlmsThierFilms,SatyajitRay,Orient Black Swan, 2011.
18. https://www.nfdcindia.com/company-profile/
19. https://www.dff.gov.in/NFA.aspx
20. https://www.ksfdc.in
21. Chalachitra Academy-Kerala. https://www.keralafilm.com/
22. Chalachitra Academy-Karnataka- https://kcainfo.com/
23. Chennai International film festival. https://www.chennaifilmfest.com/
24. Ibid-6. P 10-Para.3.10.
25. Ibid-6. 2P-13- Para3.23.
26. https://filmsdivision.org/nmic.html
27. Seeing is Believing. By Chidananda Das Gupta, Viking, 2008. P. 91.
28. Ibid- 27.P- 91.
29. https://www.ndtv.com/india-news/nadav-lapid-iffi-2022-someone-had-to-speak-up-israel-filmmaker-on-the-kashmir-files-remarks-3565136

# 9

# Do Film Societies Have a Future in the Digital Era?

## Pandemic and Changes in Film Viewing Habits

The pandemic years of 2020 and 2021 saw community activities, including film screenings, getting stalled. There was a serious crisis in the film sector, with filmmaking coming to a halt, physical screens closed, and digital screens getting unlocked. People found digital avenues to continue their activities, which included online video meetings, social media and other digital means to reach out with their products and services. Films, too, changed their human interface. From television broadcasts, online media like YouTube and OTT brought films and videos onto the ever-expanding bandwidth of smart mobile phones, not just smart television sets, which are now called home theatre screens. These digital developments completely changed the viewing habits of people across the world, including Indians. Film viewing habits changed from communal to personal.

## Is the Digital Revolution Challenging Film Societies?

The changes in viewing habits hit the film societies, already overwhelmed with the ongoing digital revolution and free availability of film in various formats, from CDs to internet downloads. The two pandemic years saw most of the film societies shutting shop. The FFSI is yet to list a formal count of the surviving official film societies post the pandemic years.

As theatres opened in 2021, it was heartening to see that audiences returned in significant numbers–clearly showing that the "cinema experience is something that is cherished. Accordingly, we expect the filmed entertainment segment to recover its 2019 levels–assuming there is no further impact of the pandemic–by the end of 2023.

Digital/OTT rights could grow to 32 per cent of segment revenues due to increased uptake of OTT platforms (refer to the digital media section of this report) and growing consumption of dubbed and subtitled content on OTT platforms," FICCI's annual 2022 report on media and entertainment industry compiled by Ernst and Young, the global consultancies, recorded the change in media habits of Indians post-pandemic year of 2020.

"TV became connected and interactive, films released online, news went hyper-local, 390 million Indians gamed online, over 150 billion songs were streamed, subscription OTT scaled to 40 million households, and digital media cemented its position as the second largest segment of Indian M&E. In doing so, digital and other technologies played a large role–and consequently, changed the power equation in favour of consumers. Consumer data became the crux for all decision-making, and media companies started to make more and more data-backed decisions. The media company of yesterday became the media-science company of today.

Also, the year saw an explosion in the Indian creator economy where more than half a million bloggers, vloggers, content creators, artists, educators, musicians, influencers etc. were actively posting content on their various social media channels to directly build an audience around their niche," the FICCI report which is considered as the most reliable media overview of the year 2022 pointed out.[1]

Most of the media habits began to change in the urban centres of India, which were the playground of Indian film societies and their film appreciation experiments. The middle-class professionals who were the patrons of film societies in the 1970s and 1980s were the most affected by this change in viewing habits, according to industry statistics.

Though there is a comeback trend in the regular film-going crowd, consisting of low-income groups, most surviving film societies were seriously affected as the majority followed the old formats of screening films. In Delhi, the India International Centre and India Habitat Centre film clubs continue their screenings, but in a subdued way. Kolkata film societies are struggling to survive, as they all complain of a lack of enthusiasm from young people. The only major film society which is not much affected appears to be *Suchitra* of Bangalore, as they have developed themselves into a Cultural complex with various other activities and a film education centre. In Thiruvananthapuram, though the FFSI lists 25 odd film societies, only one or two are visible with their activities.

### Pandemic and Online Film Groups

However, the arrival of online film groups points to different digital film societies. India's most successful online film society is the Talking Films Online (TFO) initiated by two academics, Gita Viswanath of Baroda, Gujarat, and Nikhila HS of Hyderabad. They, too, have over 300 members on their list. They operate through online and social media platforms to screen a selected film for a week and, at the end of the week, a Zoom discussion on the films, sometimes with the participating filmmaker, which makes these discussions more meaningful. I was part of such a discussion with filmmakers Adoor Gopalakrishnan and Aparna Sen.

The weekend discussion goes on for two hours, sometimes late into the night and throws us various interesting insights into the films and the filmmakers' approach and craft in each of these films. The beauty of this format is that after the sharing of the film on a Monday, the members have one full week to see it at their convenience before discussing it on Saturday. Discussions are initiated by an academic with a detailed analysis of the film before throwing it open to the logged-in members of TFO on the Zoom video meeting platform.[2]

### Online Groups as the World Order

Having found the format easy on digital lifestyle, I asked Dr. Swarnavel Eswaran,[3] a Professor in the Department of English and Department of Media and Information at Michigan State

University, whether such groups are vague in the most digital-savvy country like the USA. I was surprised to hear his views, as he pointed out that Michigan University itself had a group namely "The MSU Film Collective," which not just had the participation of his department students, but others interested in films. The website link to the group said, "We are the professors, students, filmmakers, screenwriters, and *cinéphiles* at MSU, who gather weekly in the course FLM 200 to watch and discuss good films. In the spirit of the *Cinémathèque française* and the generation of film critics and French New Wave directors it inspired, our collective abides by the principle that good film writing and good filmmaking (and just plain good living) begin with serious film watching."[4]

According to Dr. Swarnavel, there were many such groups specialising in various genres of films of interest. There were professional groups that communicated through WhatsApp and Facebook and initiated and conducted discussions on subjects of importance to each of them.

I realised I was a member of a few such groups in India, on Facebook groups like The Film Society, Film Critics Circle of India, Swayamvaram Fifty, TFO, etc. Most international film festivals have a Facebook page and a group attached to them. There are groups of filmmakers of yesteryears like Ingmar Bergman, Andrei Tarkovsky, Akira Kurosawa, Ritwik Ghatak, etc. WhatsApp groups are also there in each of the genres, and people are aplenty, too, depending on people's interests. A regular search on Google reveals many more groups on social media, not necessarily film appreciation, but each of their functions, from casting calls to the announcement of a new production to crowdfunding.

Digital platforms and habits thus have made the old film society formats obsolete, making it a habit of senior citizens. "We hardly find any young people in our screenings," admitted filmmaker Goutam Ghosh, President of the FORUM, the alternate group to FFSI in Kolkata. FFSI Secretary Amitav Ghosh admits changing its mandate is a long-winding process. "The last major change was initiated ten years ago, and it got approved by the general body recently," said Ghosh who is in his late 70s. He admitted to the organisation's inability to match the expectations of the digital age, making it a body of senior citizens who are carrying on with a legacy organisation.

**Have Analogue Film Societies Turned Obsolete?**

Surprisingly, cinema, though much celebrated today, was neither considered a form of art nor a legitimate pastime in India till the 1950s; rather, it was looked down upon as a low form of entertainment. None of the prominent cultural figures, writers, painters, or musicians associated with it wholeheartedly till films like *Pather Panchali* began to make headlines nationally and internationally. A close look at the history of the development of films as a medium reveals that it was the Film Society Movement (FSM), institutions like FTII, NFDC, NFAI and New Cinema which changed this social attitude, giving films a respectable social status along with other art forms, if not accord it a glamorous status, which it enjoys today. This is not to take into account the occasional sparks created by films like *Dharti Ke Lal* by K. A. Abbas or Guru Dutt's films as far back as in the 1940s and 1950s.

Behind the FSM was a few groups of professionals from various sectors in many urban centres in India, starting from Usha Bhagat, Social Secretary of Prime Minister Indira Gandhi, Vijaya Mulay (*Akka)*, who was friends with both Indira Gandhi and Bhagat to Narahari Rao, a public sector engineer in Bangalore and film personalities like Basu Chatterjee, Khalid Mohammed, K.A. Abbas in Mumbai to Satyajit Ray, Chidananda Das Gupta to now Goutam Ghosh and Samik Bandyopadhyay in Kolkata. They worked hard to procure world-class films over the years to create the right audience who appreciated them like any other art.

After a retrospective of his films to commemorate 50 years of his first film, at Hyderabad, by Moving Images Film Society in February 2023, Adoor Gopalakrishnan said, "There were some very good people in that film society."

The analogue way of procuring a film, screening it and discussing it still happens in many corners of the country, despite the ongoing digital revolution and change in the viewing habits of young people. It is indeed these small groups which encouraged the offbeat-art films as they were called in the 1950s and 1960s, and even celebrated the *New Wave* in Indian films through the creations of FTII graduates in the 1970s and till today through their repeated screenings creating excitement among the filmgoers as well as the popular film sector. From Guwahati to Thiruvananthapuram, these film boxes travelled to be screened in these small groups. Many of the filmmakers, writers, critics and academics who spoke, wrote and studied these films made them part of the wider cultural mosaic.

These groups across the country appeared to be holding to the old 'analogue' format of physical screenings and a discussion, formal or informal, almost limiting the activity to senior citizens among the population. As the younger generation had already entered the digital era and even seeing films on mobile screens, the question arises, has the old 'analogue' format of film society gone obsolete? The question remains even while emphasising the role of a meaningful appreciation of different layers of creative work in a film through the individual prism of the human mind conditioned by their immediate surroundings, education and grooming into various arts including films."

## Films as a Crass to Class Act

To find the right answer to whether the 'analogue' format of film societies has become obsolete, one has to look at the changing social positioning of films over the years. Chronicling the New Indian Cinema, Aruna Vasudev, the eminent film writer, narrated the makeover of films in the Indian society:[5]

> In the vibrant atmosphere of the 50s, the cinema began to be viewed as a possible art form. Cinema, until this time had been treated, as worst as, a reprehensible, though unavoidable, social catastrophe, at best a barbarous pastime for the uncultured.

Filmmaker Adoor Gopalakrishnan, speaking at a convocation ceremony at Ahmedabad University, observed that in those initial days, films as a medium had no social standing.

> Cinema from the very beginning enjoyed a very low esteem or no esteem at all. Even professional prostitutes

had refused to act in films, although the roles offered were that of the virtuous *Sati Savitri* and the like. They feared it would tarnish their image. Dada Saheb Phalke—the father of Indian cinema—had to settle for a man who looked manly every inch to enact Queen Chandramati's role in *Raja Harishchandra*. Fortunately, the film was silent, and the man's voice could not kill the role. It was a long time ago and the stigma attached to cinema refuses to wash away after a century.

**Figure 9.1.** Still from film Raja Harishchandra

From 1947 to 2023, the Film Society Movement and institutions like FTII, NFAI and NFDC established by the Central Government, have given the sector, once considered "uncultured", a façade of respectability and a glamorous positioning, making many writers get onto the bandwagon. The world recognised the *New Wave* in Indian films with films like *Pather Panchali* and a host of filmmakers went on to win awards in various International Film Festivals abroad. "Retrospectives and Film Weeks of Indian films have been held at a number of international forums and today India can justly claim to have several filmmakers of international status," the Dr. Shivarama Karanth committee report observed.[7] *Pather Panchali* itself was a cinematic adaptation of a popular Bangla novel by Bibhutibhushan Bandyopadhyay opening a new vista of adaptation of fictional works into films, a trend which is still popular across Indian languages.

The best example of this change of positioning and improved social standing is reflected in none other than Amitabh Bachchan, the Hindi film superstar. His name has often cropped up in discussions as a potential candidate for the post of President of India. Even the thought of such an honour for any film actor being considered for the top post in the country would not have been the wildest dreams of Indians till the 1970s and 1980s. The closest they could get to Parliament in the 1970s was with a Rajya Sabha nomination, like Nargis Dutt, who happened to be in the former Prime Minister Nehru and Indira Gandhi's charmed circuit, and she had a huge admirer in Egyptian President Gamal Abdel Nasser, courtesy, the film *Mother India*. Nasser not only ensured that a remake of the film was made in Egypt but even attended a *Filmfare* Award Ceremony to catch up with his favourite star in the early 1960s. Since then, many film stars and directors have been nominated to the upper house of Parliament–Rajya Sabha—over the years.

### The Box Office Versus Meaningful Films

The inherent contradiction of the situation of 'not-so-cultural' mass films made for the box office and its obsession with100s of crores of rupees in collections, and a cultured cinema promoted by the government till 2000, manifested as a clash between commercial and art films for years. The reason for the exorbitant entertainment taxation of films in India is a legacy of the "uncultured past."

Commenting on the films of those years, Vasudev pointed out that the strict censorship and lack of institutional financing were a part of this social stigma on films. "It has been allowed to go its own way, but subjected to stern censorship and more damagingly, to exorbitant taxation and a series of vexatious rules and regulations," she noted, though she added that despite all these negative conditions, 319 films were made in India in 1960.[8]

B.K. Karanjia, the editor of *Filmfare* magazine, noted the sad state of affairs of Indian cinema in the 1960s and 1970s. He focused on it in every issue of the magazine. In his autobiography *Counting My Blessings*, Karanjia categorised the 'evils': "First was the prevalence of black money deals, which was like a cancer eating into the industry's vitals from within. The second evil was black marketing in cinema tickets, spreading through the country like a prairie fire. And the third was the shameful practice of wholesale plagiarism from Hollywood films."[9]

**Figure 9.2.** B. K. Karanjia with Sivaji Ganesan

Karanjia, who campaigned against such evil practices in mainstream cinema, also had clear solutions in his mind. "What Indian films needed then was to cultivate the values of narrative strength and clarity, living characters and real situations. The perennial theme of love, so naive in current films, had to achieve a certain maturity. Producers had to learn to come to grips with the abiding theme of poverty which, with the outstanding exception of Satyajit Ray, had never been more than a platitude in our cinema."[10]

Karanjia will be known in history as one of the few journalists who could administer his advice in real life and make a difference. In 1968, Karanjia was appointed Chairman of the FFC—now NFDC—and he continued till 1975 when the national Emergency was declared. In his seven years as Chairman of FFC, Karanjia presided over the changeover of Indian cinema from a low cultural form to a higher art, called *New Wave Cinema of India*.

The *New Wave* films of India, which even took Satyajit Ray by surprise, were mainly the product of the FTII-trained filmmakers, apart from Ray's contemporary Mrinal Sen. Under

Karanjia's Chairmanship, the films of Mrinal Sen, Adoor Gopalakrishnan, Mani Kaul, Kumar Shahani, Avtar Kaul (*27 Down*) and M.S. Sathyu were financed by FFC to make films, giving a new genre to Indian Cinema, which was described as the *New Wave* Indian Cinema to the world.

Most of these filmmakers were products of the Film Society Movement or the FTII. They gave a new idiom and outlook to cinema as a medium, which was appreciated nationally and internationally in various film festivals, thus changing the older image of a barbarous pastime for the uncultured.' The new wave films/Parallel Cinema, as these films are called, also gave much-needed confidence to the Film Society Movement as the harbingers of 'art and culture' in Indian films. The media and the box office film industry began to describe these films as "art films" and *Parallel Cinema*, attracting the attention of not just the other practitioners but even the government of the day, as some of these films began to be honoured in international film festivals, making India proud.

Commenting on these films, he financed to create a *New Wave* in Indian Cinema, Karanjia wrote: "Their work held out the promise of the kind of personal perspective, provocative and socially committed cinema that we had admired in European films ever since the first International Film Festival of India."[11]

The government of the day should have been content with these statements and international honours since most of the films were produced by the FFC and later NFDC, the public sector corporations established specifically to raise the standards in filmmaking and films.

## Policy Withdrawal by the Government

The government support for the film society movement, which precipitated these films by creating a group of culturally oriented film appreciators, should have been another brownie point to those like Prime Minister Indira Gandhi, who extended political patronage to the movement all her life. The FTII and non-FTII filmmakers of the *New Wave* cinema admire the mentoring role of film societies for their kind of films, which were the toast of the film society circuit of the 1970s and 1980s.

Mrinal Sen, one of the leading figures of New Cinema, admits (in an interview in 2012) that he is a product of the Calcutta Film Society and the film society culture of the city.

"Actually, I learned cinema from watching films through the Film Society Movement," the veteran filmmaker said and went on to call the film societies the parents of good filmmakers. "Parents are very important for a child to grow. Film societies have been very important for me to grow," the senior most Indian filmmaker said after Ray admitted his love for film societies. Mrinal Sen's *Bhuvan Shome*, produced by FFC, ushered in the New Cinema in Hindi and *New Wave* in Indian films.[12]

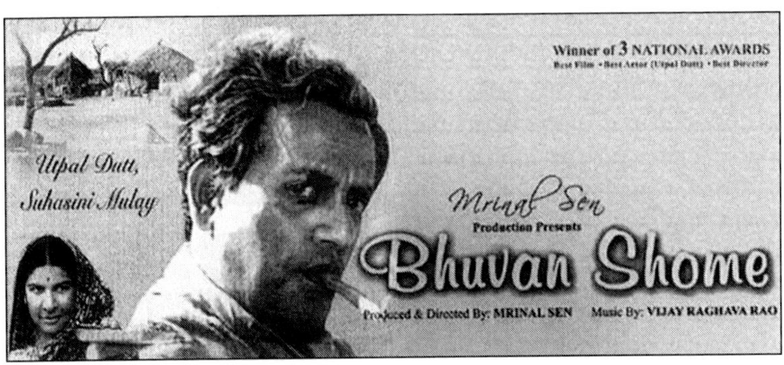


**Figure 9.3.** Poster of Bhuvan Shome

The Dr. Shivarama Karanth Committee on films, appointed by the Central Government in 1980, too placed on record the role of the film society movement in raising the level of film appreciation in the country. "While the film society movement has made a distinct contribution in the propagation of film consciousness, the movement has largely confined to major urban centres," the committee noted, and went on to add, "it is obvious that the film society movement has a very important role to play in 'initiating' audience in the appreciation of good cinema."[13]

Kumar Shahani has had the unique privilege of being known as a filmmaker whose first film *Maya Darpan* was celebrated in the film society circuit but never got a commercial release. The film was produced by FFC. Mani Kaul, too, comes in this category with his films *Ashad Ka Ek Din and Uski Roti*, both produced by FFC. Most of these films never got a theatre release and hence were a commercial flop, though celebrated across the world for their artistic merits.

In the Nehruvian view, culture was important for creating a new nation and needed equal attention as economic growth. In recognition of his stature as a filmmaker, Satyajit Ray was made the president of the FFSI. Indira Gandhi served as the vice president and Inder Kumar Gujral as the treasurer. Later, as the Minister for Information and Broadcasting, Gandhi ruled that a certification of the artistic merit of a film by Satyajit Ray, in his capacity as president of FFSI, would suffice to exempt the film from examination by the Censor Board. Many great and even controversial works of cinema thus found their way to film society screenings. India was indeed "...the great success story of political gradualism—of a kind of 'evolutionary independence,' where cultural movements like the film society in the Nehruvian perspective were an important and integral part," Anil Srivastava, a pioneer of the movement, summed up those days of evolution of Indian culture in films.[14]

With the merger of NFAI, Films Division, CFSI and DFFI with NFDC, the Central Government in 2023 has withdrawn its patronage in effective direct intervention in film culture. Film Societies have vanished from the government's film policies, and even FTII–NFAI summer residence started in 1967 has become a few days event in a few cities, that too as an orientation programme for film students. In short, the Central Government has withdrawn from direct intervention in the film sector, leaving it to corporations and two surviving film institutes funded by the government, whose future is also uncertain, going by various policy formulations to privatise them.

## *Margi* Impregnating the *Desi*

The success of the film society movement and the advent of *New Wave* films also created a sharp debate on art films and commercial films, which almost divided the industry vertically. The debate on films, which have had artistic content, but with mass appeal, always had its detractors. The '*Margi*' (classic) and '*Desi*' (popular box office) division is sacrosanct for them. Film critic TG Vaidhyanathan calls it the "confusion between the conflicting claims of art and commerce," in his book. He made a sharp division between the two streams and said: "The champions of art are invariably cosmopolitan intellectuals (who have probably spent their formative years in the capitals of Europe) frightened at the prospect of encroaching indigenisation. The champions of commerce, on the other hand, translating their box-office anxieties into the new, fashionable language of alienation, talk glibly of 'Indian-ness' and the need for Indian Cinema to have an 'identity."[15]

This sharp debate was created by Kumar Shahani and Mani Kaul, whose films rejected the Ray model of narrative in films. They went the Marxian and Brechtian (Bertolt Brecht) way and were literally banished by the regular theatres. "Kaul and Shahani may be regarded as the outer limit of the *margi* cinema, meant solely for the aficionado," Chidananda Das Gupta commented.[16] The regular film circuit developed such an antipathy for them, so much so that a humorous film of Mani Kaul did not even find a distributor years later, as they got scared by his very name, goes the legend associated with them.

There are bitter critics of Kaul and Shahani in the film society circuit too. Film scholar, Partha Chatterjee, credits the two of them as having brought the entire meaningful cinema movement to a halt. "They never grew out of their classroom," says Chatterjee, reminding us that they were FTII students when filmmaker Ritwik Ghatak was the Vice Principal there. Ritwik, though a proclaimed Marxist in his approach, never adopted the Brechtian narrative in his films and always wanted to be closer to the taste of his evolving audience, Chatterjee pointed out.[17]

Mani Kaul happened to be a nephew of a popular Hindi film star but never ventured into his uncle's way of filmmaking. Kumar Shahani and Mani Kaul remain the enigma among the *New Wave* Indian filmmakers. "At my age I am forced to explain my contribution to films, a disappointed Kumar explained his predicament of not getting funds for his films.[18] Mani Kaul ended up lecturing and promoting a film festival during the last phase of his life. However, both remain the finest theoreticians of films among the FTII products, as few like them have shown such depth in understanding film theories and experimented with the medium.

While the Ray model of the narrative had found its own path in India with its proponents finding private financers for their films, commercial films, too, have been moving to this narrative in search of global acceptance. "Yet while commercial cinema remains a window to India's popular English-speaking, globalised intelligentsia, a certain ambivalence persists," observed Vinay Lal and Ashish Nandy.

Pointed out the contradiction in the popular cinema, Vinay Lal and Ashish Nandy said:[19]

> It is a cinema that appears terribly flawed by the canons of the global film theory and almost entirely disjunctive which the globally dominant aesthetics and concept of good cinema. Its principal attractions—the carnivalesque atmosphere, the centrifugal storyline, the larger-than-life characters and stilted dialogue—also mark it out as flawed art and a curious intrusion into the world of modern art forms.

However, Chidananda Das Gupta sees this phenomenon as "signs of a rapprochement between art films and commercial cinema." Noting the films of Mani Ratnam, *Roja* (1992) and *Bombay* (1995), Kamal Haasan's *Hey Ram* (2000), Aamir Khan's *Lagaan* (2001) and Shah Rukh Khan's *Asoka* (2001), Das Gupta observed: "The lessons of all positive developments—the impact of technical and artistic growth centres, the success of many serious films in the regions, their winning of prestigious prizes in India and abroad, the emergence of the documentary and of television, the increasing emphasis on realism—cannot have been altogether lost in the mainstream film industry despite the hostile noises it often made about these trends."[20]

Ray himself refused to be drawn into a debate on art and commercial cinema in one of the last questionnaires of Das Gupta and said he believed in the art of storytelling and ensuring return on investment to the producer for his films, according to critic and writer Samik Bandyopadhyay who claimed to have seen the document.[21]

Documenting a lifetime of work, Das Gupta in his last book's chapter *Precursors Unpopular Cinema* noticed the "impregnation" of art cinema into commercial cinema, heralding a closing of the gap between art cinema and commerce. The impregnation empowered the commercial cinema in terms of: "concepts and techniques and qualifying it for international acceptance at World forums".[22]This was a big development for the popular films which began as a variety show mode of *Parsi* theatre. In effect, the new film culture which the Film Society Movement stood for, and New Indian Cinema, had made its own influence on the crass commercial cinema, giving it a better *rasiks* appeal.

**Figure 9.4.** Shooting still of Piku

The success of *Piku* (2015), a film made by a director from the film society circuit, Shoojit Sircar, is the latest example of this impregnation, making the observation of Das Gupta that, "the coexistence of *margi and desi* within the ambit of film industry may also become more peaceful," a prophetic one. *Piku* reportedly grossed over Rs100 crores at the Box Office too, apart from the fact that it has been acclaimed as a film well made with one of the best performances from popular actors Amitabh Bachchan, Irrfan Khan and Deepika Padukone.

"I have grown up watching these films and it has a great influence on your life and that is important to you," said Shoojit Sircar.[23] He remembers seeing *Rosa Luxemberg*, an award-winning German film and a US Documentary on the Vietnam war, where the film is about letters from US soldiers serving in Vietnam in diplomatic missions, in his early days as a film buff in Delhi. Shoojit is a filmmaker of repute in Hindi films in 2023, though his films are not internationally celebrated yet.

### Film Societies in the Digital Era

The pioneers had positioned the Film Society Movement as an act of cultural renaissance. A medium which was considered as less than art was elevated to a respectful cultural phenomenon by showcasing the best of the art forms and promoting such productions in India. From the *Desi* cultural form, films got elevated to the *Margi* form as described by veteran film theoretician, Chidananda Das Gupta and pioneering film society organiser.

Gautam Kaul, president (2015) of FFSI pointed out:[24]

> The FS movement has been the nursery of directors of film festivals in India. This is a breed apart. It has people who cannot write a good essay on films and yet they work to create a whole film festival of decent standards. They like their films, though they have come from disparate jobs totally unrelated to their hobby. All had one common gene. They were good managers of facts and material.

His list of such managers who enriched the Indian film festival management field included the following: U. Radhakrishnan of the Delhi Malayalee Film Society—for India Habitat International Film Festival, B.B. Nagpal, a journalist, for Prism International Film Festival and Children Film Festival in Hyderabad; Niranjan Desai and an IFS officer, from Osian International Film Festival, Malti Sahay, a housewife, from Directorate of Film Festival, S. Narayanan, a former Directorate of Film Festival staff from Mumbai International Film Festival, Shanker Mohan, an FTII alumnus, H. N. Narahari Rao, Bangalore International Film Festival, engineer and founder of *Suchitra* film society, E. Tanga

Raj, an RBI officer, Madras International Film Festival through Madras Film Society, George Mathew, an officer from the Indian Space Research Organisation, of Chalachithra, and one of the artistic selector to Bangalore Film Festival and officials of Cine Central, Kolkata, associated with Kolkata International Film Festival, constitute this elite club of people, running film festivals in India.

There are about 21 International Film Festivals being conducted in India in various parts of the country on an annual basis and four are licensed internationally. One can say that most of these film festivals are sustained by the Film Society Movement of the area and its leadership, though the State governments have come in to support them in a big way. Gautam Kaul sees film societies as a feeder channel for film students for all major film studies institutions and film critics. "It is still a feeder channel to FTII, SRFTII Kolkata, Adayar Film Institute. It is an open classroom for most of the better-known film critics in India in all languages."[25]

Going by the number of delegates to the International Film Festival of Kerala (around 10,000) one can safely say the 100-odd film societies and various film studies departments of public and private institutions are also feeder organisations to the annual film jamboree. It was at the touring IIFI in the capital of Kerala, where the concept of 'Open Forum', where the filmmakers, festival organisers and delegates were introduced by FFSI. This gave a "club-society," feeling for the organisers and the participants, enriching the experiences at the film festivals. From then, an 'Open Forum' has become a must in all the film festivals across India.

The former FFSI president also admits the elitist bias of the Film Society Movement.

Kaul observed:[25]

> It has had its limitations mainly because it was not a people's movement. It remained an elitist's interest, an evening exercise for students of serious studies in other vocational subjects. In its early years, it was the only

> window to the cinema of the West. Even today, access to classical cinema is only through FSM activities.

He and his team were focusing on IIT and IIM campuses across India to resurrect the waning Film Society Movement, without realising that the digital groupings had already taken over such 'analogue', groupings.

Sudhir Nandgaonkar, the former FFSI secretary also subscribes to the view that a serious study of films can help sustain the movement in future. "It is a general feeling of the public outside the fold of the Film Society Movement that due to 24x7 channels screening films, DVD, downloads from the internet and now on mobile, film societies have become irrelevant today. But it is not true. Take an example of literature; the books are available in bookshops and libraries, even then the languages are taught at the graduate and post-graduate level. This helps readers to understand the nuances of literature. The same thing is about film society. It is not irrelevant in today's time. But a Film Society should give emphasis on study of cinema besides screening films every month. The future of the movement lies in the study of cinema. So, the Film Society should give more emphasis to the study of cinema. Those societies that adhere to it will only survive," Sudhir*ji* who is keeping the movement's flag flying in India's film capital pointed out in 2012. He passed away in early 2023.[26]

However, H.N. Narahari Rao, the doyen from *Suchitra* Film Society, Bangalore, the only film society with its own cultural complex, says there is a need to redefine the concept of film society itself. "Film society concept has to be redefined; there is a need to accept the right to see what the members want to see. Just as in music, there must be a choice for the film-goers to see what they want. Use of advanced digital technology can lead us to such a situation," Rao pointed out.

Rao further pointed out:[27]

> From showing films, film societies have to change to curating films for the audience. They need to be in the selection process with active involvement of the youngsters. There are communications departments in all universities,

and they need to be involved in film studies and the Film Society Movement, with localised film clubs. The booming real estate sector has also shown interest in localised film clubs. It leads to the choice of the viewers, though copyright laws can be an impediment. Ultimately, the film clubs have to go local.

The only ray of hope for the film society movement to stay alive is the Film Studies departments as part of the Mass Communications courses across India to float University Film Clubs, an unfulfilled dream of the pioneers. An RTI query from the UGC revealed that there are over 200 campuses which offer film studies in India.[28] This is apart from the numerous Film Institutes which have sprung up over the years in many parts of the country. Though most of these institutes and campuses are supplying manpower to television channels across the length and breadth of the country, they have been identified as the next fertile ground for keeping the flag of the Film Society Movement flying, as film appreciation is part of the curriculum of these institutes.

Professor Mihir Bhattacharya, of Jadavpur University, Kolkata, who started the first Film Studies department offering post-graduate studies in films, admits that most of his students end up with television channels. "We have a filmmaking and production paper with practicals and hence, they find it useful to get employment in television channels," Professor Bhattacharya added.

After a wait of three years, UGC approved his department's plan to start a fully-fledged film studies department offering PG courses in 1991 for the first time in India, and the department admits around 40 students every year. The other university which offers PG courses in Film Studies is the Kolkata-based West Bengal University along with many others spread across India, going by the list from the UGC, which oversees the academic curriculum of higher education centres in India.[29] It is not accidental that the city which has a rich tradition of the Film Society Movement also pioneered film studies in Universities with its Film Studies departments. Though the Film Society Movement is at its lowest in the Eastern region, the route of looking at films with a *Margi* tradition carries on in Kolkata in the universities of the city.

Apart from focusing on campuses, there is also a suggestion to focus on states on the lines of Kerala and Maharashtra model of organisation of the film society movement. "One intervention can be further decentralisation of the Federation of Film Societies in India. At present FFSI has five regions combining three to four states in each region. An honorary worker cannot cope up with his present workload of the organisation. So, instead of a Regional Council we should have a State Council, based on regional languages. Secondly, all these years' film societies were using English as a medium of communication. Now it should do so in a regional language. Even film appreciation courses must be organised in regional languages," Sudhir Nadgaonkar pointed out. He also wants increasing involvement of the state governments in activities of FFSI, just as in Karnataka and Kerala.

"The government can play a major role in promoting the Film Society Movement in general and film culture in particular. Kerala and Karnataka have already started this. Other states are far behind," the Film Society Movement veteran pointed out.[30] The Dr. Shivarama Karanth committee of 1980 had already recommended such a step". Federation of Film Societies should set up organisations at the State level so that it can properly liaise with the State Governments for obtaining financial help and facilities for the film societies in the State."[31]

The Mumbai Film Festival's former executive Srinivasan Narayan says, in most metro cities the film viewing culture is changing and he calls it, "not organised, but widespread." He attributes the availability of DVDs and the widespread downloading of films by youngsters, for this new phenomenon. Most of them run their own blogs and social media pages which build communities around it and exchange views and ideas. Srinivasan, who started his career with the Directorate of Film Festivals in Delhi, was credited with the success of the Mumbai International Film Festival and has over three decades of experience in organising film festivals.[32]

In Chennai, film enthusiasts have many options to see world films. The auditorium of the South Indian Film Chamber of Commerce is open to film enthusiasts, mainly the ICAF to screen films from across the world as weekend morning shows. ICAF along with the State Government conducts the Chennai International film festival annually. In Hyderabad, a group of film enthusiasts have an arrangement with the studio preview theatres to screen quality world films for the *rasiks*. In Thiruvananthapuram, film societies run by young professionals, like the Banner Film Society has weekend screenings, with eminent filmmakers and film personalities choosing their favourite films. This is apart from the regular film societies; screenings at 15 KSFDC cinema halls and the annual film festivals in various parts of Kerala.

In New Delhi, the Directorate of Film Festivals, now NFDC, which runs the Siri Fort theatre, uses a small auditorium to screen films which it procures for various film festivals. This is in addition to the regular shows at Italian Cultural Centre, Alliance Francaise, Max Muller Bhavan, and the Spanish Embassy's Instituto Cervantes which screens films from all Spanish-speaking regions including Latin American films. The India International Centre and the India Habitat Centre, the places where the capital's decision-makers from the government, corporate and social sector hangout, have their own film clubs organized in the good old analogue film society way.

In Kolkata, where the Film Society Movement took the shape of an all-India movement, the situation is not glossy. The Calcutta Film Society has been revived and they celebrate the annual release of *Pather Panchali* every year. The annual Chidananda Das Gupta Memorial lecture is now conducted by the CDG Foundation. "There are enough finances available for all kinds of films in the city," pointed out Sandeep Ray in a conversation with the author in 2012.[33]

The number of FFSI-affiliated film societies is at an all-time low in the Eastern region now with only 65 remaining from close to 100 in the 1970s and early 1980s. However, the younger population among film buffs have already got their own digital groupings with various social media and digital platforms. "As the country talks about big investments in broadband to the village and a Digital India, we need to think of an effort at sustaining our film culture, the moving image re-telling of stories that bridge all cultural divides. I am not being facetious in my hope for a ubiquitous cinema as the next incarnation of the film society in the new India," Anil Srivastava, the movement's pioneer and a technologist based in the USA pointed out.[34] Increasing bandwidth of the digital infrastructure with 5G technologies is leading the digital groups of film buffs into more and more avenues to experience films and discuss them.

### Wither away FFSI?

In June 2015, the leaders of the Federation of Film Societies of India (FFSI) assembled at Thiruvananthapuram at Malayalam filmmaker KR Mohanan's residence. The late Mohanan was then the vice president of Kerala FFSI. The occasion was a discussion on the Film Society Movement as the Kerala Unit was about to celebrate its Golden Jubilee in July 2015. The Kerala unit happens to be one of the richest and largest of the FFSI, with patronage from the state government, as well as from the organised Left parties of the state.

The discussion on the way forward was a closed one and a second of the sort in the year. The leadership was unanimous in targeting the young people. Suggestions for University Film Clubs had total consensus from all of them. "We had a similar meet at Nagpur in the first half of 2015 and each of the regional leadership was assigned to groom a young person each in their respective areas to hand over the mantle of FFSI," according to Gautam Kaul, who was among the founding members of Lucknow Film Society.[35] The former IPS man turned Film Society activist is also devising various programmes to enlist top educational establishments like IIT and IIMs to the Film Society fold. However, in 2023, after the pandemic years, FFSI itself appears to be in the doldrums as most of the existing film societies prior to the pandemic are inactive, and FFSI has not yet purveyed itself to the digital groups, as current leadership appeared to be legacy one with their 'analogue' operations.

**Film Societies Affiliated to FFSI in India 1959-2014.[36]**

| Year | North | East | West | South | Kerala | Total |
|---|---|---|---|---|---|---|
| 1959 | 3 | 1 | 1 | 1 | | 6 |
| 1964 | | | | | | 23 |
| 1967 | | | | | | 108 |
| 1971 | | | | | | 111 |
| 1980 | | | | | | 216 |
| 1984 | | | | | | 94 |
| 1998 | | | | | | 98 |
| 2009 | 10 | 70 | 32 | 47 | 70 | 229 |
| | | | | | | |
| 2014 | 11 | 65 | 45 | 54 | 118 | 292 |

The numbers say that the Film Society Movement in India has grown over the years till 2014. However, in 2023 FFSI is still counting how many units survived the pandemic. The Calcutta Film Society which brought out a Satyajit Ray bulletin recently was shocked that after the pandemic a senior critic wrote its epitaph.

## Are State Units, Universities and Digital Groupings the Future?

In Kerala, a few societies have already started subtitling world films in Malayalam, making them available to the masses. In Maharashtra, many film appreciation courses are conducted in Marathi. There appears to be a crying need for going local with the medium of language, and the organisation for the FFSI to take the movement forward. Going by the focus of activity, so far, the FFSI leadership appears to target the same educated liberals in the metro cities, who were the patrons of the movement in the 1970s. However, most of them appeared to be happy with watching such films in easily available digital formats from the comfort of their homes. The opinion makers in the society appear to have changed from the government and public sector professionals to the corporates and NGOs and there is hardly any interest in film societies in these sectors though, many classics from the film society circuit have entered corporate training modules. Typical of such a film is the Akira

Kurosawa film *Seven Samurai*[37] shown and discussed to showcase teamwork and its effectiveness.

The hot favourite target audience of FFSI to expand in today's scenario appears to be educational institutions. "FFSI has plans to set up campus film societies in universities and colleges to take international cinema to the student community. Instead of 35 mm film prints, FFSI will focus on providing film DVDs to these societies to ensure smooth functioning", the official website announced in 2015. The Kerala unit of FFSI has moved forward in targeting the Universities, with a workshop for the trainers for university film appreciation courses. In 2023, FFSI's own website is under construction and details of their activities are not available.

Going by the UGC's list of affiliated universities and institutions which offer Film Studies at post-graduate and graduate levels or as an additional subject, the FFSI can easily plan University Film Clubs, provided there is a committed staffer in each of the institutions. However, with copyright issues of available films becoming an issue many a times, it will be a herculean task for anyone trying to organise public film screenings for young people, as the grey market and downloads are targeting the very same young people. Even to attempt this, FFSI leadership must be handed over to the academics from the present analogue era ones.

The effort to build a next-generation leadership is also in the doldrums, as the old guard in many places is seen harbouring vested interests. "In most places where the film societies ran successfully, there were one or two dedicated persons and when they shifted or lost interest, the society also died," Gautam Kaul pointed out. "Wrong people went to the leadership in Delhi as the DFS membership had become a status symbol in the city," recalled Deepak Roy, filmmaker and one of the life members of the society. "In many places, the old leadership refused to give way to the new," added U Radhakrishnan, former secretary of the Northern region of FFSI. Groups like Celluloid, and Jodhpur Society became history when its pioneering leaders died. Clearly, there is a crisis of leadership in the movement, which the FFSI leadership is grappling with. Unless the digital era leadership arrives and takes over the activities, one cannot see any future for FFSI as an organisation post-2023.

There are exceptions like *Suchitra* of Bangalore where the second-generation leadership has taken over the cultural complex, giving hope for the future. *Suchitra's* success in Bangalore can be attributed to a smooth leadership transition. Founder president Narahari Rao resigned from the Trusteeship of a Cultural Academy in 2003 and handed over the leadership to another set of leaders." However, my association still continues as a patron. I just go there whenever they call me. I also functioned as the Artistic Director of the Bengaluru International Film Festival for *Suchitra* for the first six years till 2014," said Rao.

Though family membership was in vogue among film societies, with the rush of members who were connoisseurs of uncensored films, the film societies lost women members in the 1970s and 1980s. With television serials becoming a popular flavour of evenings, it is now difficult to get women in general to film screenings. Though the diplomatic cultural centres are patronised by women in numbers, they are yet to look at the good old film societies.

In the history of the Film Society Movement, there were only a few women leaders. Marie Seton, Vijaya Mulay, Ammu Swaminadhan, Usha Bhagat and former Prime Minister Indira Gandhi herself immensely contributed to the Movement. In the era of women empowerment, the Film Society Movement must make it attractive to women as a group too, to make its future plans realistic and successful. It is heartening to know that new groups like TFO, the online film society, were established by two women academics.

For any and everyone who wants to develop a 'taste' for the language and art of cinema, they need an ambience, be it an individual act of seeing films or a collective movement, like the Film Societies. Despite the changing socio-cultural mosaic in the digital age, film societies and screenings of classics in formats of your convenience are still a must for film buffs in their search for grooming and mastering the film language. "Now we seem to prefer a more mechanistic view of socio-cultural development. Technology is transforming the way moving images are created and projected. Gone are the days of the rickety projector, the noise of the moving sprockets, the celluloid. The iconic Kodak is no longer pivotal. Recording a moving image is as simple—and often better in quality—as pointing your iPhone. You can stream *Battleship Potemkin* or find *The Louisiana Story* from Netflix on your television or even your tablet. All of this is making possible a new culture of cinema where everyone can participate," observed an optimistic film society pioneer and techno evangelist Anil Srivastava.[38]

Film Societies in the digital era are seen as legacy 'analogue' outdated groups by the new emerging digital generation of film buffs. With no political or governmental patronage, barring in Kerala and Karnataka, it will be a herculean task for the FFSI and film societies in general, to continue its activities in any form in the coming years. Unless of course the digital generation takes over FFSI and adopts digital formats with the support of ever-expanding bandwidth and internet technologies facilitating seamless film viewing. There are too many digital platforms to facilitate these viewing, be it any genre of films or historic ones. There is an internet archive which houses most of the old classics. There are US channels like *Criterion* which curates and digitises films across the world from its 120-odd year's history. *Mosfilm* of the erstwhile Soviet Union has digitised and uploaded Soviet-era films on YouTube, as Russia has now adopted them as part of their cultural history. Any Google search can source one of the films of interest in minutes, and they can watch it on home theatre screens or even smartphones.

Availability of films is not an issue and communal viewing has become history, but interactions between interested parties are a must for understanding the various nuances of a good work of art always, and that is where groups like film societies are needed in the digital era. But it is up to the digital generation how they format such groups, with or without legacy organisations like FFSI or not, which is a question to be answered by future events and actions.

## What Film Makers Say About FSM

The best commentators on Film Society Movement and its future are the filmmakers who made films which needed an audience such as the *rasiks*, who have some exposure to films shown in film societies. Let me quote the big three who were also associated with the film societies from their initial days of filmmaking.

**Figure 9.5.** Mrinal Sen

Mrinal Sen: "You cannot expect a large number of people to see your films. Any sensible filmmaker, when he makes films, his films are not that reachable to everyone. For instance, fiction, if you read novels. Not all novels are very popular. Popular novels are very different... Even then I want to be popular... But I am a popular failure most of the time... in the box office. But then that is why my arithmetic is very simple... I make low-budget films. People say filmmaking is an expensive process. I do not agree with them... Not all agree with them... Films can be made at a low cost. I have been making low-cost films. If you make low-cost films and if you can get to the larger minority audience scattered across the world... the larger minority audience... who would be seeing your film...and that way I keep going...That is in spite of the fact that I am a popular failure at the box office I keep going..." (in an interview when he turned 90 in 2012. He passed away in 2018.[39])

**Figure 9.6.** Adoor Gopalakrishnan

**Adoor Gopalakrishnan:** "As for the future course of film societies, it should change its character. It should grow into the Academy of cinemas where selected outstanding films are screened regularly for the interested public and discussed. It would become possible with the institution of a chain of such cinemas in the metropolises and big towns of the country. This is an area where the Government can step in and act positively. Even an enterprising distributor can do wonders to take notable cinema around the country and screen it profitably. The only way to save and foster a film culture is to introduce the young audiences in schools to the charm and beauty and worthiness of good cinema. Like good literature and good taste, they need to imbibe it early in their lives. Instead, what are we feeding them on?"[40]

**Figure 9.7.** Shyam Benegal

**Shyam Benegal:** "The relevance of the Film Society Movement today is to encourage young people to look at Cinema as an artistic activity rather than simply as a distractive entertainment. Campus Film Societies was an initiative I took as the president of the FFSI. This does not simply mean showing films but showing them as subjects for discussion and debate among the members."[41]

**Figure 9.8.** Aparna Sen, with father Chidananda Das Gupta

**Aparna Sen:** "The film viewing culture imparted to me a better taste in films (by her father Chidananda Das Gupta who used to take her to film society screenings). Think about the kids growing in a musician's home, they will have an inherent awareness about the ragas. Film is almost like that. New varied viewing of films gives fresh visual experiences. That moulds one's taste for films. This is applicable to all filmmakers. No one can make you a good filmmaker. One can learn the technology of filmmaking. But in the end, it is your worldview which makes you a good filmmaker.... But here, a good taste in films developed over the years comes handy."[42]

## References

1. https://assets.ey.com/content/dam/ey-sites/ey-com/en_in/topics/media-and-entertainment/2022/ey-ficci-m-and-e-report-tuning-into-consumer_v3.pdf p 151

2. https://www.facebook.com/groups/talkingfilmsonline
3. https://comartsci.msu.edu/our-people/swarnavel-eswaran-pillai
4. https://filmstudies.msu.edu/filmcollective/
5. The New Indian Cinema by Aruna Vasudev, - Macmillan 1980. P-2.
6. http://indianexpress.com/article/cities/ahmedabad/varsities-in-india-have-always-kept-cinema-out-of-bounds-adoor-gopalkrishnan/
7. Report of the Working Group on National Film Policy, Ministry of I&B, GOI, May 1980-P9. Para-3.2.
8. Ibid-5.
9. Counting My Blessings, by BK Karanjia, Penguin–Viking, 2005. P-182.
10. Ibid-5-P. 191.
11. Ibid-5. P. 192
12. http://vkcherian.blogspot.in/2012/06/mrinal-sen-at-90-riding-wave-of.html?view=timeslide
13. Ibid- 7. P13.Para.3.23 &3.24.
14. http://cherianwrites.blogspot.in/2016/03/on-fsm-by-anilsrivastava-pioneer-and.html
15. Hours in the Dark by TG Vaidyanathan-OUP - 1996.-P 86.
16. Seeing is Believing by Chidananda Das Gupta, Viking, 2008.P.95
17. Interview with Partha Chatterjee.
18. Interview with Kumar Shahani.
19. Finger printing Popular Culture —The Myth and the Iconomic in Indian Cinema by Vinay Lal and Ashish Nandy. OUP – 2006-introduction.
20. Ibid-16-P. 93.
21. Interview with Samik Bandyopadhyay.
22. Ibid-16.
23. Interview with Shoojit Sircar.
24. Interview with Gautam Kaul, president, FFSI.
25. Ibid-24.
26. http://cherianwrites.blogspot.in/2016/02/interviewwith-sudhir-nandgoanker.html
27. Interview with HN Narahari Rao.
28. http://cherianwrites.blogspot.in/2016/03/universities-with-film-studies.html
29. Interview with Prof. Mihir Bhattacharya

30. Ibid -26
31. Ibid- 7-P.13. Para-3.27.
32. Interview with Sreenivasan Narayanan.
33. Interview with Sandeep Ray.
34. http://cherianwrites.blogspot.in/2016/03/on-fsm-by-anilsrivastava-pioneer-and.html
35. Interview with Gautam Kaul.
36. Compiled from available FFSI documents.
37. https://en.wikipedia.org/wiki/Seven_Samurai
38. Ibid-34
39. https://cherianwrites.blogspot.com/2016/06/mrinal-da-interviewed.html
40. http://cherianwrites.blogspot.in/2016/02/adoorgopalakrishnan-on-film-society.html
41. http://cherianwrites.blogspot.in/2016/02/interview-with-benegal.html
42. ChalachitraVicharam- Malayalam VC books- 2021 V K Cherian p.151

# Annexures

## ANNEXURE 1

### Genesis of Indian films

India was one of the few countries to be an early witness to the birth of the new medium called cinema, invented by the Lumière Brothers, Auguste and Louis in 1895. The first of the screenings by the Lumiere Brothers was on March 22, 1895, at 44 Rue de Rennesin Paris at an industrial meeting where a film, *Workers Leaving the Lumière Factory*, was shown especially for the occasion.

Louis photographed the world around him. Some of his first films were 'actuality' films, like the workers leaving the factory. The brothers began to open theatres to show their films (which became known as cinemas). In the first four months of 1896, they had opened *Cinématographe* theatres in London, Brussels, Belgium and New York.

*The Celluloid Train Steams into Bombay* on July 7, the announcement for the first film show was made in 1896, at the Watson's Hotel Bombay. The city's elite, including the British officials and their *memsahebs*, paid a rupee each and braved inclement weather to witness Lumiere's *Marvel of the Century, Wonder of the World*. As the large grainy images flickered back to life and the locomotive made its first appearance in a Parisian parlour barely six months earlier and steamed into the Bombay hotel room, the audience broke into an enthusiastic applause. This event remained a historic one, as it kickstarted an entirely new medium of entertainment called cinema in India.

The development of the Indian film industry—as one of the world's largest—is as old, as varied, and as exciting as the history of the medium itself. The first short film in India was directed by Hiralal Sen, starting with *The Flower of Persia* in 1898. The first Indian feature film *Raja Harishchandra*, however, was made much later in the year 1912 and coincided with the appearance of the first full-length features in the United States. The first Indian talkie hit the screens in 1931, two years after the first British and French 'all-talkies' were made.

> At the turn of the century–when cinema dawned–India was poised for a major social and political reform. Technological innovations, such as cars, planes and gramophone records which took classical music to the masses, were transforming a society that had remained unchanged for centuries. A new force in the formation of public opinion, the press, was making its presence felt. (wrote film historians Rani Day Burra and Maithili Rao, *Source NFAI*)

Encouraged by the response, the exhibitors moved the cinema shows to Novelty Theatre and introduced a broad set of prices for both patrician and plebeian. The cheapest tickets were for four *annas* (a quarter of a rupee)—creating the four*anna* class audience that in decades to come would dictate the form and content of Indian commercial films and the rise and fall of its stars.

Though the initial stories for films were mostly from the epics of India, there was hardly any literary or cultural figure getting involved in films. The conventional literary and cultural traditions did not accept cinema as a medium of expression, though there was an effort by modernists like Prime Minister Jawaharlal Nehru to give it acceptability. However, the leader of the freedom struggle, Gandhi, had dismissed the new medium.

During the early days, the patron of the 'bioscope' was the literate urban ruling class, while the average Indian found the imported films (*The Queen's Funeral Procession, Assassination of President McKinley*) shown in the tents of Calcutta and Bombay too exotic. Enterprising young Indians began to cover local events, such as the celebration of Edward VII's coronation with cameras from London. With the rise of exhibitor magnates in India like Jamshedji Framji Madan and Abdulally Esoofally, films from all over the world were jostling for a slice of the Indian market, as recorded by film historians.

The first Indian movie released in India was *Shree Pundalik*, a silent film in Marathi by Dadasaheb Torne on May 18, 1912, at the Coronation Cinematograph in Mumbai. Torne is also considered the 'Father of Indian Cinema'.

However, the first full-length motion picture in India was produced by Dadasaheb Phalke. Dadasaheb was the pioneer of the Indian film industry. He was a scholar on Indian languages and culture who brought together elements from Sanskrit epics to produce *Raja Harishchandra* (1913), a silent Marathi film with inter-titles in English and Hindi. The female roles in the film were played by male actors.

The story of how the first film was made is as follows: "Phalke appeared to have visited every cinema show, studying films, experimenting with his cheap camera for twenty hours a day till his health failed. Pledging his life insurance policies, Phalke sailed to England trained there for a week with *Cecil Hepworth*, and returned with a Williamson camera, a film perforator, processing and printing machines, and raw stock. He was all set to make India's first feature film; all he needed was money. His wife Saraswati Phalke, who supported him throughout, allowed him to mortgage her ornaments. Interestingly, almost five decades later, Satyajit Ray would pledge his wife's ornaments to make *Pather Panchali*, the first film to put Indian cinema on the world map.

The first Indian chain of cinema theatres was owned by the Calcutta entrepreneur Jamshedji Framji Madan, who oversaw the production of 10 films annually and distributed them throughout the Indian Subcontinent.

In South India, Raghupathi Venkaiah Naidu pioneered the production of silent movies, and later talkies. Starting from 1909, he was involved in many aspects of the history of Indian cinema and travelled to different regions in Asia to promote film work. He was the first to build and own cinema halls in Madras. The Raghupathi Venkaiah Naidu Award is an annual award incorporated into the Nandi Awards to recognise people for their contributions to the Telugu film industry.

During the early twentieth century, cinema as a medium gained popularity across India.

In 1927, the British government, in order to promote the market in India for British films over American ones, formed the Indian Cinematograph Enquiry Committee (ICEC). The ICEC consisted of three Britishers and three Indians, led by T. Rangachariar, a Madras lawyer. The committee introduced censorship and ensured that only British and US films entered the Indian market.

Yet, these governmental policies did not stop Indian filmmakers from experimenting with new developments in the technology of cinema. Ardeshir Irani released *Alam Ara,* which was the first Indian talking film, on March 14, 1931. H. M. Reddy produced and directed *Bhakta Prahlada* (Telugu), and released it on September 15, 1931, and *Kalidas* (Tamil) was released on October 31, 1931. Kalidas was produced by Ardeshir Irani and directed by H. M. Reddy. These two films were Southern India's first talkie films to have a theatrical release. As sound technology advanced, the 1930s saw the rise of music in Indian cinema. *Indra Sabha* and *Devi Devyani* marked the beginning of the song-and-dance routine in Indian films. Studios emerged across major cities such as Chennai, Kolkata and Mumbai as filmmaking became an established craft by 1935, exemplified by the success of *Devdas*, which had managed to enthrall audiences nationwide. Bombay Talkies came up in 1934 and Prabhat Studios in Pune had begun production of films to cater to the Marathi language audience. Filmmaker RSD Choudhury produced *Wrath* (1930), which was banned by the British Raj in India as it depicted actors as Indian leaders, an expression censored during the days of the Indian Independence Movement. *Sant Tukaram*, a 1936 film based on the life of Tukaram (1608–50), a *Varkari* saint and spiritual poet, was screened at the 1937 edition of the Venice Film Festival, the first Indian film to be screened at an international film festival. The film was subsequently adjudged as one of the three best films of the year.

The Indian *masala* film—slang used for commercial films with song, dance, drama and romance—came up following the Second World War. South Indian cinema gained prominence throughout India with the release of S. S. Vasan's *Chandralekha*. During the 1940s, cinema in Southern India accounted for nearly half of Indian cinema halls and cinema came to be viewed as an instrument of cultural revival. The Partition of India following its Independence divided the nation's assets and as a result, a number of studios went to the newly formed Pakistan. The strife of Partition became an enduring subject for filmmaking during the decades that followed.

The Indian People's Theatre Association (IPTA), an art movement with a Leftist inclination, began to take shape through the 1940s and the 1950s. A number of realistic IPTA plays, such as Bijon Bhattacharya's *Nabanna* in 1944 (based on the Bengal famine of 1943), prepared the ground for the solidification of realism in Indian cinema, exemplified by Khwaja Ahmad Abbas's *Dharti Ke Lal* (Children of the Earth) in 1946. The IPTA movement continued to emphasise reality and went on to produce *Mother India* and *Pyaasa*, which are among India's most recognisable cinematic productions.

## ANNEXURE 2

### Memorandum of Association: FFSI

The Memorandum of Association of FFSI was as follows:

1. The name of the Society shall be the Federation of Film Societies of India, hereinafter referred to as the 'The Federation'.

2. The registered office of the Society shall be situated in the State of West Bengal in the city of Calcutta.

3. The objects for which the Federation is established shall be:

   (a) To promote the study of film as an art and social force.

   (b) To encourage the production of films of artistic value.

   (c) To promote public appreciation of films of artistic value.

   (d) To promote and coordinate the activities of film societies towards the achievement of the above aims, particularly in the matter of organisation of showing film classics and outstanding current films from all over the world.

(e) To promote research on the cinema.

(f) To co-operate with national and international organisations having similar objects.

4. The above objects will be realised through the following activities:

(i) To enrol individual film societies as its members.

(ii) To promote the formation of film societies and the development of the film society movement all over the country.

(iii) To raise funds and/or loans from member societies and from other sources and receive and pay grants, bequests, donations, subscriptions, etc.

(iv) To establish and maintain museums, collections, libraries, auditoria etc., and to translate, compile, collect, publish, purchase or sell any literature bearing upon any subject relating to films.

(v) To organise and participate in film festivals, lectures, seminars, conferences etc., in India and abroad.

(vi) To establish and maintain liaison with national and international organisations having similar aims and objects.

(vii) To own, buy or sell or purchase, hire or mortgage all property.

5. At the time of the adoption of this Memorandum of Association, the committee of Administration of the Federation consisted of the following members:

President : Satyajit Ray

Vice Presidents : (Smt) Ammu Swaminathan, Robert E. Hawks, S.Goplan

Joint Secretaries : (Smt) Vijaya Mulay, Chidananda Das Gupta

Joint Treasures : D. Pramanik, Abdul Hassan.

Members : (Smt) R.Anatharaman, (Smt) Rita Ray, K.L. Khandapur, Jag Mohan, A. Rehman, A.Roy Choudhary.

*Source*: FFSI

## ANNEXURE 3

### Presidents of FFSI- 1959-2016

1. Satyajit Ray (1959-92)
2. Mrinal Sen (1992)
3. Anil Chatterjee (1992-96)
4. Chandran Nair (1996-2000)
5. Vijaya Mulay (2000-2001)
6. Moinul Hasan (2001-04)
7. Shyam Benegal (2004-10)
8. H. N. Narahari Rao (2010-12)
9. Kiran V Shantaram (2012-14)
10. Gautam Kaul (2014-16)
11. Kiran V Shantharam-(2016-23)

(*Source*: FFSI)

# Bibliography


Abhija Ghosh, *Celluloid in Transit: Film Society Cultures in India*, (M. Phil dissertation)

Adoor Gopalakrishnan, *Cinemayudelokam (The World of Cinema)*, (Kerala Bhasha Institute, 1983).

Annette Kuhn and Guy Westwell, A Dictionary of Film Studies (OUP, 2012).

Aruna Vasudev, *The New Indian Cinema* (New Delhi: Macmillan India, 1986).

B D Garga, *Art of Cinema* (Penguin UK, 2005).

Calcutta Film Society, *CFS Bulletin-Pather Panchali Day*, Special Issue-2012.

Chidananda Das Gupta, *Seeing Is Believing: Selected Writings on Cinema* (Penguin India, 2008).

Chidananda Das Gupta, *The Cinema of Satyajit Ray* (NBT, 2001).

David Page and William Crawley, *Satellites Over South Asia: Broadcasting, Culture and the Public Interest* (SAGE Publications Pvt. Limited, 2001).

Dipankar Mukhopadhyay, *Mrinal Sen-60 Years in Search of Cinema*, (Harper Collins, 1996)

Gautaman Bhaskaran, *Adoor Gopalakrishnan: A Life in Cinema* (Penguin UK, 2017).

H.N. Narahari Rao (ed.), The Film Society Movement in India, (The Asian Film Foundation, 2009).

https://assets.ey.com/content/dam/ey-sites/ey-com/en_in/topics/media-and-entertainment/2022/ey-ficci-m-and-e-report-tuning-into-consumer_v3.pdf

Indira Gandhi, *Selected Speeches of Indira Gandhi: January 1966-August 1969*, 1971.

John W. Hood, The Essential Mystery: The Major Filmmakers of Indian Art Cinema, (Orient Black Swan, 2009).

*Kerala Grandhashala Sangham-Rajata Jubilee Suvaneer (Kerala Library movement–Silver Jubilee Souvenir* 1971, Malayalam.

Khwaja Ahmad Abbas, *I Am Not an Island: An Experiment in Autobiography* (New Delhi: Vikas, 1977).

Marie Seton, *Portrait of a Director: Satyajit Ray* (Penguin Books India, 2003).

Marie Seton, *The Film as an Educational Force in India* (Ministry of Education, 1956).

Mihir Bhattacharya, *Cinema and the Bad New Times: Foundation Day Lecture at Gauhati Cine Club*, 26 April, 2013.

Peter Sutoris, *Visions of Development: Films Division of India and the Imagination of Progress, 1948-75*, (OUP, 2016).

Publications Division, *Jawaharlal Nehru Selected Speeches: Volume-2: 1949-1953* (Publications Division Ministry of Information & Broadcasting, 2017).

Publications Division, *Jawaharlal Nehru's Speeches Vol. 3 (1953-1957)* (Publications Division Ministry of Information & Broadcasting, 2017).

R. M. Ray, *Indian Cinema in Retrospect*, (Hope India Publications, 2009).

*Report of the Working Group on National Film Policy*, Ministry of Information & Broadcasting Ministry, (Govt of India, May 1980).

Satyajit Ray, *Deep Focus: Reflection on Indian Cinema*, Ed. Sandip Ray (Harper Collins, 2011).

Satyajit Ray, *Our Films, Their Films* (Bombay: Orient Longman, 2011).

Suranjan Ganguly, *Satyajit Ray: In Search of the Modern*, (Penguin Books, 2000).

T. G. Vaidyanathan, *Hours in the Dark: Essays on Cinema*, 1996.

Utpal Datta, *On Cinema* (Seagull Books Pvt Ltd, 2009).

Vijaya Mulay, *As Others See it*, NFAI Project.

Vinay Lal and Ashis Nandy, *Fingerprinting Popular Culture: The Mythic and the Iconic in Indian Cinema*, (OUP, 2006).

# Index

## C

## F

## G



## H



## I

## N

## O



## P

## R



## S

## T

## U



## V



## W



## Y



## Z